CANADA AMONG NATIONS 1999

CANADA AMONG NATIONS 1999

A Big League Player?

Edited by
Fen Osler Hampson, Martin Rudner,
and Michael Hart

OXFORD
UNIVERSITY PRESS

OXFORD
UNIVERSITY PRESS

70 Wynford Drive, Don Mills, Ontario M3C 1J9
www.oupcan.com

Oxford New York
Athens Auckland Bangkok Bogotá Buenos Aires Calcutta
Cape Town Chennai Dar es Salaam Delhi Florence Hong Kong
Istanbul Karachi Kuala Lumpur Madrid Melbourne Mexico City
Mumbai Nairobi Paris São Paulo Singapore Taipei Tokyo
Toronto Warsaw

and associated companies in
Berlin Ibadan

Oxford is a trade mark of Oxford University Press

Canadian Cataloguing in Publication Data
The National Library of Canada has catalogued this publication as follows:
Canada among nations

Annual.
1984–
Produced by the Norman Paterson School of International Affairs at
    Carleton University.
Each vol. Has also a distinctive title.
Published: Ottawa : Carleton University Press, 1990–1997; Toronto :
Oxford University Press, 1998–   .
ISSN 0832-0683
ISBN 0-19-541458-6 (1999)

1. Canada—Foreign relations—1945–   —Periodicals.   2. Canada—
Politics and government—1984–   —Periodicals.   3. Canada—Politics and
government—1980–1984
Periodicals.   I. Norman Paterson School of International Affairs.

FC242.C345   327.71   C86–031285–2
F1029.C3

Cover Design: Brett J. Miller

CONTENTS

CONTRIBUTORS

Keith Acheson is a professor in the Department of Economics, Carleton University.

Louis A. Delvoie is a senior fellow in the Centre for International Relations, Queen's University.

William A. Dymond is Director, Policy and Planning Bureau, Department of Foreign Affairs and International Trade.

Heather Forton is Director, Services Trade Policy Division, Department of Foreign Affairs and International Trade. She served in Canada's Permanent Mission to the World Trade Organization, responsible for legal affairs, 1994–8.

John Graham is an international election consultant, a former Director of Academic Relations, Department of Foreign Affairs and International Trade, and a former ambassador.

David G. Haglund is Director, Centre for International Relations, Queen's University.

Fen Osler Hampson is a professor in The Norman Paterson School of International Affairs, Carleton University.

Michael Hart is a professor in The Norman Paterson School of International Affairs, Carleton University.

Robin Jeffrey Hay is a senior partner, Global Affairs Research Partners.

David M. Malone is president of the International Peace Academy, New York, and former Director-General of the Global and Human Issues Bureau, Department of Foreign Affairs and International Trade.

Christopher Maule is a distinguished research professor in the Department of Economics and in The Norman Paterson School of International Affairs, Carleton University.

Ernie Regehr is director of Project Ploughshares at the Institute of Peace and Conflict Studies, Conrad Grebel College.

Dane Rowlands is an assistant professor in The Norman Paterson School of International Affairs, Carleton University.

Martin Rudner is a professor and Director of The Norman Paterson School of International Affairs, Carleton University.

Pierre Sauvé is an adjunct lecturer at the John F. Kennedy School of Government, Harvard University, and a non-resident senior fellow at the Brookings Institution, Washington.

Grace Skogstad is a professor in the Department of Political Science, University of Toronto.

J. Christopher Thomas is a senior partner of Thomas & Davis, Vancouver/Ottawa.

ABBREVIATIONS

AAFC	Agriculture and Agri-Food Canada
ACCC	Association of Canadian Community Colleges
APEC	Asia-Pacific Economic Co-operation
AUCC	Association of Universities and Colleges
Cancon	Canadian content
CAP	Common Agricultural Policy (EU)
CBC	Canadian Broadcasting Corporation
CBIE	Canadian Bureau of International Education
CCFPD	Canadian Centre for Foreign Policy Development
CIC	Citizenship and Immigration Canada
CICAD	Inter-American Drug Abuse Control Commission
CIDA	Canadian International Development Agency
CIIA	Canadian Institute of International Affairs
CMAG	Commonwealth Ministerial Action Group
CRTC	Canadian Radio-television and Telecommunications Commission
CTBT	Comprehensive Test Ban Treaty
CYAP	Canada's Year of Asia Pacific
DFAIT	Department of Foreign Affairs and International Trade
DSB	Dispute Settlement Body (WTO)
EC	European Community
ECOSOC	United Nations Economic and Social Council
EPG	Eminent Persons Group
EU	European Union
FAIR	Federal Agriculture Improvement and Reform Act (US)
FIPA	foreign investment protection agreement
FIRA	Foreign Investment Review Agency
FRELIMO	Mozambique Liberation Front
FSO	foreign service officer
FTA	Canada-US Free Trade Agreement
FTAA	Free Trade Agreement of the Americas
GATS	General Agreement on Trade in Services
GATT	General Agreement on Tariffs and Trade
GDP	gross domestic product
HIPC	highly indebted poor countries
HRDC	Human Resources Development Canada
IANSA	International NGO Action Network on Small Arms
IMF	International Monetary Fund

IFOR	UN Implementation Force (in former Yugoslavia)
MAI	Multilateral Agreement on Investment
MFN	most-favoured nation
MNE	multinational enterprise
NAB	New Arrangements to Borrow
NAFTA	North American Free Trade Agreement
NATO	North Atlantic Treaty Organization
NPT	Non-Proliferation Treaty
NG	Negotiating Group (MAI)
NGO	non-governmental organization
NORAD	North American Aerospace Defence Command
NTI	National Treatment Instrument
OAS	Organization of American States
OCHA	Office for the Co-ordination of Humanitarian Affairs (UN)
ODA	official development assistance
OECD	Organization for Economic Co-operation and Development
OSCE	Organization for Security and Co-operation in Europe
POP	persistent organic pollutant
REIO	regional economic integration organizations
SADF	South African Defence Force
SAGIT	Sectoral Advisory Group on International Trade
SDR	Special Drawing Rights
SPLA	Sudan Peoples Liberation Army
SPS	Sanitary and Phytosanitary Measures Agreement
SWAPO	South West African People's Organization
TRIMs	Trade-Related Investment Measures
UN	United Nations
UNDC	United Nations Disarmament Commission
UNEP	United Nations Environment Program
UNESCO	United Nations Educational, Scientific, and Cultural Organization
UNGASS	UN General Assembly Special Session on the World Drug Problem
UNHCR	United Nations High Commission for Refugees
UNPROFOR	United Nations Protection Force (in former Yugoslavia)
WEOG	Western Europe and Other Group (UN Security Council)
WTO	World Trade Organization
WUSC	World University Service Canada
YES	Youth Employment Strategy

Preface

The 1999 volume of *Canada Among Nations*, entitled *A Big League Player?*, is the fifteenth in this annual series produced by The Norman Paterson School of International Affairs, Carleton University.

The coming of the millennium provides a convenient occasion to review Canada's performance in key areas of international relations and to contemplate future challenges to which Canadian foreign policy will be called upon to respond. Canada is distinct in its international persona—a member of the G–7, a recently re-elected non-permanent member of the United Nations Security Council, an actively engaged member of international alliances and multilateral organizations, and yet a relatively small-population country with an open, vulnerable economy. If Canada's international interests and objectives tend to range globally, its capabilities are rather more limited. Canadian foreign policy must deal with the profound challenges of a small, enthusiastic player playing in the biggest of the big leagues.

This tension between Canadian foreign policy goals and capabilities is, arguably, most readily apparent in the three issue-areas of human security, economic security, and cultural diplomacy that represent the subject matter of this book. Canada's promotion of human security, which became the defining theme of Canada's presidency of the Security Council during February 1999, will have the formidable task of responding to a complex world of subnational conflict, unstable states, and nuclear proliferation. Canadian concern for economic security will have to address the very difficult trade and investment policy questions on the agenda for the forthcoming round of multilateral trade negotiations. Cultural diplomacy remains a weak 'third pillar' of the Liberal government's foreign policy, but may command increasing policy attention in order to resolve the ongoing Canadian quandaries regarding such key issues as international education and cultural industrial policy.

An analysis of these issues can present significant lessons learned from Canadian foreign policy experience while also having important bearing on the future conduct of Canada's international affairs.

We gratefully acknowledge the generous support of the Donner Canadian Foundation, which enabled an editorial workshop to take place at which contributing authors came together for a detailed discussion of the policy issues and analytical approaches at stake.

We are also grateful for the continued support of The Norman Paterson School of International Affairs for this endeavour. This annual initiative involves a number of people whose efforts should be acknowledged. Brenda Sutherland was responsible again this year for the supervision and inputting of the initial text with her usual care and flair. Janet Doherty organized the editorial workshop and administered the book project. Susan Johnston and Greg Maruszecka provided research assistance to the editors, prepared the list of abbreviations, and assisted with the editing. We are grateful to Richard Kitowski and his staff at Oxford University Press for their editorial support and involvement in the production process.

It has been a pleasure and a privilege for all three editors to work together, and with our contributing authors and editorial support people, on this 1999 volume of *Canada Among Nations*. We hope that *A Big League Player?* will play its part in informing Canadians and providing ideas to policy-makers as they grapple with resolving the tensions in Canada's approach to these salient issues of international concern.

Fen Osler Hampson
Michael Hart
Martin Rudner

Ottawa, March 1999

1

A Big League or Minor League Player?

FEN OSLER HAMPSON, MICHAEL HART,
AND MARTIN RUDNER

Several years ago it looked as if Canada had no foreign policy focus other than on trade promotion. Critics chastised the Chrétien government for having an overly narrow view of Canadian national interests and for paying scant attention to human rights when doing business abroad with questionable regimes through the highly publicized and much-touted Team Canada missions. Now the pendulum appears to have swung the other way. With the growing prominence of Foreign Minister Lloyd Axworthy's 'human security' agenda following the successful conclusion of the Anti-Personnel Landmines Treaty campaign, critics argue that the national interest is being suffocated by 'soft power' and humanitarian crusades that are antagonizing many of Canada's allies, most notably the United States.

As the essays in this fifteenth volume in the *Canada Among Nations* series emphasize, trade policy remains the locus of Canadian foreign policy as a new set of pressing issues looms large on the multilateral trade agenda. Given the central importance of trade promotion to Canada's national interests, much of the responsibility for the management of Canada's international trade relations and linkages continues to lie where it has for the past two decades—with the Prime Minister's Office. But we find that political leadership on trade policy is lacking at a time when Canada wants to play in the big leagues.

Foreign Minister Axworthy's vaunted human security agenda grabs most of the headlines and public attention these days both at home and abroad. But the 'human security' slogan invoked by the minister in his after-dinner speeches has evolved into a series of somewhat more substantial—if none the less still controversial—policy initiatives and undertakings. Although Axworthy's agenda remains a work-in-progress whose foundations still lie in his exhortations from the 'pulpit', it has generated sufficient bureaucratic and political momentum that its impact on Canadian foreign policy is growing, as is the attention it is gathering abroad.

What are the key elements of the 'Axworthy doctrine', as it has been called by some? What are the new issues and choices that confront Canadian policy-makers on trade policy, investment, and international finance? Where does cultural policy fit into the rubric of 'soft power' and the projection of Canadian national interests and values abroad? These are the questions that are considered here.

The volume is organized thematically across these three themes. The essays in Part One deal with the trade and investment agenda of Canadian foreign policy, particularly as they pertain to Canada's economic security and participation and involvement in multilateral economic institutions. The essays in Part Two address what is surely the weakest—if not tottering—pillar of Canadian foreign policy, namely, that of culture, academic relations, and the projection of Canadian 'values' as distinct from 'interests' abroad. The essays in Part Three focus on the meaning and content of Foreign Minister Axworthy's human security agenda and how DFAIT (Department of Foreign Affairs and International Trade) has organized itself to deal with the panoply of issues that fall somewhat untidily under the human security label. The discussion that follows in this chapter is

intended to introduce the reader to some of the main themes and
issues covered by this volume.

PURSUING ECONOMIC SECURITY

In 1998 some Canadians celebrated and others lamented the tenth
anniversary of the Canada-United States Free Trade Agreement
(FTA) and the fifth anniversary of the North American Free Trade
Agreement (NAFTA). Whether celebrating or lamenting, Canadians
had become increasingly aware of the large role external trade and
investment flows had come to play in their lives. Ministers have
always been quick to claim Canada's role as a 'trading' nation, but
only in the last decade has the full import of this phrase become
apparent to most Canadians. During this decade, as the Cold War
underpinnings of postwar foreign policy steadily waned, the trade
and economic basis of our relations with the rest of the world waxed.

The Liberals, while initially strongly opposed to the FTA and NAFTA
before coming to power, were not shy about claiming their benefits
and pursuing their opportunities. More than any other Prime Minister
in modern times, Jean Chrétien has made Canada's trade welfare a
central element of his foreign policy, personally leading major 'Team
Canada' missions and using every occasion to advance Canada's trade
profile. Unlike many of his predecessors, he was content to let his
Foreign Minister dominate the traditional foreign policy agenda while
he devoted his energy to the economic agenda. By 1998, however,
the political and commercial pay-offs from Team Canada missions
had become less apparent while policy decisions about Canada's role
in the further evolution of the global economy and its governing
institutions had become more demanding. Neither the Prime Minister
nor the key international players in his cabinet seemed wholly comfortable with this dimension of the foreign policy agenda. Chrétien
decided to give the fiftieth anniversary celebration of the multilateral
trading system in Geneva in May 1998 a miss. Attended by world
leaders from Bill Clinton and Tony Blair to Nelson Mandela and Fidel
Castro, Canada was content to be represented by its Trade Minister.

Consciously or unconsciously, the Prime Minister was wrestling
with the new reality of post-Cold War international relations. The
'high' politics of military security that had long held pride of place
as the foundation of interstate relations was beginning to be crowded

by the 'low' politics of economic security. The inexorable march towards a more integrated global economy was creating both headaches and opportunities that leaders were reluctant to delegate to their subordinates. They were beginning to appreciate that a global economy needed global governance. Institutions and procedures that had been sufficient in the 1960s seemed to be strained to the breaking-point, even those that had been considerably beefed up in the 1980s and early 1990s.

Canada's experience over the past 15 years in negotiating and implementing new international rules has been generally satisfactory and positive, but it has required some painful adjustments. It has also raised strident opposition from ultra-nationalists and other groups. The risk-averse government of Jean Chrétien, therefore, has tended to be reluctant to go further. Although ready to negotiate free trade agreements with marginal trading partners such as Chile and the remaining members of the European Free Trade Association, it has been less prepared to exercise leadership in more challenging areas. Its reticence about the ill-conceived OECD (Organization for Economic Co-operation and Development) Multilateral Agreement on Investment (MAI) was understandable. As Bill Dymond explains in Chapter 2, the MAI had few friends and many enemies and might have fared better had it been pursued within the World Trade Organization (WTO) as part of a larger agenda.

Although perhaps unimportant in its own right, the MAI contributed to weakening ministerial willingness to pursue difficult policy choices. At the WTO's second ministerial meeting in May 1998, for example, Trade Minister Sergio Marchi advanced the notion of 'cluster' or 'mini' negotiations limited to only one or two issues, fearing that larger negotiations might expose Canada to politically difficult choices. For the rest of the year, as the MAI floundered, Canada concentrated its resources in the relatively safe preparatory work for the Free Trade for the Americas initiative, the quixotic pursuit of free trade around the Pacific through the Asia-Pacific Economic Co-operation conference, and a perpetual transatlantic dialogue. Missing was a clear commitment to a new round of multilateral negotiations and a willingness to explore the challenges posed by deepening global integration.

At the WTO's third ministerial meeting in Seattle at the end of November 1999, ministers are likely to launch a new, full-fledged round of negotiations. Canada remains tentative in its approach, waiting to see if anything threatening may emerge, rather than considering Canadian objectives that could be realized with early, creative initiatives. During the Uruguay Round of multilateral negotiations, Canada distinguished itself by the boldness of its vision and the determination and skill of its coalition-building leadership. There was little evidence of this in 1998. The wind seemed to have gone out of Canada's trade policy sails. Certainly, Canada's vaunted leadership position in Geneva seemed to be waning.

The tougher rules and more reliable dispute settlement procedures of the WTO seem also to have made life more difficult for the Chrétien government. After a number of important victories vindicating Canada's championing of strong dispute settlement provisions, Canada suffered some reverses, particularly on the split-run magazine issue, which exposed some chinks in Canada's arsenal of cultural protection programs. Other disputed issues on the horizon for decision in 1999, including the provision of subsidies to the aerospace sector, seem further destined to make the trade file more controversial.

One of the issues that appears to both inspire and spook Canada's political leadership is the claim to be heard by so-called civil society groups. Negotiations used to be matters of primary interest to export-oriented and import-competing industries. The political key to success lay in finding a balance between these two groups. Now virtually all business interests are committed to liberal, rules-based trade around the world. Opposition to trade negotiations now comes from a much wider spectrum of voices, claiming that liberalization threatens other societal values or should be harnessed to achieve non-trade objectives. This development has both positive and negative dimensions. These claims recognize the tremendous progress made in opening up markets, resolving disputes, and making markets more predictable and stable. For some, the very success of the trade regime suggests that there may now be sufficient room to ensure that the equity side of governance gains greater recognition in international trade negotiations. For others, the values and foundational assumptions of the open, multilateral trading system are suspect. Governments have yet to work out a satisfactory approach to these complementary but profoundly different voices.

It is one thing to insist that governments should give greater weight to human, social, and environmental concerns in negotiating and implementing international economic agreements. It is quite another to reject such agreements and insist that trade liberalization and economic integration are responsible for addressing human, social, and environmental problems. From one perspective, there is scope for consultation and for finding mutually acceptable solutions; from the other, there is only scope for a dialogue of the deaf. The current government has shown ambivalence about where it stands. Until it decides, leadership on the emerging agenda of trade and economic issues, many of which reach deep into national economic life, will continue to be difficult.

The stresses and strains of globalization and governance were evident on a number of fronts during 1998. Dane Rowlands, in Chapter 6, illustrates the extent to which the combined impact of globalization and more liberal world capital markets can affect the Canadian economy and limit the choices available to Canadian policy-makers. He identifies three specific issues raised over the past year as Canada weathered the effects of the Asian financial crisis:

- the extent to which offshore trade and investment developments can affect Canadian currency values and policy efforts to support those values;
- the need to come to terms with the costs and benefits of an open global economy and liberal capital markets; and
- a greater need to find a balance between Canada's domestic and international economic objectives.

Canada's relatively small, open economy is more vulnerable to global economic turmoil than larger economies and the Asian financial crisis brought this home to policy-makers to a greater extent than ever before. What happens abroad matters to Canada. The Asian crisis, by undermining investor confidence and by reducing demand for commodities, helped to put downward pressure on the value of the Canadian dollar, which in turn led to a range of unanticipated domestic and international results. Rowlands indicates that while it is conventional to look to domestic and US factors to explain Canadian economic developments and policy choices, the past year underlined the extent to which non-US foreign developments impacted on the performance of the Canadian economy. They can also affect the choices available to Canadian policy-makers in setting interest rates or determining budget priorities.

Canada has traditionally considered itself a leader in pushing for institutional reform at the multilateral level and for greater certainty and stability in the operation of the international trade and payments system, but the Asian crisis made Canada more hesitant and less certain in its approach. Rowlands argues that Canada's enthusiasm for liberal capital markets may have been tempered somewhat by the experience of the past year. Officials in the Department of Finance appear more willing to see an increase in the international supervision of the financial system, if only to dampen the turmoil flowing from crises such as the one triggered by the fall in Asian currency values. They have become interested in establishing mechanisms that would allow international and national authorities alike to anticipate such crises and take steps to calm markets more quickly.

If Rowlands chronicles a relatively successful response to international crisis, Bill Dymond, in Chapter 2, tells a quite different story of the interaction between international and domestic forces. Dymond had the unenviable task of leading Canada's team at the OECD negotiations to forge a Multilateral Agreement on Investment— the ill-fated MAI. He candidly observes that Canada was never convinced that the OECD was the best place to pursue this goal, but Canada could ill afford to absent itself from such a politically important negotiation. Ultimately, the venture proved to be as ill conceived and ill pursued as Canadian officials had feared. Not surprisingly, it failed. Many have attributed this failure to the stalwart opposition of civil society groups. Dymond demonstrates quite convincingly that, while such groups certainly added a new and not always welcome dimension to the negotiations, the reasons for failure were both more complex and related to internal opposition. The absence of a clear reason for strengthening investment rules among OECD members, leading to lukewarm business support, as well as turf considerations within some of the delegations, were more pertinent in dooming the negotiations from the start. While few tears will be shed over the MAI, the failed OECD negotiations do leave a bitter legacy for future negotiations at a more appropriate forum, such as the WTO.

If civil society groups do not deserve either opprobrium or applause for the demise of the MAI, their ubiquitous presence throughout the negotiations did raise challenges for governments and officials charged with negotiating international agreements. Dymond, relying on his experience as MAI negotiator and as a veteran of more than 30 years as a trade official, offers some advice on what governments need to do to accommodate the more moderate voices among these groups. The Canadian government must be ready and willing to sit down and listen to any group in Canadian society. It must also be prepared, within limits, to address their concerns and criticisms. It is very difficult for any government to respond to critics who reject the benefit for Canada of co-operative action among nations within the framework of international law and institutions.

As a relatively small, open economy, Canada can try to help shape the evolution of the global trade and payments regime, but it can neither dictate the final product nor afford to absent itself from the results. The record clearly demonstrates that Canada has been relatively influential in determining the contours of the current system and has also been one of the major beneficiaries of that system. Canada's ability to influence future negotiations will require that Canada, more than ever before, come to the table with ideas that have been fully thought through and represent a broad consensus within the country. That challenge is becoming more difficult.

In Chapter 4, Grace Skogstad indicates that even when there is broad support for international agreements, it is difficult to find the narrow zone of agreement acceptable to all participating governments. More than any other sector of the economy, the agriculture community—government and private sector alike—is already gearing up for the next round of negotiations. Implementation of its Uruguay Round commitments proved to be less problematic for Canada than some had feared, in part because Canada had already made a head start for domestic policy reasons at rolling back income and price support programs. Indeed, fiscal reality forced Canada to go well beyond its Uruguay Round commitments. Canada is thus well placed to pursue further reforms and, having moved beyond quota-based supply management, can concentrate on trading better access for its export sector for gradual increases in import exposure for other sectors.

The economic analysis is clear; the problem is political. The challenge remains to pursue Canada's agricultural trade interests by finding middle ground between the import-sensitive supply management sectors and the export-oriented grains and red meat sectors. Skogstad estimates that Canada will continue to be a strong supporter of rules-based systems and will support efforts to strengthen rules about the use and abuse of sanitary and phytosanitary measures, subsidies, trade remedies, and more, but it will also remain cautious about the pace and extent of liberalization. Canada has little left to give in opening its market for non-sensitive sectors and is reluctant to move too quickly to open up its market for sensitive sectors.

Skogstad concludes by suggesting that while Canadian farmers as a whole have become more dependent on market-based outcomes, domestically and internationally, they also have modest expectations of limited reform and consolidation in the next round. Reflecting these ambiguities, Canada will support continued movement in the direction set by the Uruguay Round, but will be reluctant to exercise any leadership.

Whichever way the next round of agricultural negotiations conclude, they will need a large dose of help from the WTO's dispute settlement provisions. To date, some of the most difficult issues these procedures have had to address have arisen in the agricultural area, many involving Canada as a complaining party, a respondent, or an interested third party. As Heather Forton traces in Chapter 3, the success of the WTO in its first four years is not unrelated to the success of the dispute settlement process. Between 1 January 1995 and 31 December 1998, members of the WTO invoked the dispute settlement provisions 155 times on 118 distinct matters. Canada was involved in 22 cases as either a complainant or respondent and in many more as a third party. The process has given members a unique new confidence in the efficacy of the rule of law, a confidence that has been evident both in the implementation of the more than 20 agreements administered by the WTO and in the willingness of members to enter into further negotiations to deepen and extend the rules and procedures.

Forton, who was directly involved in the implementation of the dispute settlement process from her vantage point as the legal affairs officer in the Canadian Permanent Mission to the WTO in Geneva, explains not only the extent to which the system has worked, but also the extent to which it has experienced growing pains and will need some adjustment. It needs both to accommodate the heavy demand placed on its limited resources and to work out some of the quirks and shortcomings experience has brought to light. At the same time, she cautions against being too quick to make changes. Members have made a major commitment to make the system work; as a result, the need for changes are likely to be addressed 'patiently, thoughtfully, cautiously, and incrementally'. Of course, should the next round result in major new commitments that both deepen and extend the WTO's scope, the need for changes may become more pressing.

The kinds of new commitments that might lead to expansion and strengthening of the dispute settlement provisions are discussed by Chris Thomas and Pierre Sauvé in Chapter 5. In their view, trade, investment, and competition policies should be approached in a coherent and integrated manner to achieve the international 'contestability' of markets. This concept represents an important qualitative deepening in the nature and degree of liberalization, a deepening whose foundations may be laid during the next round of negotiations. Their paper explores some of the forces that underpin the concept of contestability, highlights the possible architectural or rule-design implications of anchoring competition values and principles within the multilateral trading system, and reflects on a number of political economy considerations that a competition-oriented trade agenda might generate.

They make the point that despite 50 years of steady trade liberalization and deepening integration, the assertion of jurisdiction by national customs authorities has hardly diminished. Tariffs, for example, may decline to zero under a trade agreement, but customs authorities then busy themselves monitoring compliance with rules of origin. Producers are better able to organize complex streams of input and achieve greater economies of scale in free trade areas, but many trade barriers and differences in national law enforcement persist. Thomas and Sauvé compare trade negotiations to the process of peeling an onion. The removal of one layer of barriers and distortions reveals another. In addition, due to rapid change in the way corporations do business internationally, multilateral trade negotiations play 'catch up' to the changes being wrought by economic actors.

They further caution that the legal and policy issues raised by deeper integration are complex. Trade and investment agreements tend to be drafted in general terms and lack the specificity of domestic legislation and regulations. As a matter of general principle, international law imposes the obligation upon states to take only such action as is necessary to ensure that effect is given to the international obligations they have undertaken. Substantial differences in national legal systems, legislative practice, administrative law, and constitutional frameworks, let alone political, socio-economic, developmental, and other factors, inevitably lead to differences in how broadly drafted international agreements are implemented in national laws.

In their view, these developments suggest that it is timely to consider whether greater governance at the international level is feasible
and desirable. One reason for doing so is the desirability of promoting as much coherence as possible between domestic and multilateral policy objectives. Indeed, the increasing emphasis on
market-based approaches and competition values at the domestic
level would appear to be equally desirable at the international level.
Moreover, the lack of—or constraints on—market competition has
the potential to create significant international friction and national
competition law may not always effectively reach transnational anti-
competitive practices, or may consider some of the market access
issues in a different light, emphasizing domestic over global welfare
considerations. The objective of preserving competition in the global
marketplace may not be achievable with reliance solely on the operation of national competition policy regimes. It may need to be more
firmly rooted in the multilateral trading system.

The 'contestability' agenda gives rise to a series of discrete, albeit
interrelated, policy challenges:

- how to raise the prominence of competition values and principles in the design and operation of the multilateral trading
  system;
- how to strengthen the multilateral trading system through the
  development of a comprehensive set of investment protection
  and liberalization disciplines;
- how to address public policies and government actions that
  affect or distort the conduct of international business and, in
  particular, those competition-restricting measures that arise
  from the domestic regulatory conduct of nations;
- how to deal with private practices and market structures having the same effect;
- how best to strengthen public support for, and enhance confidence in the benefits from, an open, competition-oriented, and
  rules-based trading system.

The focus of their paper is global, but it is of great significance
for Canada to delineate the direction for changes in the rules and the
prospect for further negotiations between Canada and the United
States. For example, the potential for a customs union between
Canada and the United States is largely a matter of determining

whether Canada wants to move forward on the contestability agenda on a bilateral basis, both to pursue Canadian objectives and to build experience for possible wider application in the future.

The ideas advanced by Thomas and Sauvé will not necessarily inform, let alone dominate, negotiations during the next round of multilateral negotiations. Rather, they will bear fruit over a longer period of time and probably only after a period of experimentation at the regional and plurilateral level. Nevertheless, it is important for Canadians to get their minds around these issues as they prepare for and participate in the next round of multilateral negotiations and think through how best to advance the Canada-US negotiating agenda.

Whatever direction the next round of multilateral negotiations should take, Canada seems uncharacteristically unprepared to participate. With the notable exception of the agriculture file, Canadian officials seem to have sharpened their regional negotiating skills while ignoring the multilateral dimension. As the United States and Europe prepare to test the waters for widening and deepening the ambit of the WTO, the governing Liberals in Ottawa seem to have developed an appetite for the very emphasis they found most objectionable a decade ago. While this may not be a new development, it is a direction that seems at odds with the government's stated policy preferences of only a few years earlier. Rather than leading, the government seems to be following the beat of an earlier drummer.

PROJECTING CANADIAN VALUES AND IDENTITY ABROAD

In Chapter 7, on the 'third pillar' of Canadian foreign policy, John Graham reviews the ebb and flow of Canada's experiences in international cultural diplomacy. Designated as one of the three goals of Canadian foreign policy under the current Liberal government's foreign policy framework, *Canada in the World*, the projection of Canadian values abroad was defined as encompassing cultural products and international education as well as such normative elements as democracy and human rights. Earlier initiatives, in particular those relating to promoting Canadian higher education internationally, came up against policy indifference in DFAIT and resource constraints in government generally. Because the constitution assigned culture and education to provincial jurisdiction, the federal government had no particular departmental commitment to these policy domains.

Canada is one of the few countries in the world without a national education department, so that the federal government's involvement in international educational and cultural affairs remains fragmented and divided among a host of departments, agencies, and programs.

Whereas the renewed emphasis on cultural diplomacy appears to signal a revitalized, more ambitious approach to international education, until now this area has suffered from fiscal and bureaucratic neglect. While the federal and provincial governments dithered, Canada lagged further behind in the global competition for market share in the emergent trade in knowledge-sector services.

More recent organizational initiatives, both in DFAIT and among non-governmental educational organizations, point to an enhanced awareness of the opportunity costs to Canada of its deteriorating competitive advantage in international education. Deepening concern over Canada's lagging international performance at the ministerial and bureaucratic levels, and in the educational community, prompted an attempt to define a national strategy for promoting Canadian 'exports' of higher educational services. John Graham expresses concern about the sustainability of this renewed momentum, and proposes organizational alternatives both outside and inside the Department of Foreign Affairs and International Trade to administer the implementation of Canada's international cultural and educational programs.

Christopher Maule and Keith Acheson, in Chapter 8, consider Canada's trade policies in the cultural domain. Their discussion bridges two of the so-called 'pillars' of the contemporary Canadian foreign policy framework—trade promotion and cultural diplomacy, or the projection of Canada's culture abroad. Up to the present, Canadian policy regarding the cultural industries has tended to be highly protectionist in an effort to encourage Canadian ownership and enhance Canadian content. This protectionist impulse emanates from the Department of Heritage Canada. It reflects a tradition of cultural nationalism coupled with, and reinforcing, the vested interests of certain elements in the cultural industries concerned. Not all of Canada's cultural industries are dependent on protection; indeed, Canadian talent and cultural enterprise have succeeded in attaining an important and prominent presence internationally. It is paradoxical that some of those advocating cultural protectionism are firms that actually are also involved in the import of cultural products, and thus manipulating trade restrictions to their own commercial advantage.

The arguments for cultural protection, which are examined in detail, are seen to emphasize the relatively small size of the Canadian market, the narrow scope for distinctive Canadian content, and the high degree of import penetration already attained in the various media. When subjected to empirical analysis, however, most of these claims are demonstrated to be spurious or overstated. The authors then consider the arguments in favour of a more open approach to trade in cultural products, based on the demonstrated competitive advantages of Canadian cultural industries. A survey of recent international trade disputes involving cultural products would seem to indicate that domestic Canadian protectionism may place in jeopardy the successful extension of Canadian talent and cultural enterprise to international markets.

PURSUING HUMAN SECURITY

A careful reading of the human security agenda suggests that some of its key thematic elements are also not all that new. During the prime ministership of Brian Mulroney, Canada was actively committed to the promotion of human rights abroad. Canada, after all, took the lead in establishing an activist stance against the apartheid regime in South Africa. At the 1985 Commonwealth Heads of Government Meeting in Harare the establishment of an Eminent Persons Group (EPG) was a Canadian-led initiative. When the EPG mission failed, Canada was quick to implement sanctions. At the 1987 Commonwealth meeting in Vancouver, it was again Mulroney himself who stood up to Britain's Margaret Thatcher on the issue of sanctions (Brown, 1990). The Progressive Conservative leader also played a key role in focusing global attention to the emerging issues of environmental security and sustainable development at the 1992 Rio Conference on the Environment and Sustainable Development. By resisting US pressure, Canada was able to save the biodiversity treaty, one of the key achievements of the conference (Runnalls, 1993). Likewise, Mulroney's Foreign Minister, Barbara McDougall, took the lead in Organization of American States (OAS) efforts to restore democracy in Haiti following the military coup led by General Raoul Cedras (McDougall, 1999). These and other initiatives bore the hallmark of 'human security' in all but name.

Within DFAIT, major bureaucratic reforms were introduced by Gordon Smith, the former deputy minister, which led to the establishment of a bureau for global issues that has helped implement Axworthy's human security agenda. As David Malone writes in Chapter 10, this internal bureaucratic reorganization took place under Axworthy's predecessor, André Ouellet, but reflected a growing awareness within senior ranks of the bureaucracy about the importance of a whole new set of functional issue-areas—human rights, rule of law, peacebuilding, terrorism, drugs, and governance—that were not easily addressed by existing departmental structures. These new structures have proven to be critical to the implementation of Foreign Minister Axworthy's human security agenda.

Since his major 1997 address on the subject, Axworthy's human security approach has evolved and developed along three somewhat unique and distinct tracks. They include the following elements, which are discussed at greater length below: (1) initiatives to focus international attention on direct threats to individuals, such as the campaign to ban anti-personnel landmines or to curb the production and sales of small arms and light weapons; (2) focused activities such as the Canadian Peacebuilding Initiative, the creation of an International Criminal Court, and the integration of human security concerns in the work of the international and regional organizations; and (3) innovative partnerships with like-minded countries and civil society (DFAIT, 1999e).

Initiatives to Focus Attention on Direct Threats to Individuals

As a follow-up to the Anti-Personnel Mines Ban Convention signed by 122 countries on 3–4 December 1997, Canada created a five-year, $100 million fund to support the full implementation of the Convention. In addition, on 21 September 1998, Axworthy launched the Mine Action Outreach Program, in co-operation with Mines Action Canada and the Red Cross. Mines Action Canada received $300,000 to help sustain its activities in the campaign to ban anti-personnel landmines. Six youth mine action ambassadors were also appointed to work with local mine action groups to broaden public awareness of the issue (DFAIT, 1998l).

A number of specific initiatives also were important to the anti-personnel landmines campaign. In the aftermath of Hurricane Mitch, which through mudslides and flooding displaced anti-personnel landmines into previously cleared areas, Canada announced that it would contribute funds to support an assessment mission of the OAS to evaluate the effects of Hurricane Mitch on existing mine action programs.

Another $3.6 million are to be allocated over five years to support various community-based rehabilitation programs in Nicaragua, El Salvador, Guatemala, and Honduras. Canada also announced a $1 million contribution to the International Trust Fund for Demining and for the Assistance of Mine Victims in Bosnia and Herzegovina by the government of Slovenia (DFAIT, 1998h).

The issue of light arms and how Canada is dealing with this highly complex issue is the subject of Chapter 13. Ernie Regehr argues that Axworthy's December 1997 public expression of interest in the issue 'did not represent the introduction of the small arms issue to the Department of Foreign Affairs and International Trade.' In fact, Canada had already participated in a UN panel exploring ways in which UN peacekeeping missions could become more effective in post-conflict disarmament and weapons collection in war-torn societies. Since 1995 Canada was also in the process of changing its internal gun control laws, which included preventing civilian access to any military-style weapons as well as a comprehensive registration system. Some of these ideas were already being carried into international discussions by DFAIT, with the assistance of the Department of Justice.

However, the success of the landmines campaign gave new energy to small arms control efforts. As Regehr notes, '[s]hortly after the landmines conference, in early 1998, Canada co-sponsored resolutions in the Commission on Crime Prevention and Criminal Justice and the Economic and Social Council (ECOSOC) calling on states to work towards the elaboration of an international instrument to combat the illicit manufacturing of and trafficking in firearms, their parts and components, and ammunition within the context of a United Nations convention against transnational organized crime.' Duplicating the success of the landmines campaign and subsequent treaty will not be easy, though. Regehr argues that as yet there is no international consensus on what an effective, global small arms campaign might best focus on. Furthermore, because of the complex set of interlocking interests and motives involved in curbing the sale and international flow of light arms and weaponry, achieving such a consensus will be an uphill battle.

Another noteworthy group of initiatives undertaken by the government concerns the plight of children in situations of armed conflict. These are described at greater length by Robin Hay in Chapter 11. But it is worth noting that Canada has already pledged $400,000 to the trust fund established to support the work of the Olara Otunnu, special representative of the UN Secretary-General for Children and Armed Conflict. Canada is also seeking ways to ensure that the plight of children is addressed in such fora as the OAS and the OSCE. To spur greater domestic attention to this problem, the minister supported the creation of a joint Committee on War-Affected Children, which has brought together non-governmental organizations (NGOs) and government officials to work on the issue. Canada also strongly supports the Optional Protocol to the Convention on the Rights of the Child, which would raise to 18 years old the age of recruitment and participation in hostilities. Canada was the first government to provide resources to the international NGO Coalition to Stop the Use of Child Soldiers. Canada supports inclusion of child protection specialists in UN peace-support operations and has also expressed support for the notion of rapid-response mediation teams to advocate on behalf of children in conflict zones (DFAIT, 1999d, 1999e).

The past 12 months have also seen greater attention being paid to the Western hemisphere dimensions of human security. Canada proposed the creation of a dialogue group of foreign ministers to study the impact of the drug trade on the human security agenda, including such issues as governance and rule of law, health, social development, environment, and cross-border conflict. The purpose of the group is to strengthen the political commitment to existing conventions, declarations, and the Hemispheric Drug Strategy. Canada also supports the efforts within the OAS to develop an Inter-American Declaration on the Rights of Indigenous People and appointed its first Counsellor for International Indigenous Issues (DFAIT, 1998c).

Axworthy's official visits to Cuba, Jamaica, Mexico, and Nicaragua in early January 1999 were directed at strengthening hemispheric co-operation on drug-trafficking, anti-personnel mines, and human rights (DFAIT, 1998j). He used his visit to Jamaica to announce his dialogue on illicit drugs and a meeting to be held later in the spring to bring together participants from the hemisphere to discuss drugs and human security. The dialogue would initially focus on the relationship between drugs and governance; small arms and firearms; development and trade; education and health; and public engagement (DFAIT, 1999a).

Even so, his long-term ambitions for the hemisphere in the realm of human security appear unlimited. In a speech he gave to the annual conference of the Canadian Institute of International Affairs in October 1998, Axworthy argued for an approach to human security on the continent that would not be just limited to trade and commerce. He called for broader co-operation and joint efforts on education and the development of human resources, the environment, and the movement of goods and peoples. To this end, Canada would support the creation of an Alliance on Higher Education and Enterprise in North America by the North American Institute. Axworthy also suggested that the concept of 'continental transport corridors' warranted 'serious investigation'. A '"Murmansk to Monterrey corridor" could enhance North America's global competitiveness' and serve as the 'lifelines of an emerging North American community', he said (DFAIT, 1998g).

Focused Activities

On 18 July 1998 Lloyd Axworthy signed the Statute establishing the framework for the International Criminal Court. The Court will be the first permanent international tribunal empowered to prosecute individuals accused of genocide, war crimes, crimes against humanity, and eventually crimes of aggression. The Statute was signed after five weeks of negotiations with a final vote of 120–7, with 21 countries abstaining. Canada played a leading role in the negotiations: chaired a group of like-minded states at a preparatory commission that worked for over two years on the framework legislation. Canada also provided assistance to some of the least-developed countries to allow them to participate in the preparatory meetings and subsequent negotiations. The ICC will eventually be presided over by 18 judges from 18 countries. It will have automatic jurisdiction over international crimes. States that ratify the Statute automatically accept the jurisdiction of the Court. An Independent Prosecutor is to be elected by secret ballot by those states that have ratified the Statute. Cases can also be brought before the Court by the UN Security Council and the Independent Prosecutor. As soon as 60 states ratify the Statute the Court will come into existence (DFAIT, 1998k: 1–2).

Canada also took the lead with Norway in developing a draft declaration on the right and responsibility of individuals, groups, and institutions to promote and protect universally recognized human rights and freedoms (otherwise known as the Declaration on Human Rights Defenders). The draft was approved at the 54th session of the UN Human Rights Commission. At the UN Commission on Human

Rights, Canada took the lead on more human rights resolutions than any other single country (DFAIT, 1998k: 2).

Innovative Partnerships

On 11 May 1998, Axworthy and the Foreign Minister of Norway, Knut Vollebaek, signed the Lysoen Declaration committing the two countries to a 'framework for consultation and concerted action in the areas of enhancing human security, strengthening humanitarian law, preventing conflict, and fostering democracy and good governance'. The agreed agenda for action covers issues such as landmines, the establishment of an International Criminal Court, human rights, international humanitarian law, women and children in armed conflict, small arms proliferation, child soldiers, child labour, and northern and Arctic co-operation. Under the framework for consultation and co-operation, there will be annual ministerial meetings to review progress and set priorities and bilateral teams to develop and implement joint ministerial initiatives (DFAIT, 1998a). Efforts are also under way to expand this bilateral undertaking by assembling a bigger multinational coalition committed to advancing the human security agenda—what has already been dubbed the Humanitarian 8—comprised of Canada, Norway, Switzerland, Austria, Chile, Thailand, South Africa, and Sweden (Spencer, 1999).

With its election, on the first ballot with 131 votes, to a Security Council seat on 8 October 1998 to serve along with the Netherlands as representatives of the Western Europe and Other Group (WEOG) for a two-year term, Canada re-entered the big league—at least as far as the key decision-making body of the United Nations is concerned. This was the sixth time Canada had been elected to serve on this high-level body and the minister wasted no time impressing on Canadians the importance of the result through his series of highly publicized public consultations managed by the Canadian Centre for Foreign Policy Development.

There is no doubt that we were off to a running start once we took our seat. The Security Council voted on 30 January 1999 to accept a Canadian proposal that would allow the Council to move forward on the issue of Iraq. The Security Council had been deadlocked over a French proposal calling for the removal of sanctions against Iraq following the December attack by British and American warplanes on Iraq. The Canadian proposal called for the establishment of three panels to assess key issues concerning Iraq and to provide recommendations to the Council. The first panel would assess the status of Iraq's compliance with the disarmament provisions of the UN Security Council. The second panel would assess the humanitarian situation in Iraq. The third would review the status of Iraq's compliance on the issues of missing POWs and Gulf War compensation (Milner, 1999).

Although the Security Council has traditionally been concerned with a rather narrow set of security concerns, Canada used its position as President of the Council in February 1999 to push for a broader security agenda that would embrace 'human security' considerations. Axworthy's address to the Security Council on 12 February 1999 called for a focus on the growing threats to human security, particularly those arising from the increased 'civilianization' of armed conflict. The minister reminded his colleagues that 80 per cent of casualties in armed conflict are civilians and that this problem must not be a sideshow for the Council. Specifically, he called on the Council to strengthen its role in the prevention of conflict through improved early warning, strengthened human rights institutions, renewed efforts to control the flow of arms, and 'having the capacity to act quickly' (DFAIT, 1999f).

In spite of Axworthy's obvious embrace and enthusiasm for the concept of 'soft power', events in the late spring of 1998 on the Indian subcontinent served as an all-too-brutal reminder of the continued value that some nations place on the hard power currency of nuclear weapons. As Louis Delvoie discusses in Chapter 12, Canada's response to Indian and Pakistan nuclear tests was to recall its High Commissioners, cancel CIDA consultations, ban military exports, oppose non-humanitarian multilateral aid, and stop non-humanitarian development assistance (DFAIT, 1998b). He characterizes this policy as one of 'cuts and condemnation'. The response might not have been the right one under the circumstances, as Delvoie notes, and Canada unfortunately chose to ignore the real 'soft power' lessons that emerged from the nuclear proliferation experiences (e.g., Ukraine, North Korea) of the 1980s, i.e., to engage the parties rather than isolating them.

The current crisis over Kosovo and the NATO response are subjects of major public concern and further demonstrate that 'soft power' or negotiations frequently have to be backed up by 'hard power', i.e., the threat or use of force. Canada announced last October that it would participate in NATO air operations against Yugoslavia, should they be necessary to end the conflict (DFAIT, 1998f). In late January 1999, the Prime Minister announced that Canada would also send ground troops to Kosovo if needed. This statement provoked a small firestorm of controversy about whether Canadian soldiers should be committed without formal parliamentary debate and the backing of the United Nations (Blanchfield and McCabe, 1999: A1).

The release of the House of Commons Standing Committee on Foreign Affairs and Trade Report on Canada and the Nuclear Challenge was not as controversial as some had anticipated because it stopped short of endorsing a no-first-use nuclear policy for NATO. The key recommendations call for substantive moves towards eventual disarmament, the de-alerting of all nuclear forces, an open debate on NATO's nuclear policy, aid to bolster the Russian missile early warning system, and increased transparency of nuclear weapons stockpiles, fissile materials, and doctrine (DFAIT, 1998i). Although the report was welcomed in some circles, it made official Washington cringe, fearful that Canadian support for a renewed debate about the role of nuclear weapons in the alliance would open Pandora's box. Such a debate, in Washington's eyes, would be counter-productive now, particularly since NATO is in the process of admitting new members and redefining its own strategic concept (Carnegie Endowment for International Peace, 1998: 2).

Canada was one of the first countries to ratify the Comprehensive Nuclear Test Ban Treaty, which it had signed on 24 September 1996, when it enacted the Comprehensive Nuclear Test Ban Treaty Implementation Act (DFAIT, 1998e). Canada abstained on a key vote in the UN on 13 November 1998 that called on nuclear weapons states 'to demonstrate an unequivocal commitment' to the elimination of nuclear weapons through negotiations and practical steps. The abstention marked a policy shift, as Canada had previously never opposed the US policy on nuclear weapons. Axworthy reportedly wanted Canada to vote on the affirmative side of the resolution to save the Nuclear Non-Proliferation Treaty, but heavy lobbying from the United States, the United Kingdom, and France prompted Canada to moderate its position (Roche, 1998: A21). As David Haglund argues in Chapter 9, in spite of the fact that Canada is still formally wedded to its transatlantic partnerships, its actions and growing ambivalence about NATO strategy are raising questions abroad about the depth of its commitment to the alliance. There are also brewing complications between Ottawa and Washington about the renewal of the North American Aerospace Defence Agreement, which expires in the year 2001, because the Americans are keen to develop ballistic missile defence technologies that, Ottawa fears, could undermine the existing Anti-Ballistic Missile Treaty (1972) and spur a new arms race (Sallot, 1999: A4).

What are we to make of Foreign Minister Axworthy's new human security agenda? It is clearly more than just a sideshow to what some regard as the 'core' issues of Canadian foreign policy—trade and economic security. But the moral content of this agenda strikes some as being removed from vital Canadian national interests, particularly when we set ourselves on a collision course with our major trading partner. Some commentators have uncharitably referred to Axworthy as a latter-day Howard Green—the self-righteous Secretary of State who served under Prime Minister John Diefenbaker (Martin, 1998: B5). Media baron Conrad Black, another outspoken critic, has accused the government of spreading 'clouds of humbug about soft power, which in practice almost always means the absence of any power at all' (Knox, 1999a: A14). In some respects, the most balanced assessment comes from the inventor of 'soft power' himself, Harvard's Joseph Nye, who points out that 'Canada has always been good at punching above its weight in world politics.' But, says Nye, 'to keep doing so in the global information age requires not just good ideas in speeches but also an extraordinary degree of political and diplomatic coordination.' Nye believes that Canada should also pay close attention to its 'hard-power resources' and not forget that there are other dimensions—including the military and the economic—to world politics (Nye, 1999: 30).

CONCLUSION

Playing in the big leagues at the close of the twentieth century is more than a matter of pursuing 'popular' human security issues. It also requires a willingness to take leadership roles in the definition and evolution of the broader foreign policy agenda, including in trade and the global eonomy. Exercising innovative leadership has the added bonus of providing Canada with a voice it would not otherwise enjoy. Followership, on the other hand, has the unpalatable result of becoming captive to the agenda of other players. As the MAI episode so well illustrates, Canada has little choice but to participate in the negotiation of major international economic agreements but has limited influence on the final outcome of those negotiations. What influence Canada has must be exercised early and must rely on superior preparation, far-sighted analysis, inspired ideas, and skilful coalition-building. The deployment of these traditional tools of Canadian 'statecraft' will be called upon in 1999 and beyond if Canada is to keep its big league status.

REFERENCES

Blanchfield, Mike, and Aileen McCabe. 1999. 'Chrétien offers troops to Kosovo', *Ottawa Citizen*, 30 Jan., A1.

Brown, Chris. 1990. 'Canada and Southern Africa: Autonomy, Image, and Capacity in Foreign Policy', in Maureen Appel Molot and Fen Osler Hampson, eds, *Canada Among Nations 1989: The Challenge of Change*. Ottawa: Carleton University Press, 207–24.

Carnegie Endowment for International Peace. 1998. 'Canada Aims to Shift Nuclear Policy', *Proliferation Brief* 1, 18 (16 Dec.).

Department of Foreign Affairs and International Trade (DFAIT). 1998a. 'Canada and Norway Form New Partnership on Human Security', Press Release No. 117, 11 May.

———. 1998b. 'Notes for a Statement by the Honourable Lloyd Axworthy, Minister of Foreign Affairs, to the Standing Committee on Foreign Affairs and International Trade, "India's Nuclear Testing: Implications for Nuclear Disarmament and the Nuclear Non-Proliferation Regime" ', Statement 98/40, 26 May.

———. 1998c. 'Notes for An Address by the Honourable Lloyd Axworthy, Minister of Foreign Affairs, to the 28th Session of the Organization of American States General Assembly', Statement 98/OAS, 1 June.

———. 1998d. 'Axworthy Launches Landmine Outreach Program', Press Release No. 217, 21 Sept.

———. 1998e. 'Canada to Implement Comprehensive Nuclear Test Ban Treaty', Press Release No. 219, 23 Sept.

———. 1998f. 'Canada to Participate in NATO Military Enforcement Action in Kosovo', Press Release No. 242, 12 Oct.

———. 1998g. 'Notes for an Address by the Honourable Lloyd Axworthy, Minister of Foreign Affairs, to the Canadian Institute of International Affairs 1998 Foreign Policy Conference', Statement 98/67, 16 Oct.

———. 1998h. 'Canada Announces $3.7 Million for Mine Action in Central America in Aftermath of Hurricane Mitch', Press Release No. 268, 20 Nov.

———. 1998i. 'Axworthy Welcomes Parliamentary Committee Report on Nuclear Policy', Press Release No. 291, 10 Dec.

———. 1998j. 'Axworthy to Visit the Caribbean and Latin America to Highlight Human Security Issues', Press Release No. 296, 23 Dec.

———. 1998k. 'The International Criminal Court Agreement bears strong Canadian imprint', *World View* No. 1.

———. 1998l. 'The Ottawa Convention and Public Participation', *World View* No. 1.

————. 1999a. 'Axworthy Launches Hemispheric Dialogue on Drugs During Visit to Jamaica', Press Release, 8 Jan.

————. 1999b. 'Axworthy Addresses National Forum on Canada's International Relations', Press Release No. 6, 22 Jan.

————. 1999c. 'Axworthy Announces $1 Million Toward Re-establishing Peace and Security in Sierra Leone', Press Release No. 14, 27 Jan.

————. 1999d. 'Axworthy Announces Initiatives Aimed at Protecting Children in Armed Conflict', Press Release No. 27, 12 Feb.

————. 1999e. 'Notes for an Address by the Honourable Lloyd Axworthy, Minister of Foreign Affairs, to the Conference at Columbia University on "The Protection of Children in Armed Conflict"', Statement 99/9, 12 Feb.

————. 1999f. 'Notes for an Address by the Honourable Lloyd Axworthy, Minister of Foreign Affairs, to the United Nations Security Council, "The Protection of Civilians in Armed Conflict"', Statement 99/8, 12 Feb.

Knox, Paul. 1999a. 'Black Savages Axworthy's "soft power"', *Globe and Mail*, 24 Feb.

————. 1999b. 'Prospects for UN-led peace missions darken', *Globe and Mail*, 23 Jan., A16.

Martin, Lawrence. 1998. 'Axworthy's policies are no easy sell', *Ottawa Citizen*, 21 Nov., A5.

McDougall, Barbara. 1999 'The OAS Intervention in Haiti', in Chester A. Crocker, Fen Osler Hampson, and Pamela R. Aall, eds, *Herding Cats: The Management of Complex International Mediation*. Washington: United States Institute of Peace Press.

Milner, Brian. 1999. 'Multiple agendas face Canada at UN', *Globe and Mail*, 3 Feb., A19.

Nye, Joseph S., Jr. 1999. 'The Challenge of Soft Power', *Time* 153, 7, (22 Feb.): 30.

Roche, Douglas. 1998. 'How Canada bucked the U.S. line on nuclear arms', *Globe and Mail*, 23 Nov., A21.

Runnalls, David. 1993. 'The Road from Rio', in Fen Osler Hampson and Christopher J. Maule, eds, *Global Jeopardy: Canada Among Nations, 1993–94*. Ottawa: Carleton University Press, 133–53.

Sallot, Jeff. 1999. 'Missile plan may complicate NORAD renewal', *Globe and Mail*, 26 Feb., A4.

Spencer, Christina. 1999. 'It's a new world or so Canada says', *Ottawa Citizen*, 25 Jan., A9.

2

The MAI: A Sad and Melancholy Tale

WILLIAM A. DYMOND

'This is a sad and melancholy tale', dictated Churchill to a new stenographer.
'Oh sir, I am so sorry', he said. 'Just take it down', growled Churchill.

Three years of negotiations to conclude the Multilateral Agreement on Investment (MAI) at the Organization for Economic Co-operation and Development (OECD) came to an ignominious end on 20 October 1998. This was the date scheduled for relaunching the negotiations following a six-month pause, but a few days before the meeting France formally withdrew from the negotiations. Without France, European Union (EU) member states would not continue the negotiations and, without the EU, there was no point in continuing. The negotiations were over. At a subsequent meeting on 3 December, US and OECD secretariat efforts to resuscitate the MAI were firmly rebuffed. What had begun with high optimism and an ambitious agenda in

1995 shuffled quietly off into a footnote of history, accompanied only by sighs of relief from beleaguered governments.

Some will argue that the failure of these negotiations marks the first successful revolt of civil society groups against the forces of globalization. Others will insist that an impasse on the essential negotiating issues accounts for the failure. Civil society opposition to the MAI was certainly a factor, but by any measure its penetration of public consciousness paled compared to the free trade debate in the 1980s. As for the impasse at the negotiating table, again the issues were for the most part neither new nor critical to the economic interests at stake. The reasons for failure must lie elsewhere. This paper will argue that the fundamental cause of failure lay in the attempt to negotiate an investment agreement among countries with well-established, liberal, and transparent foreign investment policies and the consequent choice of the OECD rather than the World Trade Organization (WTO) as the negotiating forum. OECD proponents argued with great conviction that OECD countries should have little difficulty in transcribing their current regimes into a high-quality agreement. Negotiating at the WTO, strongly promoted by Canada, would yield a low-quality agreement riddled with exceptions necessary to accommodate developing countries. Moreover, OECD countries, after four years of detailed preparatory work, were ready to proceed to negotiations. Since there was no consensus in the WTO to negotiate investment rules, many years might pass before a multilateral investment agreement would be signed, ratified, and implemented.

The OECD rationale contained a fatal weakness. OECD countries had few investment barriers whose removal was negotiable or worth the effort. The MAI would thus offer few new benefits to investors. In these circumstances, negotiators would come to the table determined to offer nothing beyond the maintenance of current regimes. Governments would be unable to demonstrate the economic benefits flowing from an MAI and would be deprived of a supportive constituency to combat the barrage of public criticism that, increasingly, attends most international trade and investment negotiations. Not surprisingly, faced with a sharply negative political gain/pain ratio, governments seized the opportunity to abandon the negotiations offered by French reluctance to resume the project.

This chapter delineates the main events of the negotiations from their early preparatory phase to conclusion, analyses the main negotiating issues, discusses the role Canada played and the public debate in Canada, and concludes with some observations on the lessons learned.

BEGINNINGS AND ENDINGS

The OECD embarked on the negotiation of the MAI at its 1995 annual ministerial council meeting. Ministers called for the 'immediate start of negotiations for a Multilateral Agreement on Investment . . . which would provide a broad multilateral framework for international investment with high standards for the liberalization of investment regimes . . . [and] be a free-standing international treaty open to OECD and non-OECD member countries.'[1] Ministers stated that agreement should be reached by the 1997 ministerial meeting. The decision was part of the usual package of decisions reached at the ministerial council, ranging across the whole of the OECD's programs, from macroeconomic co-ordination to the environment. It attracted scant media attention.

In launching negotiations for an MAI, the OECD drew on its long history in developing principles governing the treatment of foreign investment, beginning with the 1961 Codes on the Liberalization of Current Investment Transactions and on the Liberalization of Capital Movements through the 1976 National Treatment Instrument (NTI), a voluntary undertaking to accord no less favourable treatment to foreign than that accorded to domestic corporations. Neither the Codes nor the NTI contains investment protection undertakings relating, for example, to the expropriation of investments or to any binding enforcement mechanisms. Furthermore, Canada and a number of other countries excepted broad sectors from the Codes and the NTI to permit the maintenance of discriminatory restrictions on invisible transactions and capital movements. Canada, for example, exempted transport, energy, culture, telecommunications, and fisheries.[2] The Codes and the NTI constituted embryonic investment instruments that captured a given policy consensus on the treatment of foreign investment without trying to enshrine that consensus into a set of legally binding rights and obligations. They provided useful models for the elaboration of bilateral investment agreements and a test for new OECD members, such as Korea and Mexico, determining their suitability for membership in the club. However, these instruments remained of limited scope and engaged only the members of the OECD (Hart, 1996).

In 1991, OECD members embarked on a study of the need for a broader investment instrument. Four years of preparatory work yielded a broad consensus favouring the negotiation of a legally binding instrument, open to non-OECD countries and containing provisions for liberalization, protection, and dispute settlement. In their report to ministers, the Investment Committee declared: 'The time is ripe to negotiate a multilateral investment agreement (MAI) in the OECD', comprehensive in scope, covering all sectors under a broad definition of investment, and based on a 'top-down' approach in which exceptions would be listed and be subject to progressive liberalization.[3] (Such an agreement would set high standards of investment protection and liberalization, be legally binding, be applied to all levels of government, deal with measures taken by regional economic organizations, provide for dispute settlement, and take account of other international agreements. The committee observed that a major effort would be required to conclude the agreement by the time of the ministerial meeting in 1997. Prescient words indeed (Smythe, 1998).

As the pace towards launching negotiations quickened, momentum favouring negotiations at the OECD rather than the WTO grew irresistible. Canada argued the case for the WTO but the absence of a WTO consensus to take up investment, owing to the unreadiness of many key developing countries to engage in investment protection and liberalization negotiations, weakened the case. It was clear that OECD countries were ready to negotiate in 1995 and conclude by 1997. Waiting for the WTO could have meant a very long delay. Institutional factors and bureaucratic preferences also played an important role in the decision to proceed at the OECD. In the United States, the OECD is a State Department fiefdom; the MAI presented an opportunity to champion the OECD as a body where serious US objectives could be achieved and thus enhance State's reputation. The EU dynamic also played strongly in favour of the OECD. In the OECD, EU members negotiate in their own name, while in the WTO the European Commission negotiates for the EU as a whole. There was little appetite to enlarge the Commission's mandate by going to the WTO prematurely. These bureaucratic prerogatives were fed by an ambitious OECD secretariat that perceived an opportunity to steal a march on the WTO by becoming the prime organization for negotiating international investment rules.

In September 1995, the MAI Negotiating Group (NG) under the chairmanship of Frans Engering, a senior Dutch official, met for the first time and set briskly upon its task. Between September 1995 and April 1998, the NG met 23 times in Paris. Numerous working and drafting groups were created to examine detailed provisions and draft articles based on the results of discussions in the Negotiating Group. In the spring of 1997, the chairman, representatives of the G–7 countries (with the addition of a Swiss delegate who chaired one of the OECD investment committees), and the OECD deputy secretary-general began to meet over dinner during each session in an effort to identify areas for possible compromise. These meetings provoked considerable discomfort among non-participating countries, who masked their natural complaint of exclusion with lofty statements about the collective will and decision-making that was the tradition of the OECD.

By January 1997 the secretariat produced a first draft consolidated text[4] of the MAI that accurately captured the state of the negotiations after 15 months of work. The basic provisions had been borrowed from the ample number of models in the some 1,300 bilateral and regional investment protection agreements to which OECD members individually are party. They covered national and most-favoured-nation (MFN) treatment, expropriation and compensation, transfers of funds, other standard investment protection provisions, and dispute settlement mechanisms encompassing both state-to-state and investor-state provisions. While there were unresolved issues in each of these areas, OECD countries had accepted such provisions in other agreements, and their incorporation into a multilateral instrument represented no new departures. When the text dealt with such issues as the definitions of investment or the treatment of exceptions to the MAI, or was silent on issues such as culture or extraterritoriality, it was clear that on a large number of critical matters no common pattern had emerged in OECD practice. The reality was and remained that the NG had proved adept at borrowing standard texts from other agreements but inept at addressing the hard issues that, unless resolved, would mean failure.

As evidence of progress achieved between September 1995 and January 1997, the consolidated text proved deceptive. With February came the submission of draft exception lists to the MAI. These lists were necessarily preliminary since they would define the carve-outs from the specific MAI obligations each country would require and that could not be finalized until the text of the MAI itself was final. In style and substance, the lists ranged from the precise lists of Canada and the United States, which defined in great detail the legislation and measures that would not be covered by the MAI, to generally worded lists submitted by most of the EU members and a number of other countries. Some lists omitted references to sectors where investment barriers existed on the grounds that measures not covered by specific exception would be covered by general exceptions.[5]

At the March 1997 meeting, the chairman, with little consultation but no disagreement from the Negotiating Group, concluded that the negotiations could not be concluded by the time of the spring ministerial meeting in May, as promised in the mandate. He announced at a press conference in Paris that a one-year extension to the negotiating mandate would be sought. Neither this announcement nor the subsequent agreement by the 1997 ministerial council to extend the mandate received any media attention.[6]

In June, the painstaking and ultimately fruitless effort to find the formula for agreement began in earnest. These efforts continued into early 1998, when all serious negotiation came to an end. The primary focus was on the structure and ultimately the balance of exceptions. At issue was not only the substance of exceptions but whether and to what extent countries would undertake obligations not to broaden or deepen them (standstill) and commit to their elimination (rollback). A secondary focus was the development of measures on environment and labour issues responding to the rising clamour in public opinion that the MAI would induce a race to the bottom among countries anxious to attract foreign investment and ready to weaken domestic labour and environment regulation to this end. This work was given particular force by a meeting held on 30 October 1997 with some 60 representatives of non-governmental organizations (NGOs) who called for a suspension of the negotiations pending a full examination of the environmental and social implications of the MAI (Smythe, 1998: 251–2). The rising prominence of labour issues on the agenda was due to ever stronger signals from labour unions in a number of countries that they would oppose the MAI if progress were not made on their objective of incorporating a social clause into trade and investment agreements.

As 1998 began, the Negotiating Group had scheduled four meetings with a view to concluding before the annual ministerial meeting on 30 April. Five observer countries, Brazil, Argentina, Hong Kong, Slovakia, and Chile, had signalled their readiness to become signatories. The three Baltic countries were also anxiously pressing at the door. The potential for having 35 or more countries as signatories seemed within reach. Since there would not be time to complete a full legal text for signature by ministers, it was agreed that the objective should be to arrive at a 'political settlement' on all the outstanding issues to be presented to ministers. The legal text would be completed over the succeeding months with a view to opening the MAI for signature in the autumn of 1998. To generate negotiating momentum, the chairman scheduled the February NG session as a 'high-level' meeting, hoping to attract sub-cabinet officials to ensure that the negotiators on the ground got the political kick necessary to conclude the political settlement in time for ministerial approval.

Reality intervened, rudely. At the first meeting of the new year, the United States startled the NG by stating that the range and complexity of issues remaining on the table would require considerably more time to resolve than had been envisaged. It was thus unrealistic to work for even a political settlement by April 1998; the negotiating mandate would need to be extended. While it was plausible to argue that the time available was insufficient to permit a conclusion of the negotiations,[7] the real reason lay elsewhere, specifically in the failure of the US administration to obtain fast-track trade negotiating authority from the Congress in 1997. The MAI had been pulled from the fast-track proposal in a vain effort to insulate it from the gathering domestic opposition to the OECD negotiations. With fast-track withdrawn and with the onset of a US election year, the administration clearly wanted no controversy over its trade policy. Hence it wished neither to conclude nor to terminate the MAI negotiations in 1998.

The February, March, and April meetings of the NG witnessed no serious effort to close any of the gaps. With the United States effectively off the dance floor, there was no incentive for any delegation to search for compromise. Rather, the NG resigned itself to finding a formula for extending the mandate. This somewhat desultory exercise seemed well on course until mid-April, when the French demanded a formal suspension of the negotiations for a period of six months to allow time for public consultations and to devise a new basis for carrying forward the negotiations. While the French proposal was rejected, ministers saw little point in continuing an intensive schedule of negotiations in circumstances where, given the US position, nothing could be achieved until late autumn. It was agreed that the next meeting of the NG would not occur until October. Ministers, nevertheless, issued a robust statement that the aim was to reach a successful and timely conclusion of the negotiations,[8] but they set no new deadline for completion. Frans Engering chose this moment to withdraw from the chair, citing the pressure of other duties, and it was widely expected that a senior German official, Lorenz Schomerus, would take over.

Negotiations were set to resume on 20–1 October. There was a broad view that this meeting would trigger an intensive effort to conclude the negotiations and present a package to ministers by May or June of 1999. Clearly, the time for closure was fast approaching. Negotiating fatigue was growing among the major delegations; the negotiations had been running for three years and were not making much progress. The slow pace left many countries exposed to withering public criticism with no effective counter-arguments. A decision by the WTO, expected by the end of 1999, to launch a new round of comprehensive multilateral trade negotiations, which could well include investment, meant that if the MAI were not concluded soon, there would be very little interest in continuing at the OECD. Again, reality intervened. French Prime Minister Lionel Jospin torpedoed the negotiations. Rising in the National Assembly on 14 October, Jospin announced that France was withdrawing from the negotiations on the grounds that the French requirements had not been and could not be met. The absence of an agreed upon cultural exception, voluminous US exceptions, and US insistence on the right to apply its laws extraterritorially were all cited as reasons that made the MAI irremediable. The real reason for withdrawal was the need to appease the Communists and the Greens in the Jospin coalition. With no significant support for the MAI from French business and noisy public opposition, especially from the French cultural sector, Jospin's coalition could be reinforced at little cost. With such political factors at play, it was evident that France's withdrawal was definitive and final.

Faced with this *coup de tonnerre*, the secretariat transformed the 20 October negotiating session into an informal consultation. The crucial question was the readiness of EU members to continue the negotiations in the absence of France. For all the member states, the critical issue was not the fate of the MAI but the withdrawal of France. The most urgent task was to ensure French participation in any future discussions on investment. This could not be rushed; time and patience were paramount; no decisions should be reached that would foreclose this possibility. Once again, EU solidarity overrode any other objectives. The United States (i.e., the State Department) was anxious to find some way to continue the OECD discussion and address the French worries. Informal meetings should be arranged in December by holding a seminar with business, labour, and NGOs. Options should be discussed, such as developing non-binding investment principles, designing a model agreement, or downsizing the MAI by stripping it of its enforcement mechanisms. Japan, a consistently strong MAI proponent, was prepared to continue the negotiations but acknowledged that the French position made that clearly impossible; it had to be recognized that the MAI had provoked a debate on globalization; the OECD should not be too ambitious; and work could continue on investment guidelines or a model agreement but negotiations for a treaty should not continue. Canada argued that the negotiations were clearly over and that closure should be brought to the exercise. The secretariat should prepare a paper identifying the areas of agreement and posing the tough questions that would need to be answered in any investment agreement. Canada would continue its effort to seek negotiations on a global investment agreement in the WTO, the forum where real gains could be achieved. Similar arguments were echoed by other OECD countries.

The funeral on 20 October was long, the mourners few, and the pallbearers many. In the park behind the OECD conference centre in Paris a small but triumphant demonstration of NGOs beat out victory on steel drums. At the subsequent press conference, enlivened by a young woman protester marching across the tables of the room shouting anti-MAI slogans, the OECD deputy secretary-general argued that there was a consensus on the need for a multilateral framework on investment and the informal consultations would continue. A few weeks later, the secretariat produced a paper[9] that attempted to create a basis for restarting the negotiations. Apart from the United States, there was no support for any such effort and the paper was roundly rejected. The OECD will revert to its prime role of policy analysis and development, leaving the task of negotiations to the WTO.

THE ISSUES

The mantra of the MAI was 'a high-quality investment agreement'. It was inspired by the conviction that the OECD countries would create the international benchmark for investment protection and liberalization and intimated the superiority of the OECD in negotiating such agreements. This was the philosophy of the like-minded assembled to achieve a common purpose. Like-mindedness[10] could carry the negotiations some distance on the common principles underlying investment protection, such as national treatment. It quickly dissolved when the negotiations moved into terrain where the philosophy and practices of OECD member countries had produced distinctly uncommon principles, especially in investment liberalization. This terrain proved to be a thickly seeded minefield of issues from which there was no easy escape. Six major issues were unresolved when negotiations ceased: exceptions, culture, the coverage of subnational levels of government, extraterritorial measures, labour and environment, and definitions, as well as a range of unresolved secondary issues. However, any real gains for investors in OECD countries flowing from resolving such issues were hardly apparent. By the spring of 1998, seemingly intractable negotiating issues, elusive benefits, and a withering public debate formed a poisoned chalice. Not even chanting the mantra in the last ministerial review could help. In negotiating terms, the mantra proved to be words without meaning.

Exceptions

Exceptions were the most difficult issue. At stake was the overall balance of the MAI since exceptions would effectively establish the extent to which the MAI rights and obligations of each signatory would bite. While there was a broad consensus to provide the standard exceptions for any measures necessary to defend national security or to fulfil United Nations Charter obligations relating to peace and security, the hardest nut to crack was the question of country-specific exceptions. The chairman and many European countries took the view that the ministerial mandate to negotiate a high-quality agreement meant that specific exceptions should be subject to an obligation not to make any investment restriction more severe and progressively to remove them. Moreover, rollback of a barrier by a signatory would not require reciprocal action by others but would be achieved through the time-honoured OECD peer-pressure negotiating technique. Canada and the United States argued that standstill or rollback obligations attached to exceptions were negotiating issues, not overriding principles to be incorporated into the agreement. As in the North American Free Trade Agreement (NAFTA), two types of exceptions were necessary: list A, constituting exceptions generally fixed in legislation and practice, for example, percentage limitations on the level of foreign ownership in a sector;[11] and list B,

covering sectors such as social services or preferential economic policies for Aboriginal people and minorities whereby Canada and the
United States required the flexibility to discriminate against foreign
investors in respect of not only current measures but any measures
that might be adopted in the future. As for list A exceptions, requests
for liberalization might be entertained but the concept of unrecipro-
cated liberalization achieved through peer pressure was fantasy. List
B exceptions were non-negotiable.

While claiming the moral high ground on exceptions, the EU countries also demanded the right to exclude non-EU countries from the
benefits of any internal liberalization. This was called the REIO clause,
meaning regional economic integration organizations, Eurospeak for
the EU and no one else. The United States, Canada, and Japan
objected that the clause constituted a giant, imprecise exception for
the EU to escape its obligation to provide most-favoured-nation treatment to all MAI signatories.[12]

Culture

The treatment of cultural industries in the MAI seemed tailor-made for
a titanic struggle among the G–7 countries: Canada, France, and Italy
joined by Belgium, Portugal, Greece, and Australia, facing the US,
UK, Japan, and Germany joined by the Netherlands, New Zealand,
and the Nordic countries. From the outset, it was agreed that cultural
industries would be excepted from MAI coverage. However, the
breadth and depth of the exception and its general or country-specific character would probably require arduous negotiations. In the
end, culture failed to live up to its billing as a defining issue primarily because the United States and its allies understood that a hard core
of countries would reject any MAI, whatever its benefits, that did not
satisfy their needs for a cultural exception.

In June 1996, France proposed[13] a general exception for any measure regulating foreign investment to preserve and promote cultural
and linguistic diversity. In October 1996, the NG chairman attempted
to focus discussion on the controls required to prevent abuse of a
cultural exception.[14] The French proposal was never discussed, since
the concept of a general exception was palpably unacceptable to the
United States as it would have created a precedent that international
trade and investment agreements would henceforth deprive US entertainment and media interests, the second or third largest US export
industry, of any benefit. The chairman's approach was anathema to

Canada, France, and others because the need to insulate the cultural sector from MAI disciplines, especially the right to discriminate against foreign investment, was permanent in time and unlimited in scope, and could not be made subject to standstill or rollback obligations.

The potential solution originated in an EU proposal to adopt a bottom-up instead of a top-down approach for culture, whereby MAI signatories would accept only the specific obligations for culture they would list in a separate schedule. In this approach, a signatory would be free to list no cultural sectors for coverage. It might even be possible for groups of signatories to exchange MAI rights and obligations without imposing any obligation on other signatories. Neither a general exception nor country-specific exceptions would be needed. The solution was not without problems. Given the symbolic importance of culture, some countries might need a bold cultural industry exclusion or exception clause, which then would need some complicated architecture to achieve the desired result. The technical feasibility and politically saleability of this approach were never put to the test.

Subnational Levels of Government

The majority of OECD members have unitary governments constitutionally empowered to implement all the obligations of trade and investment agreements. As OECD countries have generally removed or substantially reduced the most significant national trade and investment barriers, unitary states are increasingly demanding that the obligations undertaken by federal states apply to their subnational jurisdictions.

The United States and Canada adopted superficially different positions on the coverage of state and provincial measures. In reality, the positions were identical and based on NAFTA. The United States declared that its states would be automatically bound by the MAI as a matter of US treaty practice. However, its list of exceptions for US states' measures excluded the states as a practical matter from any meaningful MAI obligations. Canada stated that the application of the MAI to matters under the jurisdiction of the Canadian provinces should not be assumed and would depend on a satisfactory balance of rights and obligations.[15] In that event, a package of exceptions applicable to provincial measures would be required, as under no circumstances would the MAI exceed the level of obligations imposed on Canadian provinces by NAFTA. Australia described a long procedure of consultation with its states respecting all international agreements touching state jurisdiction, and hence no commitments could be taken in advance of the coverage of its states' measures. European federal countries such as Germany, Austria, and Belgium appeared to have few problems with the concept that the MAI would be automatically and fully applicable to their subnational jurisdictions. No doubt membership in the EU has allowed them to develop ways and means of covering these jurisdictions in deep integration agreements.

The EU was the most insistent on the coverage of subnationals. Its position seemed driven for the most part by theoretical rather than practical concerns. Only one subnational measure was identified, and that only for the United States. In the last months of the negotiations, EU members insisted that US states be obligated not to discriminate against EU-owned, US-based companies in the grant of investment subsidies,[16] a request flatly rejected by the United States. No request was made for the removal of any Canadian provincial measure. It is reasonable to suppose that the end result on this issue would have closely tracked the General Agreement on Tariffs and Trade (GATT), which imposes an obligation on federal governments to take all reasonable measures to ensure compliance with its terms by subnational jurisdictions.

Extraterritoriality

The US Helms-Burton and Iran-Libya Acts enacted in 1996 posed a direct threat to the success of the negotiations. The Helms-Burton Act contained a range of measures aimed at discouraging investment in Cuba, including a right for US citizens to sue foreign companies with investments in the United States for damages if they trafficked in property in Cuba that had been expropriated from these owners. Another provision, suspensible by the President for periods of six months, would extend the same rights to persons who had become US citizens after their property was seized. It also banned the executives and members of their families of companies trafficking in expropriated property from entry into the United States. The Iran-Libya Act penalized foreign companies with investments in the petroleum sector of either of these two countries, for example, by denial of US Export-Import Bank export credits and insurance. Beyond the wave of international outrage that US claims or exercises of extraterritoriality normally arouse, both Acts ran directly counter to the central purpose of the MAI: high-quality protection for foreign investment and investors. In response, Canada tabled two proposals: one to prevent any country from taking action against a signatory or its investors because of the investment of its nationals in a third country; the second to give primacy to the laws of the host-country investor in the event this investor's activities in a third country brought it into conflict with the laws of an MAI country. These proposals were subsequently slightly amended by the EU and became, in effect, joint proposals.[17]

The US refused to discuss these proposals but engaged in separate consultations with the EU that produced an agreement in April 1997. This agreement envisaged the development of disciplines governing transactions in so-called illegally expropriated property and disciplines on extraterritorial measures for eventual incorporation in the MAI. Informal consultations in which Canada participated on the margins of the next several MAI negotiating sessions made little progress. In May 1998 at the annual US-EU summit meeting, a skeleton text of disciplines on expropriated property was agreed to, subject to permanent waivers of the sanctions in the Helms-Burton and Iran-Libya Acts. It was also agreed to incorporate a provision on conflicting requirements into the MAI, but there was no question of the United States accepting any limits to refrain from hostile extraterritorial action on foreign investment. Canada was not party to the EU-US agreement and was not committed to accepting the disciplines or the US-EU undertaking on conflicting requirements as a satisfactory limitation on US extraterritoriality. Hostile statements on the US-EU deal from the congressional sponsors of the Helms-Burton Act also cast considerable doubt on its political viability. In any case, the solution may have been worse than the problem. It was open to the criticism that it was selectively retroactive, multilateralized US extraterritoriality, and made other countries party to its effective administration while providing no concrete rules to prevent US extraterritorial measures in the future.

Labour and the Environment

Labour and environmental issues slowly crept onto the agenda and by the latter half of 1997 had attained status as major negotiating issues. A consensus quickly formed among the major countries[18] that without a credible labour and environment package there would be no answer to the claim that the MAI was a charter of duties for governments and rights for corporations. The package became known as the 'three-anchor' approach, comprised of preambular references to relevant international declarations on the environment and labour (for example, the Rio and Copenhagen Declarations on Environment and Social Development, respectively), a commitment to maintain environment or labour standards to attract an investment modelled on NAFTA (article 1114), and the association of the OECD Guidelines for Multilateral Enterprises, adopted in 1976, with the MAI. The preamble would, as customary, aim to push the right combination of emotive and political buttons.[19] The third anchor prompted little controversy since the Guidelines that set out labour, environmental, and social objectives for multinational enterprises (MNEs) impose no binding obligations on either MNEs or their host governments.

The negotiations focused on the second anchor, specifically whether the commitment not to lower standards would be binding on governments or remain a largely hortatory statement, as in NAFTA. Environmentalists were not impressed with a hortatory article but worried that a binding obligation could effectively chill environmental regulation if each regulatory act were subject to legal challenge under the MAI. Their prime objective, if the MAI could not be killed, was a general MAI exception for any investment measure taken for environmental reasons. Labour saw value in a binding obligation but attached higher priority to making respect for core labour standards a condition of membership in the MAI. Business groups grew increasingly alarmed that the attractiveness to developing countries of an MAI would be weakened by environmental and labour clauses.[20] The Negotiating Group struggled over many months to respond to these concerns in a manner compatible with the central purpose of an investment agreement. EU members stated their interest in binding provisions. The US wanted extensive but non-binding language. The Canadian position, developed through extensive consultations with environmental and labour groups and in federal-provincial consultations, had not yet crystallized but was tending away from binding provisions and towards issues such as ensuring that national treatment did not mean identical treatment, given that environmental regulations can legitimately be different, and respect for core standards on labour issues.

Environmental and labour issues raised the central issue of reconciling the regulatory power of government over investment with the protection of investors and investment from expropriation without compensation. At issue was whether regulations that impose costs on investors, for example, through compliance with environmental regulations, constitute expropriation and justify a claim for compensation. The filing of a NAFTA investor-state case by a US company alleging that a Canadian environmental regulation constituted expropriation called into question the power of governments to regulate without incurring significant financial liability and seemed to substantiate the claim of opponents that the MAI threatened to subject state sovereignty to multinational corporations. It was quickly agreed that the MAI would need to narrow the scope of expropriation provisions to insulate normal and non-discriminatory regulations from compensation claims, even if such regulations generate financial losses for investors. Resolution of this issue would have been critical to the success and saleability of the MAI.[21]

Most of the MAI negotiating issues were as familiar to investment negotiations as old clothes. Labour, environment, and the interpretation of expropriation are new issues on the international negotiating agenda.

Definitions

The coverage of the MAI would be determined by whether it employed an enterprise-based or an asset-based definition. The former would cover tangible assets such as factories and buildings, while the latter would cover portfolio investment such as equities and both tangible and intangible assets such as commercial rights under contract. While the asset-based definition commanded broad support, there was no agreement whether the definition should be open or closed. The draft definition in the consolidate text is open, listing items that are included and thus implying that non-listed items might also be covered. Such a definition could cover any area of government interface with the economy, for example, government preferences restricting public purchases to domestically owned firms. A closed definition, as in NAFTA, states what is included in the definition and what is not. This basic difference was compounded by problems over the inclusion in the definition of items such as intellectual property, public debt, and real estate.

The debate in the negotiating group had a circular quality. Until the definition was resolved, it would be difficult to reach decisions on the substantive obligations of the MAI; but the reverse proposition was equally true. An attempt by the chairman to declare the definition agreed upon was sharply rebuffed by Canada and other countries. The Canadian position was clear. In no case would

Canada exceed the coverage of NAFTA in the definition of investment in the MAI.

Other Issues
Solutions for a range of secondary issues also remained out of reach. One proposal supported by the Europeans was to prohibit most per-formance requirements, i.e., the conditions that governments may impose on investors as a condition for investment even where invest-ment incentives, such as for research and development, are in play. Another was to prevent governments from enforcing commitments voluntarily undertaken by investors. This would have gone well beyond the WTO Agreement on Trade-Related Investment Measures (TRIMs) and NAFTA and was clearly unacceptable. The application of the national treatment principle to the privatization of public assets and to the grant of investment subsidies, the coverage of intellectual property rights, the obligations on state-owned enterprises and state-authorized monopolies, and various aspects of dispute settlement (but not its central features) also provoked long and fruitless discus-sions. These were by no means central issues, and compromises, it was felt, could quickly be found once the more fundamental issues had been resolved.

CANADA AND THE MAI

Public debate often reduces complex and controversial issues into digestible but misleading sound bites. During the free trade debate in the 1980s, controversy erupted over the loss of sovereignty inher-ent in the Canada-US Free Trade Agreement (FTA), as if the concept of binding obligations constraining the sovereignty of both countries to raise barriers to trade was a radically new and untested policy. The reality that Canada and the United States had been closely bound in a sovereignty-constraining trade agreement—the GATT—for almost 40 years was lost in the heat and thunder of debate. Similarly, in the public debate on the MAI, the issue was reduced to whether Canada should enter any investment protection agreement, as if the MAI was a radical new plot hatched in secret by evil globalizers. Again, real-ity was lost, specifically that Canada has comprehensive investment protection agreements with the United States and Mexico in NAFTA and with 25 other countries in bilateral foreign investment protection agreements (FIPAs) that commit Canada to the same principles of non-discrimination and protection for foreign investment that were at the core of the MAI negotiations.

Canada's embrace of investment agreements was, however, relatively recent. It was not until 1988 that Canada entered into binding obligations of non-discrimination and investment protection in Chapter 16 of the FTA. Canada historically had refused such undertaking for fear that the unusually high levels of foreign ownership of Canadian industry left the nation highly exposed to international crisis. Accordingly, Canada needed to remain unencumbered by any international obligations to prevent the forced repatriation of investment. In the postwar years, rapidly rising volumes of foreign investment generated a deep public and political preoccupation over the costs and benefits of foreign ownership. The response was a series of measures to reinforce Canadian control over industry, notably the creation of the Foreign Investment Review Agency (FIRA) in 1974 with a mandate to review foreign acquisitions of Canadian business and the establishment of new businesses by foreign investors. Declining concern about foreign investment had led to the conversion of FIRA into Investment Canada, with a mandate to seek out foreign investments, and created a favourable environment for the negotiation of investment rules in the FTA (Hart, 1998; Hart, with Dymond and Robertson, 1994).

The words introducing Chapter 16 in the annotated version of the FTA confirmed the change in Canadian policy: 'A hospitable and secure investment climate is indispensable if the two countries are to achieve the full benefits of reducing barriers to trade in goods and services.' Canada thus recognized that the benefits of free trade with the United States could not be fully exploited without foreign investment. Maintaining the right to discriminate against foreign investment would limit Canada's ability to attract foreign investors and vitiate a fundamental objective of the FTA. Of equal importance was the recognition that Canadian firms would need to invest abroad to achieve economies of scale and specialization; thus, it was important to secure investment protection from our free trade partner. As befits a beginning, the FTA investment chapter was modest. While it provided for the non-discriminatory treatment of foreign investment and contained standard investment protection obligations, it basically applied to direct investment. NAFTA, negotiated five years later, is a much more ambitious instrument comprising a fully dressed foreign investment agreement and a vastly larger definition of investment. In the Uruguay Round, Canada accepted the disciplines of the TRIMs agreement prohibiting the use of certain performance requirements. Separately, Canada accelerated its program of negotiating FIPAs. By the opening of the MAI negotiations, Canada's conversion to the virtues of foreign investment protection agreements was complete.

Canada thus came to the MAI fully equipped to negotiate a comprehensive multilateral investment agreement. The changes in Canadian legislation affecting foreign investment and allowing Canada to accept more general binding obligations in this area had already been embedded in national policy. The FTA, NAFTA, and the growing network of bilateral FIPAs established the parameters within which Canada would enter into negotiations. Moreover, these agreements had demonstrated that investment protection and non-discrimination provisions were compatible with exceptions for sensitive sectors such as culture, health, education, and social services. They had also proven that provincial government measures could be covered in a manner consistent with Canadian constitutional practice and could be satisfactory to our trading partners. While it was likely that some Canadian investment restrictions would come under pressure during the MAI negotiations, there was a high level of confidence that these pressures could be successfully resisted. This confidence was vindicated by the negotiations.

Confidence in the strength and coherence of Canada's negotiating position was not matched by confidence in the choice of the OECD as the negotiating forum. As the preparatory process in 1994 and 1995 marched towards a negotiating mandate, Canada argued that the negotiations should be carried out in the WTO. There were few barriers of consequence in OECD countries. There were significant investment barriers in developing countries and a need for treaty-based investment protection as investments in such countries grew. However, faced with a near consensus to proceed in the OECD, Canada saw little point in holding up negotiations and every point in attempting to use the MAI as a springboard into eventual WTO negotiations. Canada argued successfully that the negotiations be genuinely open to non-members and pressed hard for the admission of such countries as full participants so they could become founding signatories. In the WTO, Canada took the initiative in seeking the inclusion of investment in the work program emerging from the 1996 Singapore ministerial meeting. The eagerness to welcome non-members to the negotiating table, combined with Canada's aggressive

WTO posture, generated considerable suspicion in the OECD about the depth of Canadian commitment to the MAI.

The Canadian negotiating position from the beginning was to replicate the investment provisions of NAFTA found principally in Chapter 11, but also comprising elements of the chapters dealing with the movement of executive personnel and with monopolies and state enterprises. Included in this position was the requirement for complete exceptions for culture, health, and social and education services and programs for minorities and Aboriginal peoples. Canada added two objectives on the need for credible labour and environment provisions, including narrowing the scope of compensable expropriation and seeking measurable progress on US extraterritorial measures prompted by the Helms-Burton and Iran-Libya Acts.

Canada's NAFTA-rooted negotiating position irritated the chairman of the NG, the secretariat, and certain EU countries. Canada's dismissal of the hallowed peer-pressure method of OECD negotiations added to this irritation. The chairman made it clear that he was prepared to envisage an MAI without Canada. The problem was never the substance of Canada's exceptions, once a *modus vivendi* on culture had emerged. Throughout the negotiations, no country requested Canada to reduce or eliminate any investment restrictions or to open any sensitive sector such as health to foreign investment. The discomfort lay in Canada's flat refusal to override national interests in order to preserve the purity of the MAI. Once the realization sank in that the United States would not move off the exceptions incorporated in NAFTA and, moreover, had made an offer of little value on the coverage of US states' practices, the pressure on Canada eased considerably.

The public debate over the MAI, which began in the spring of 1997, confirmed the comforting permanence of public debate in Canada. Little has changed since 1911, when the Laurier government negotiated a modest free trade agreement with the United States. Sir Robert Borden, leader of the Conservative opposition, wrapped himself in the imperial flag and campaigned successfully on the theme that the agreement constituted a mortal threat to sovereignty (Dymond, 1987). The free trade debate of the 1980s was a remake of the 1911 debate, with the addition of social and environmental issues. The nationalists argued that the FTA would rob Canadians of their sovereignty, especially cultural sovereignty; social groups maintained that free trade would destroy programs; and the environmentalists insisted that free trade would lower environmental standards.

The MAI debate played the same tunes, but with some updated lyrics. Threats to Canadian sovereignty remained the dominant theme, but the source of these threats was no longer the United States but multinational corporations, which would use the MAI to overturn democratically elected government. The capacity to legislate to protect the environment, to enforce labour laws, to foster a distinct national culture, to require investors to provide jobs, or to maintain national health and education systems would give way to corporate power.[22]

There were, of course, some differences. One was that the impact of the MAI on public opinion was considerably less than had been the case with free trade in the 1980s. While the FTA ranked as the item of greatest national concern in public opinion polls for months during the negotiations, and in the subsequent 1988 federal election, public awareness of the MAI never rose above 30 per cent, despite months of sustained criticism. A second difference was that the proponents of multilateral agreements over bilateral liberalization agreements now seemed opposed to all agreements. FTA opponents tried to escape the protectionist label by claiming that multilateral trade agreements presented fewer dangers to Canada because of their broad membership. The fact that Canada was now prepared to multilateralize the FTA/NAFTA investment provisions and to proceed to the WTO seemed to stimulate rather than calm opponents. A third difference was the absence of the Canadian business community. In contrast to their vigorous advocacy of the FTA, the business community was largely a silent observer in the MAI debate. It saw the MAI as a useful idea, but since it would not add to investment protection in the OECD and could not address the problems Canadian investors face in many developing countries, business leaders considered that little would be lost if the MAI failed.

The most important difference between the two debates was that the FTA would result in major changes in Canadian policies, while the MAI would lead to no changes in policy. Once comprehensive investment protection had been extended to the United States by virtue of NAFTA, covering some 55–60 per cent of inward foreign investment, there was no substantive case against extending the NAFTA investment terms to a further 20 per cent of inward foreign investment, as represented by the remaining members of the OECD. The success of the negotiations would have had the same result as their failure: no consequential changes in Canadian investment policy.

The vehicle for the debate was the consolidated text, which leaked in the United States and spread through the Internet. Although successive versions of this text were promoted as signs of progress by the secretariat (which never ceased prattling that 90 per cent of the text was already agreed to), it had a deeply counter-productive effect because it conveyed the impression that a comprehensive agreement had already been reached in 1997, leaving only minor details to be settled (Smythe, 1998: 253). Moreover, since the text did not contain the confidential draft lists of exceptions, it implied that sectors such as social services would henceforth be exposed to unrestricted foreign investment and left governments with the difficult task of proving that essential national positions had not been sacrificed.

The Canadian government response to the public debate was quick and multifaceted. A blizzard of material prepared to respond to correspondence appeared on the Internet; an aggressive campaign was launched to seek out and offer consultations to interested groups (e.g., labour, environment, Aboriginal, women's, business, and development groups); public hearings were held by the House Foreign Affairs and International Trade Committee; in addition to speeches in the House, Trade Minister Sergio Marchi made a major address in early 1998 setting out Canadian objectives and bottom lines in stark, unambiguous terms; the chief negotiator was made available for media interviews; consultations with the provinces, a feature of the MAI negotiations since before the 1995 launch, were intensified.

But these debates are difficult for governments. The benefits of trade and investment agreements are diffuse and long term; they must be presented in factual and verifiable terms and communicated in a way that responds to public anxieties. Frequently, governments are placed in the unenviable position of defending a negative, for example, that Canadian independence will not be sacrificed, a statement that can only be proved in the future. The opponents of liberalization face few similar constraints. Their craft involves drawing lurid and overstated scenarios of what could happen. Facts are unimportant and balance and circumspection a distinct disadvantage. As columnist David Frum pointed out during the FTA debate: 'protectionists have all the fun . . . since they do not consider themselves bound by the customary standards of evidence expected in controversies over matters of urgent public policy' (Hart, with Dymond and Robertson, 1994: 110).

As the MAI tottered into oblivion, opponents began to prepare their campaign against an investment negotiation in the WTO. Some of the more conspiratorially minded argued that the failure of the MAI in the OECD was no more than a plot to disarm opponents. Others took the more reasonable view that moving from Paris to Geneva did not change the fundamental character of an investment protection negotiation.[23] The difference in the WTO framework would be twofold. Investment would be but one of many issues on the negotiating table engaging a much larger set of domestic stakeholders. Second, and more importantly, an investment agreement in the WTO would in principle generate net gains of investment protection for Canadian investors. The promise of such gains should equip the government with a tool it lacked in the MAI. Whether the business community, so conspicuously invisible during the MAI debate, embraces an investment agenda at the WTO will be interesting to learn in the next months and years.

LESSONS

If victory has many fathers and failure is an orphan, it can also be observed that the lessons learned from failure are sharper than those from victory, which are often lost in the glow of achievement. The lessons of the MAI are both old and new; however, the following stand out.

First, two fundamental conditions must underpin any negotiation: the agreement resulting from the negotiations must address problems that cannot be solved by purely domestic measures, and the agreement should improve economic relations among the countries party to it. Achievement of these objectives creates the political justification to limit the scope for sovereign decision-making. In the case of the FTA, Canada sought to restructure the economy. Canada was free at any time to unilaterally remove its own barriers to US goods and investment. While such action would have benefited the economy, reciprocal action by the United States ensured the free access to the US market, which was essential to the full exploitation of the efficiencies resulting from the removal of Canadian trade barriers. Placing the trade relationship with the United States on a new and more secure, treaty-based footing enshrined in the FTA contributed to an overall improvement in the bilateral economic relationship.

The MAI was deficient in both respects. Canadian investors and investment enjoy liberal and transparent investment regimes in the OECD area. Consultations with Canadian business generated neither requests for the removal of any investment barrier nor demands to enhance investment protection beyond what OECD countries already provide. The prospect that important MAI observer countries such as Brazil and Argentina, increasingly important countries for Canadian investors, would become signatories would have been but a modest step towards generating some tangible benefits that could be presented to the public. Since there were no problems to be solved, the MAI had little scope to improve economic relations between Canada and its OECD partners.

Second, unless governments entering negotiations and the negotiators appointed to the task have a reasonable expectation of achieving something new and important, the negotiating dynamic will be defensive, focused on the protection of established positions rather than a readiness to bargain to obtain something of value. The plausibility of negotiations among the like-minded countries contains this fatal weakness. At most the MAI, as a multilateral framework of rules, could do two things. It could provide a guide for bilateral and regional investment agreements, but it was unlikely that countries would allow their arrangements to be overridden by the MAI. Canada insisted that the MAI would not supersede the investment provisions of NAFTA except in the event that the MAI represented a net gain over NAFTA, for example, in the scope of the expropriation article. The MAI could also establish a benchmark for future negotiations in the WTO. While these were laudable objectives, they were of insufficient value to persuade any country to change its long-standing positions and thereby alter the defensive dynamic that drove the negotiations.

Third, the need for transparency in negotiations has reached new heights and governments will need to devise practical ways and means of responding to the incessant public demand to be informed. The issue is more than a matter of transparency. One of the sharpest criticisms levelled at the MAI was the secrecy attending the negotiations. The charge is totally unwarranted. The negotiations were conducted in the traditional manner by national delegations comprised of diplomats and expert officials. Understandably, neither the public nor the media had seats at the table, but there was no effort to conceal the negotiations or their purpose from the public. Press statements on the launch of the negotiations, the annual reviews of progress, and regular reports issued by the OECD secretariat are hardly evidence of a desire to keep the negotiations secret. In Canada, volumes of material were made available on the DFAIT Web site, hearings were held by a parliamentary committee, and ministerial speeches set out Canadian objectives and bottom lines. Offers were made to all interested groups to consult with the negotiating team, further testifying to the readiness, indeed eagerness, for broad-based and extensive domestic consultations. The degree of transparency and public involvement in the negotiating process was unprecedented. It is fair to conclude that the charge of secrecy was, in large measure, a proxy for a more difficult issue—the acceptability of the government's international trade and investment agenda.

The MAI fell squarely within the postwar tradition of negotiating ever more liberal trade and economic agreements consistent with the steady deregulation and liberalization of economic management in the OECD countries. The groups who complained the strongest about secrecy were those most opposed to the central purposes and economic philosophy of the MAI.[24] As public pressure on the MAI grew, the Negotiating Group chairman and the secretariat persisted in the belief that an aggressive campaign to set the facts straight would remedy the huge misunderstandings and misinformation from which the MAI suffered. They missed the point. The problem was that the MAI constituted an exceptionally narrow base on which to conduct a debate about the merits of trade and investment liberalization. Opponents sought to discuss the role of MNEs, the threat to national sovereignty posed by non-discriminatory treatment, and the rationale for compensating for expropriation. They rejected the basic rationale for the WTO, the FTA/NAFTA, and other recent agreements. The more the negotiating process was opened up, the more insistent the opposition became, not to the MAI as such but rather to the fact that government regulation of foreign investment—and for that matter, of international trade and financial flows—was becoming ever lighter. As the debate increased in volume and departed from the arcane details of an investment agreement, the MAI's natural supporters in the business community remained on the sidelines, declining to lend legitimacy to a fundamental assault on the concept of a liberal and open economy. In future, governments and their negotiators will have to be prepared for a broad-ranging debate about fundamentals and resist the temptation to believe that the objectives of transparency can be secured by the provision of information and the offer of consultations on the details.

Fourth, there was a new actor on the scene, the Internet. Once the consolidated text was leaked, it and its succeeding versions spread rapidly throughout OECD countries and beyond. In the recent past, the distribution of official documents—those published and those leaked—was limited by the capacity of photocopy machines and the size of postal budgets. Now they are instantly and broadly available to anyone with a computer and an Internet connection. By one count, the negotiations spawned over 50 Web sites and news groups hostile to the MAI (Kobrin, 1998: 97). The Internet connected groups across great distances of space and constituent interests. Governments had access to the same tool and Canada was first off the mark with its widely praised Web site. The Internet has accelerated the arrival of civil society groups into the negotiating room, ending the days when negotiations were the province of expert officials working solely under political guidance from their governments. There is a certain irony in this: many opponents decried the MAI as the latest manifestation of globalization at the expense of the nation-state; they broadcast their message by using the tools of globalization to mobilize opposition against a project mandated by democratically elected governments of nation-states.

The MAI negotiations were a sobering experience for the OECD as an institution. Its traditional strengths of policy analysis and development and its operating style served it poorly when confronted with the challenge of negotiating a complex treaty text involving binding and enforceable commitments. Aggressive chairmanship, a public and intrusive role for the institution in contacts with delegations, the media, and civil society, and peer pressure have long been highly effective modes of operation enabling the institution to make a significant contribution to the efforts of member countries to address cutting-edge economic, environment, and social issues. However, peer pressure cannot replace the careful balancing of competing agendas and delicate and patient bargaining; the sensitivities of key countries, for example, those of Canada and the United States on the imperative of unbound reservations, cannot be ignored; stimulating momentum towards preferred outcomes through contacts with the media and business and civil society groups can prove counter-productive; and the constant chanting of a mantra cannot telescope the arduous task of treaty-making. Patient repairs are required to the reputation of the OECD in order to refocus its work in its areas of greatest strength and to commit it to eschewing all further negotiating initiatives.

Canada was right to participate in the negotiations and to stay the course, notwithstanding the preference maintained throughout to get to the WTO as soon as possible. Even as prospects dimmed for reaching an agreement among the like-minded in the face of defensive negotiating agendas, the negotiations offered an opportunity to create the basic multilateral framework for investment rules that would have set the stage for negotiations in the WTO. The attempt pressed forward by the OECD secretariat and many European countries to go beyond a framework and the dismissal of such a framework as unfaithful to the ministerial mandate create expectations that could not be met and anxieties that could not be answered.

Fifty years ago, Dana Wilgress, the head of the Canadian delegation to the Havana conference for the negotiation of an International Trade Organization, reported to the government 'that the broad question of international investment had not yet received the collective consideration it required' (Hart, 1995: 93). The MAI effort marks an opportunity missed for that collective consideration, and herein lies its sad and melancholy tale.

NOTES

1. See OECD press release SG/PRESS (95)41. Canada was represented by Roy MacLaren, Minister for International Trade.
2. These exceptions have been maintained in NAFTA and Canada's bilateral investment agreements.
3. See OECD document DAFFE/INV/ICE(95)FINAL.
4. See DAFFE/MAI(98)REV7. This is the seventh and final version of the consolidated text, little changed from the first version. References in this chapter are to this version.
5. Canada, for example, submitted no exception for culture on grounds that our needs would be covered by a general exception such as proposed by France.
6. See SG/COM/NEWS(97)45.
7. Much of the plausibility of this argument derived from its source, the United States, an advantage the sole remaining great power continues to enjoy. However ludicrous its statements may prove on close examination, they always have a superficial ring of plausibility.
8. See SG/COM/NEWS(98)50.
9. See DAFFE/MFI (98)1.
10. Like-minded countries assembled together should beware. Reporting on a meeting of like-minded countries in the 1970s, one commentator called it a gathering of the 'lite-minded'.
11. For example, Canada limits foreign ownership of airlines to 25 per cent; no such limitation applies to airline ownership by nationals. Without an exception, this limitation would violate the national treatment rule.

12. The Europeans become quite emotional over attacks on the REIO clause, which is fundamental, in their view, to European construction, i.e., European preferences.

13. 'Nothing in this agreement shall be construed to prevent any Contracting Party to take any measure to regulate investment of foreign companies and the conditions of activities of these countries in the framework of policies designed to preserve and promote cultural and linguistic diversity.' Consolidated Text, 128.

14. See DAFFE/MAI(96)29.

15. See paragraph 3 of the headnote to Canada's exceptions list.

16. This late request had all the qualities of new wine: fresh taste, easy drinking, quick headache.

17. See Consolidated Text, 122–6.

18. There was, however, a small but noisy group of dissidents, including Australia, New Zealand, and Mexico, who were opposed to any references to environment and labour on the ground that they should be treated in forums such as the United Nations and the International Labour Organization, not in an investment agreement.

19. While it may seem logical that the preamble should be the first text drafted so that the negotiators will know the guiding principles for the negotiations, in practice, the preamble is usually the last text negotiated, informed by the principles the negotiators have actually used.

20. Based on consultations held by the Canadian negotiating team with environment, labour, and business groups.

21. The chairman's proposal, Consolidated Text, 144, provided a reasonable start; it had not been discussed when the negotiations ceased.

22. See, for example, the advertisement in the *Globe and Mail*, 29 May 1997, sponsored by the Council of Canadians, the Sierra Club, the Canadian Labour Congress, and others.

23. In a letter to the *Vancouver Province*, 23 Nov. 1998, the chair of the BC legislative committee on the MAI wrote that 'it would be a serious mistake' to conclude that the MAI is dead since many countries, Canada included, are calling for the MAI negotiations to be restarted in the WTO.

24. Following a TV clip, I received an angry letter from a Catholic nun protesting the MAI as fundamentally immoral.

REFERENCES

Dymond, William A. 1987. 'Free Trade, 1911 and All of that', *bout de papier* 5, 2 (Summer): 22–5.

Hart, Michael. 1995. *Also Present at the Creation: Dana Wilgress and the United Nations Conference on Trade and Employment at Havana*. Ottawa: Centre for Trade Policy and Law.

———. 1996. 'A Multilateral Agreement on Foreign Direct Investment—Why Now?', in Pierre Sauvé and Daniel Schwanen, eds, *Investment Rules for the Global Economy: Enhancing Access to Markets*. Toronto: C.D. Howe Institute.

———. 1998. *Fifty Years of Canadian Tradecraft: Canada at the GATT 1947–1997*. Ottawa: Centre for Trade Policy and Law.

————, with Bill Dymond and Colin Robertson. 1994. *Decision at Midnight: Inside the Canada-US Free Trade Negotiations*. Vancouver: University of British Columbia Press.

Kobrin, Stephen J. 1998. 'The MAI and the Clash of Globalizations', *Foreign Affairs* (Fall).

Smythe, Elizabeth. 1998. 'The Multilateral Agreement on Investment: A Charter of Rights for Global Investors or Just Another Agreement?', in Fen Osler Hampson and Maureen Appel Molot, eds, *Canada Among Nations 1998: Leadership and Dialogue*. Toronto: Oxford University Press.

3

Defusing Conflicts in International Trade: Making the WTO Rules Work

HEATHER FORTON

The World Trade Organization (WTO) dispute settlement system is unprecedented in the context of international law in general. WTO members—sovereign governments—consented to a binding dispute settlement system allowing for the enforcement of international trade rules and disciplines. In a multilateral context, negotiators were able to develop a set of international trade rules and disciplines on an exceptionally broad range of issues and then provide for their enforcement on the basis of agreed rules and institutions. The WTO's first Director-General, Renato Ruggiero, has justifiably called the dispute settlement system 'the central pillar of the multilateral trading system and the WTO's most individual contribution to the stability of the global economy'.[1]

The WTO's legal regime is a product of the evolution of the dispute settlement system under the General Agreement on Tariffs and

Trade (GATT), combined with innovative proposals from various negotiators (see Hart, 1998). Canadian and US contributions to the development of the WTO regime were coloured by their respective experiences with the dispute settlement system established in the 1989 Canada-United States Free Trade Agreement (FTA) and replicated in the 1994 North American Free Trade Agreement (NAFTA). The FTA, in turn, had borrowed from the GATT dispute settlement system, while NAFTA flowed from developments not only in the FTA but also in the GATT and the WTO.

The NAFTA dispute settlement system is noteworthy in the international context, but with an important distinction: there are only three parties to NAFTA whereas by the end of 1998 there were 133 members of the WTO. Canada, the United States, and Mexico, as parties to NAFTA and as members of the WTO, can choose whether they want a dispute heard under NAFTA or in the WTO, assuming the matter arises under both agreements. NAFTA Article 2005 gives the complaining party the discretion to choose the forum. However, once the forum is selected, it must be used to the exclusion of the other. As the purpose of this paper is not to discuss the NAFTA dispute settlement procedures but the WTO legal regime, suffice it to say that although the dispute settlement systems of NAFTA and the WTO are very similar, there are also important differences (see Mareau, 1997).

The WTO dispute settlement system has been functioning effectively since it entered into force on 1 January 1995. While many recognize that improvements could be made to the process, most members are generally satisfied with how it is operating. WTO members agreed in December 1996 in the Declaration of the First Ministerial Conference of the WTO that:

> The Dispute Settlement Understanding (DSU) offers a means for the settlement of disputes among Members that is unique in international agreements. We consider its impartial and transparent operation to be of fundamental importance in assuring the resolution of trade disputes, and in fostering the implementation and application of the WTO agreements. The Understanding, with its predictable procedures, including the possibility of appeal of panel decisions to an Appellate Body and provisions on implementation of recommendations, has improved Members' means of resolving their differences. . . . We are confident that longer experience with the DSU, including the implementation of panel and appellate recommendations,

will further enhance the effectiveness and credibility of the dispute settlement system.[2]

This view is still widely held. Nevertheless, it is also clear that members are monitoring the system very closely, especially with regard to its implementation provisions. If members were to find significant flaws with these provisions, it would probably affect their overall evaluation of the dispute settlement process. To date, panel and Appellate Body rulings and recommendations have been implemented to the satisfaction of the complaining parties. None the less, some important disputes reached the implementation stage in 1998 and raise a number of important questions, including the Ecuador, Guatemala, Honduras, Mexico, and US complaint against the European Communities (EC)[3] with regard to the latter's regime for the importation, sale, and distribution of bananas, and the US and Canadian complaint against the EC with regard to the importation of hormone-treated beef. In the closing days of 1998, the United States also raised questions regarding Canada's implementation of the panel and Appellate Body rulings and recommendations in their dispute involving periodicals.[4]

This chapter discusses the experience of WTO members with the dispute settlement system during its initial four years and considers some of the suggestions put forward by various commentators to ensure that the system continues to serve its intended objectives: the full and effective enforcement and implementation of members' rights and obligations.

ORIGINS OF THE WTO DISPUTE SETTLEMENT SYSTEM

Although the WTO dispute settlement system may be 'unique' in public international law, it is not entirely new. It is based on the dispute settlement system that had evolved over the years as a result of the experience of the GATT contracting parties. In effect, the WTO dispute settlement system codifies those elements of the GATT dispute settlement system that were viewed as being positive and worth maintaining. Over the years, that system had developed on the basis of a unique combination of pragmatism and legalism. Initially, GATT's contracting parties demonstrated a pragmatic and flexible approach to the interpretation and application of the rules. However, as they gained confidence in the rules and procedures and negotiated ever deeper obligations, they showed an increasing willingness to use legal means to enforce them. By the time of the Uruguay Round negotiations, they were prepared to apply the rules definitively (WTO Agreement, Article XVI:4) and establish binding procedures to enforce their implementation (see Petersmann, 1997a, 1997b; Pescatore et al., 1997).

The Uruguay Round negotiators realized, however, that the codification of the GATT system would not be sufficient to meet the needs of future members of the WTO. Governments recognized that the system had to be strengthened to ensure the security and predictability of members' expectations. The negotiators had painstakingly negotiated a set of comprehensive, and sometimes complicated, trade rules covering a wide range of issues. These rules would be of little real value if they could not be enforced. The rules themselves would have no significance if they could be breached with impunity or if there were no means by which to resolve legitimate questions of interpretation. Consequently, elements were added to the GATT dispute settlement system to ensure that the policy objectives of members, as reflected in the rules of the WTO as a whole, would be secured.

BASIC ELEMENTS OF WTO DISPUTE SETTLEMENT

One of the most fundamental principles of the WTO dispute settlement system that was retained from the GATT system is that of having parties to a dispute find mutually agreed solutions to their differences. Article 3.7 of the DSU states that 'the aim of the dispute settlement mechanism is to secure a positive solution to a dispute. A solution mutually acceptable to the parties to a dispute and consistent with the covered agreements is clearly to be preferred.' Consequently, the DSU encourages parties to a dispute to resolve the issue through a mutually agreed solution and to resort to 'litigation' of the dispute only if that course of action is not possible.

Not only is this principle explicitly enunciated in the DSU, but other provisions in the DSU implicitly support this approach. For example, Article 4.7 does not require a complaining party to request a panel immediately once the 60-day consultation period is over. Lawyers, especially those not familiar with the GATT culture, tend to view the dispute settlement system as providing a rapid litigation procedure with the consultation phase being nothing but a period of time set aside for an unusual type of WTO-expedited 'discovery' process. This is not the case. The negotiators of the DSU wanted the consultation phase of the process to be more than just a *pro forma* step in the litigation procedure. Pursuant to the DSU, disputing parties may consult as long as the complaining party deems it is in its interest to continue to resolve the matter without going to a panel. In addition, Article 12.12 of the DSU allows the complaining party to ask a panel to suspend its proceedings. A complaining party would usually take advantage of this provision if it believed there was a possibility of resolving a case without going any further in the litigation process. In the past, panels have been suspended using this provision, such as Canada's case against the EC with regard to the trade description of scallops and the EC's case against the United States with regard to the Helms-Burton Act.

An important difference between the GATT dispute settlement system and the WTO legal regime is that the DSU applies to all subject areas covered by the WTO agreement. With the exception of some special or additional rules applicable in specific situations, the same dispute settlement rules apply to trade in goods, trade in services, the trade-related aspects of intellectual property rights, and the application of sanitary and phytosanitary measures. In other words, different areas do not have different dispute settlement rules; members cannot 'forum shop'. In fact, when a member is requesting consultations or the establishment of panel, it may cite the violation of several provisions from different covered agreements. The more than 20 agreements that make up the WTO form a single undertaking and are reinforced by an integrated dispute settlement system.

Another significant improvement to the GATT system is that provisions were introduced in the DSU to ensure that if a complaining party to a dispute so wished, the dispute could be resolved promptly. In other words, if the complaining party cannot resolve the matter through consultations and mutual agreement, it can quickly proceed to litigation of the matter. Very specific time frames have been introduced throughout the dispute settlement process, in particular with regard to the panel process. In theory, the various stages of the initial panel process are to be completed within six months, with a possible extension of three months, and those of the appeal process within 60 days, with a possible extension to 90 days (Articles 12.9 and 17.5 of the DSU). The system was designed to provide for the prompt settlement of disputes because promptness was recognized as important to governments as well as to business and other trading interests for whom the rules were ultimately being developed. The longer disputes took to resolve, the longer trade benefits were being nullified or impaired.

Admittedly, maintaining these time frames in practice has been extremely challenging, especially in cases involving complex issues and requiring specific expertise. There have also been significant delays because a panel report is not circulated to the members of the WTO until it is available in all of the official languages of the WTO.[5]

Also essential to the improvement of the GATT dispute settlement system was the introduction of a number of provisions that in effect removed the defending member's ability to block the process. In the GATT dispute settlement system, the defending party could easily frustrate the complaining party by not agreeing to the establishment of a panel or by blocking the adoption of panel reports. As a result, several provisions of the DSU were designed to ensure that the process would move forward despite a reluctant defendant. For example, Article 7 states that standard terms of reference will apply if the parties to the dispute do not agree to the terms of reference for the panel within a specified period of time; Article 8.7 allows any party to the dispute to refer the matter of panel selection to the Director-General of the WTO for decision if the parties do not come to an agreement within a certain period of time; Article 6 ensures that defendants are no longer able to block the establishment of a panel;[6] and, most importantly, Articles 16 and 17 effectively impede defendants from blocking the adoption of the panel report and the adoption of the Appellate Body report, respectively.[7] These last two articles of the DSU ensure that the rulings and recommendations of panels and the reports of the Appellate Body proceed to the implementation phase of the dispute settlement process.

Another significant innovation of the WTO dispute settlement system was the creation of the Appellate Body. Contrary to the GATT dispute settlement system, any party to a dispute in the WTO may appeal a panel decision. Although the 'winners' are not likely to appeal a favourable decision of a panel, they may appeal in order to clarify a point of law they deem to be important. 'Losers' are more likely to appeal the findings of a panel, but must do so on a point of law and interpretation; the Appellate Body does not provide scope for a rehearing of the original issues.[8] Some of the issues considered by the Appellate Body include: the status of prior panel reports, especially those of the GATT; the specificity required in the request to establish a panel; judicial economy; burden of proof; the scope of the appeal; the overlap between agreements such as the GATT 1994 and the General Agreement of Trade in Services; and the right to have private counsel participate as a member of a delegation at panel proceedings.

The WTO dispute settlement system also contains a number of new rules regarding the implementation of reports once they have been adopted. For example, there are provisions to determine the reasonable period of time within which a member found to be in breach of its obligations must implement the recommendations, to provide recourse to the original panel to determine if a defendant's action is consistent with the recommendations, and to authorize compensation or retaliation if the defendant does not comply with the recommendations. Several of these provisions have not yet been fully tested by the members, but evidence to date suggests significant differences of view with regard to the interpretation of some of these provisions.

In short, the WTO dispute settlement system is much more sophisticated than the former GATT system. It is designed to provide better support to the framework of international trade rules and disciplines, and it increases the security and predictability of the regime. However, contrary to the GATT, many of the new elements are legalistic in nature, and consequently it will take some time for the WTO to adjust to all these new procedures. It is also through the use of the system that elements requiring some further reflection and adjustment will become evident.

REVIEW AND PROPOSALS FOR REFORM

WTO members agreed in 1994 that they would review the operation and efficacy of the DSU in 1998. Already in 1997, this had sparked a great deal of debate and commentary regarding how the system could be improved and what were considered to be the serious challenges facing the WTO dispute settlement system. Academic commentators, while generally positive in their appraisals, singled out a range of issues that they believed merited further consideration (see, e.g., Jackson, 1996, 1998a, 1998b). The Dispute Settlement Body agreed in February 1998 that it would conduct the review after the May ministerial meeting and conclude its work early in 1999. Prior to this decision, no member had made any proposals for reform, nor did any emerge that would require formal changes at this stage.

Numberous suggestions for strengthening the functioning of the system, however, were raised during the review by both governmental and non-governmental commentators.

Before flagging some of the issues that have been raised, it is essential to note that it is unrealistic to raise the same expectations regarding the DSU as one would for a domestic legal system. Domestic legal systems have evolved over long periods of time and changes or innovations to those systems usually have been introduced only after much careful analysis by a wide variety of experts, lawyers in particular. Further, the DSU is relatively new; there has been a limited amount of experience with some of the provisions and no experience with regard to other provisions. Despite its appearance, it is not a legislative text that was laboriously drafted, studied, and reviewed by teams of lawyers. It is a text that was negotiated in a very particular multilateral context and time frame. The text contains a number of constructive ambiguities that may have satisfied negotiators at the time of drafting but are proving to be challenging for those individuals who must now apply the various provisions. Certainly, improvements can be made to the system and some issues require focused attention (see Steger and Hainsworth, 1998; Shoyer, 1998).[9] However, based on past experience and preliminary discussions during the review, it is clear that the WTO will address them patiently, thoughtfully, cautiously, and incrementally.[10]

Some of the refinements and adjustments being proposed concern such issues as:

- The lack of clarity in the language dealing with the notification of mutually agreed solutions, i.e., requirements regarding the timing and the exact content of such notifications are not outlined in detail, resulting in inconsistent application of the provision.
- Whether or not requests for consultations should be more specific in addressing every measure and every legal claim the complaining party intends to pursue (some members have already stated they favour more specificity whereas others have claimed a need for requests to be very general).
- Whether complaining parties should benefit from an accelerated dispute settlement procedure when the defendant does not respect the terms and conditions of a mutually agreed solution.

- Greater definition as to when a member does not have the 'substantial trade interest' required to be a participant in consultations requested by another member.
- How to deal with situations where procedural rules deny the benefits of the substantive provisions of the DSU; for example, a 10-day procedural requirement to place items on the agenda of the Dispute Settlement Body can delay a member exercising its right to call for the establishment of a panel on the sixty-first day after the request for consultations.
- Must the requests for the establishment of a panel be presented at consecutive meetings of the Dispute Settlement Body in order to benefit from the provision that allows for the automatic establishment of a panel the second time a request is on the agenda of the Dispute Settlement Body, or can several meetings take place between the time of the first and second requests, thus allowing the parties arguably to try to reach a mutually agreed settlement in that period?
- Should provision be made for members to become third parties to a case at the appellate stage of the dispute settlement process, i.e., there may be a dispute in which a member has no trade or systemic interest but the panel report contains interpretations that raise significant concerns the member would like to bring to the attention of the Appellate Body before it renders its decision on the matter.

One of the more fundamental issues raised by several commentators is that the dispute settlement system is not viewed as dealing suitably with multi-party complaints. It has been argued that the provisions of the DSU have to be further developed to deal more adequately with situations where there is more than one complaining party. In addition, some members have indicated a need to determine if there are disputes in which it would be appropriate to have more than one defendant and to elaborate the provisions that would be required in those circumstances.

Many members would also like to have the DSU clearly provide panels and the Appellate Body with the authority to make preliminary determinations or rulings. Although panels are increasingly being asked to make such determinations and do so on some issues, there is usually a significant amount of reluctance to address issues, such as the sufficiency of a request for the establishment of a panel, without hearing the entire case.

Members are also realizing that it is becoming more difficult to find panelists for the growing number of cases. Not only are more panelists required but the level of expertise required is also increasing. In addition, some individuals who would have readily served as panelists in the past now waiver in light of the tremendous amount of work it entails and the increased public profile such a position may have, depending on the dispute. Panelists have had to deal with submissions that are much longer, supporting evidence that is more extensive and complex, and meetings that are longer and more frequent, requiring them to devote more time and energy to study the issues and render a decision than was necessary in the past. Officials serving with the permanent missions to the WTO, the traditional source of panelists, have found the burden of serving on a panel while continuing their 'day' jobs more than many are prepared to accept.

The issue of allowing members to have private counsel participate in panel and Appellate Body proceedings appears to have been resolved by the Appellate Body's decision in the EC bananas case permitting private counsel to participate as part of a member's delegation. However, several members, developing countries in particular, would like to have this option clearly enunciated in the DSU in order not to have to debate the issue on each occasion.

Many disputes have proven far more complex than those dealt with in the context of the GATT. The evidence presented in some cases has been far more elaborate than the evidence presented by parties in the past. The growing length of both panel and Appellate Body reports—426 and 76 pages, respectively, in the recent shrimp-turtle case—illustrates the problem. Some members are calling for clear rules of evidence to ensure due process. They want rules to deal with the nature of the evidence presented, the acceptability of such evidence, and the timing within which the evidence is to be made available to the panel and the parties (Thomas, 1996, 1997).

A further issue is the public demand for greater transparency of the system. The debate revolves around the need, on the one hand, to keep various interested groups in society informed and to ensure that there is public confidence in the outcome of WTO dispute settlement system cases and the requirement, on the other hand, to ensure that commercial confidential information is protected and to maintain a system that can still recruit panelists and effectively exercise its role of safeguarding the rules (see Dunoff, 1998).

There is also the issue of the overall timing for the dispute settlement process. The time lines were designed to satisfy the demands of US Section 301 procedures and were generally in line with GATT experience. Recent experience has demonstrated, however, that the time lines may be too ambitious for all cases. Those who have been involved in cases, especially those cases requiring scientific expertise to be presented, have found that the time frames provided in the DSU are not realistic. There will certainly be attempts to adjust the time frames for specific stages of the process, if not to extend the overall time frame.

Of critical importance are the implementation provisions of the DSU. Canadian experience with them to date has been limited. Early implementation experience was positive, but several difficult cases since then, including the EU bananas and beef-hormone cases and the Canadian periodicals case, suggest that more detailed and precise rules may be desirable. It is understandable that if these provisions do not lead to the effective implementation of panel and Appellate Body rulings and recommendations, it will be a severe blow to the credibility of the dispute settlement system.

Although not crucial, some members have been disappointed with the application of the provision dealing with the determination of the reasonable period of time within which a member must comply with the rulings and recommendations. The arbitrators have tended to take a cautious approach by repeatedly deciding on the 15-month period, despite having the option of determining that a much shorter period is adequate.

The EC bananas case raised some interesting issues with regard to the implementation provisions of the DSU. There is debate regarding what the mandate is for the original panel that has to consider whether or not there is consistency or existence of measures to comply with the rulings and recommendations of the panel and Appellate Body. There is also debate as to whether the complaining party can proceed to compensation and retaliation without first asking for the original panel's view on the issue of consistency or the existence of measures to comply with the rulings and recommendations. US dissatisfaction with Canada's implementation of the periodicals decision also raises concerns regarding implementation.

There will undoubtedly be further discussion of how a member determines the amount of compensation or the amount for which it can retaliate, especially in circumstances where there was no trade prior to the introduction of the inconsistent measure or where it is difficult to quantify the trade impact of the measure.

THE PRICE OF SUCCESS

The extensive use of the WTO dispute settlement system is creating significant pressures on the resources, both financial and human, of members as well as of the secretariat. The pressures on the developing countries are particularly acute and members will have to reflect on the means through which they can assure the continued active participation of the developing countries. Members will have to find a way to address the issue of the prohibitive costs involved for developing countries. The dispute settlement system will only be respected and effective if all members can have access to it. They will need to guard against it becoming the preserve of the 'wealthy' few.

The financial and human resource pressures result not only from the increase in the number of cases but also because the submissions to the panels are generally far more comprehensive and lengthy than those presented in the context of the GATT. The disputes are often more complicated than in the past, thus requiring expertise in different fields. It has been argued that the WTO will not be able to continue to provide its high-quality assistance to panelists and the Appellate Body without additional resources, a prospect that appears slim in light of some leading members, such as the United States, maintaining that there must be zero budget growth for the WTO.[11]

The increasing number of cases being pursued under the dispute settlement system is perhaps the most telling indication of the system's success as well as of the need for review and perhaps eventual reform. It is extremely significant that the dispute settlement system is being used so extensively. Not only the developed countries but also the developing countries are making full use of the dispute settlement process. The increase can be attributed in part to the growing importance of trade to national economies. In Canada, for example, trade now accounts for 80 per cent of GDP. Members are also using the dispute settlement system because they view it as a reliable and effective means of securing market access commitments. In addition, there has been an increase in cases because members are not only dealing with traditional market-access issues, but also with a growing number of instances related to the treatment of goods and services within national economies; there are now disputes dealing with such matters as trade in services, the protection of intellectual property rights, sanitary and phytosanitary measures, and trade in agricultural products.

As of December 1998, there had been 155 requests for consultations, the first step in the dispute settlement process. The requests dealt with 118 distinct matters.[12] Most complaining parties invoked the GATT 1994 together with other agreements, particularly the Agreements on Subsidies and Countervailing Measures, Agriculture, Technical Barriers to Trade, Import Licensing Procedures, and Sanitary and Phytosanitary Measures. The most frequent complaining parties were: the United States (51 requests), the European Communities (40), Canada (13), India (8), Japan (6), Brazil (6), Mexico (5), New Zealand (4), Thailand (4), and Switzerland (3). In addition to the developing countries mentioned above, six developing countries have requested consultations twice and 13 developing countries have requested consultations once. The system is clearly not being used only by the developed countries.

The most frequent respondents were the United States (27 complaints), the European Communities (26), Japan (12), India (12), Canada (9), Brazil (8), Korea (8), Australia (6), Argentina (6), Indonesia (4), and Turkey (4). By the end of 1998, 42 distinct matters (involving 58 requests) had proceeded to the panel stage of the process. Of the 155 requests, a mutually agreed solution had been notified or announced with regard to 29 of them. That 19 per cent of the cases were settled on the basis of a mutually agreed solution is very encouraging.

Canada made 13 formal requests for consultations. It complained against the European Communities with regard to the trade description of scallops, the duties on imports of cereals, measures affecting livestock and meat (the hormones case), measures affecting asbestos and products containing asbestos, measures affecting the imports of wood and wood conifers, and patent protection for pharmaceutical and agricultural products. It complained against Japan with regard to its taxes on alcoholic beverages, against Australia for its measures affecting the importation of salmon, against Korea for its measures affecting the importation of bottled water, against Brazil for its export financing program for aircraft, against India for its quantitative restrictions on imports, and against the United States regarding certain measures affecting the importation of cattle, swine, and grain. Canada also joined five other complainants to make a request for consultations against Hungary with regard to its export subsidies.

Canada reached a mutually agreed solution in five of the above-mentioned cases. The scallops case went through the panel process but once the European Communities had seen the interim panel report, the parties moved expeditiously to negotiate a settlement. The case was resolved just prior to the issuing of the final panel report and the WTO was notified of the mutually agreed solution. Canada has also come to an agreement with the EC regarding the cereals case. In this instance, the invocation of panel proceedings was sufficient to convince the EC to respond seriously to Canada's complaint. However, the WTO has yet to be informed of the mutually agreed solution. The Korean bottled water case never went to a panel because a settlement was reached and then notified to the WTO. With regard to the Hungarian export subsidies case, unlike the other complainants, Canada decided not to request a panel. Subsequent to the request for a panel by the other complainants, a mutually agreed solution was notified to the WTO. Canada also reached a mutually agreed solution with India with regard to the issue of quantitative restrictions prior to having to request a panel.

Five cases have gone to the panel stage. After the panel and Appellate Body process, Canada's case was sustained against Japan in the liquor tax case and Japan is now implementing the recommendations. It is interesting to note that due to Japan's inability to implement fully all the recommendations within the reasonable period of time, Japan provided compensation. Again, after the panel and the Appellate Body process, Canada prevailed against the EC in the hormones case and against Australia in the salmon case. Although the two cases are at different stages of the dispute settlement process, both have yet to be implemented. The case against Brazil on export subsidies for aircraft is at the hearing stage of the panel process. Finally, a panel for the asbestos case against the EC was established in November 1998. At the end of 1998, three cases were at the consultation phase of the process: the complaints against the EC over wood and wood conifer imports and on patent protection for pharmaceutical and agricultural products, and the complaint against the United States regarding cattle, swine, and grain.

During the WTO's first four years, Canada was a respondent in nine cases involving six distinct matters. The United States complained against Canadian measures concerning periodicals. Brazil filed two different requests, both with regard to the export of civilian aircraft, but each request invoked different WTO provisions. The United States and New Zealand filed separate requests on the exportation of Canadian dairy products. The European Communities filed a complaint against the patent protection regime for pharmaceutical products and another complaint against Canadian measures affecting film distribution services. Finally, the European Communities and Japan filed separate complaints against measures affecting trade in automotive products.

Of these six distinct matters, only the periodicals case went through the complete panel and Appellate Body process. Canada's view did not prevail in this case and the government is in the process of implementing the panel's recommendations.[13] At the end of 1998, the export of civilian aircraft and the export of dairy products were both at the hearing stage of the panel process. Requests for the establishment of panels for the pharmaceutical products and the automotive industry cases were imminent. The film distribution services issue remained at the consultation stage.

In reviewing the above information, it becomes clear that Canada has been an extremely active participant in the dispute settlement system both as a complainant and as a defendant. In addition to the cases in which Canada has been either a complainant or a defendant, Canada has either requested to join consultations in complaints raised by other members or has become a third party with regard to matters that have gone to a panel in over 30 other cases. It is thus not difficult to conclude that, to date, Canada has benefited substantially from the dispute settlement process in a manner consistent with its traditionally strong advocacy of a strong, rules-based system with an effective dispute settlement system.

CONCLUSIONS

The dispute settlement mechanism has been working to the satisfaction of WTO member countries. However, members are monitoring the system very closely, particularly with regard to the implementation of the recommendations made by panels and the Appellate

Body. Members have recognized that the system is not without its flaws and improvements will be welcomed, either as a result of the 1998 review of the DSU or at some future time. What is more interesting is that the ultimate beneficiary, the business community, is gaining confidence in the system. Many sectors of the business community view the WTO dispute settlement system as a viable means through which to achieve some of their objectives. Business is beginning to realize what most members of the WTO have known for a long time—that all member countries of the WTO and their respective business communities stand to benefit from a strong rules-based international framework with an effective mechanism to enforce those rules. As one of the pre-eminent authorities on international trade law concluded recently, 'The new organization [WTO] has had a successful launch, it has engaged in a number of different activities, . . . and it has put into practice a quite remarkable set of new procedures for Dispute Settlement among nations concerning trade matters' (Jackson, 1998b: 330). Based on the first four years of experience, the WTO's capacity to defuse and resolve conflicts has been critical to making its rules work.

NOTES

The views and comments expressed in this chapter are those of the author and do not necessarily reflect the views of the government of Canada or the Department of Foreign Affairs and International Trade.

1. Statement dated 17 April 1997, reprinted at <www.wto.org>.
2. World Trade Organization, Ministerial Declaration, WT/MIN(96)/DEC/1, Dec. 1996.
3. In the context of the World Trade Organization, the European Communities (EC), rather than the European Union (EU), remains the proper designation.
4. Interested readers are invited to visit the dispute settlement section of the WTO Web site (see note 1), where full texts of the DSU, the WTO agreements, and all GATT and WTO panel and related decisions and reports can be retrieved.
5. The three official languages of the WTO are English, French, and Spanish. A panel report is usually issued to the disputing parties in one of the WTO's official languages. The panel report is only circulated to members of the WTO as a whole after it has been translated into the other two languages.
6. The defendant can only block the establishment of a panel the first time it appears on the agenda of the Dispute Settlement Body (DSB). The second time it appears on the agenda the panel will be established unless there is a consensus of all members of the WTO not to have it established.
7. Panel reports are automatically adopted by the DSB 60 days after they are circulated unless there is a consensus to block adoption or one of the parties to

the dispute appeals all or part of the ruling to the Appellate Body; a report of the Appellate Body is adopted within 30 days of its circulation unless there is a consensus to block its adoption.

8. The Appellate Body has taken a broad view of this requirement. In the periodicals case, for example, it decided that in order to 'complete the analysis' it would rule on matters that had not been raised on appeal by either Canada or the United States.

9. Steger and Hainsworth serve on the secretariat of the Appellate Body and Shoyer served in the US Mission to the WTO in Geneva.

10. Of course, should the scope of the WTO's rules expand to cover such matters as competition policy, investment, and other matters, the need for reform and improvements would become more pressing. As Pierre Sauvé and Chris Thomas argue in Chapter 5 the demands that would be placed on the DSU by competition policy alone would require major rethinking of some of its provisions. The purpose of the 1998 review, however, was not to anticipate the possible evolution of the multilateral trading system and the demands this would place on dispute settlement procedures, but to review the functioning of the DSU within the context of the current rules.

11. The items discussed above do not constitute a comprehensive list of all the 'concerns'. It is important to note that not all these concerns have to be resolved immediately to ensure the efficient functioning of the dispute settlement system. In fact, most concerns will require much reflection in order to determine how best to deal with them.

12. For example, if there have been three requests for consultations, each filed by a different member, but all three requests deal with the same issue, then it is considered as three requests for consultations but one distinct matter. The WTO maintains a detailed, up-to-date report on the status of all cases at its Web site.

13. As this article was being prepared for publication, US officials were arguing that Canada's response to the panel's recommendations does not mitigate its original complaint and are inconsistent with Canada's WTO obligations.

REFERENCES

Dunoff, Jeffrey L. 1998. 'The Misguided Debate Over NGO Participation at the WTO', *Journal of International Economic Law* 1, 3.

Hart, Michael. 1998. *Fifty Years of Canadian Tradecraft: Canada at the GATT 1947–1997.* Ottawa: Centre for Trade Policy and Law.

Jackson, John H. 1996. 'The WTO Dispute Settlement Procedures: A Preliminary Appraisal', in Jeffrey J. Schott, ed., *The World Trading System: Challenges Ahead.* Washington: Institute for International Economics.

————.1998a. 'Designing and Implementing Effective Dispute Settlement Procedures: WTO Dispute Settlement, Appraisal and Prospects', in Anne O. Krueger, ed., *The WTO as an International Organization.* Chicago: University of Chicago Press.

————. 1998b. 'Dispute Settlement and the WTO: Emerging Problems', *Journal of International Economic Law* 1, 3 (Sept.).

Marceau, Gabrielle. 1997. 'NAFTA and WTO Dispute Settlement Rules—A Thematic Comparison', *Journal of World Trade* 31, 2 (Apr.).

Pescatore, P., W.J. Davey, and A.F. Lowenfeld, eds. 1997. *Handbook of WTO/GATT Dispute Settlement*. Irvington-on-Hudson, NY: Transnational.

Petersmann, Ernst-Ulrich. 1997a. *International Trade Law and the GATT/WTO Dispute Settlement System*. London: Kluwer Law International.

———. 1997b. *The GATT/WTO Dispute Settlement System: International Law, International Organizations, and Dispute Settlement*. London: Kluwer Law International.

Shoyer, Andrew W. 1998. 'The First Three Years of WTO Dispute Settlement: Observations and Suggestions', *Journal of International Economic Law* 1, 2 (June).

Steger, Debra P., and Susan M. Hainsworth. 1998. 'World Trade Organization Dispute Settlement: The First Three Years', *Journal of International Economic Law* 1, 2 (June).

Thomas, J. Christopher. 1996. 'Litigation Process under the GATT Dispute Settlement System: Lessons for the World Trade Organization?', *Journal of World Trade* 30, 2.

———. 1997. 'The Need for Due Process in WTO Proceedings', *Journal of World Trade* 31, 1.

4

Canadian Agricultural Trade Policy: Continuity Amidst Change

GRACE SKOGSTAD

In late November 1999 members of the World Trade Organization (WTO) are scheduled to commence a new round of negotiations on agriculture. Designed to continue the reform process begun in the GATT Uruguay Round (1986–93), the scope of the negotiations is still undetermined. Whether it will extend beyond those items earmarked in the WTO Agreement on Agriculture—market access, domestic support, and export competition—will only be decided on the eve of the negotiations.[1] Although a narrow negotiation is less attractive to Canada than is a broader one, even a limited agricultural round has the potential to afford significant benefits to Canadian agriculture. Almost half of Canadian farm cash receipts are derived from agricultural exports (Vanclief, 1998: 1). Formulating a unified and credible negotiating position to present in Geneva in late 1999 is thus a major item on the current agenda of Canada's agricultural ministers and agri-food policy community.

This chapter examines the likely elements in the government of Canada's agricultural negotiating position during the next WTO Round. Canada's negotiating position will necessarily reflect the fundamental structural realities of Canada's agricultural economy, the priorities of the national and provincial governments, the interests and ideas of the Canadian agri-food sector as a whole, and Canada's experience with both the regional North American Free Trade Agreement (NAFTA) and the multilateral WTO agreement. Canada's agricultural economy continues to be bifurcated: while the most economically significant grain, oilseed, and red meat sectors rely on export markets to absorb much of their production, the supply-managed poultry, eggs, and dairy sectors continue to derive the vast percentage of their incomes from the protected domestic market. The challenge, first confronted during the Uruguay Round, of reconciling the divergent interests of export- and domestic-oriented agricultural sectors remains. The key question surrounding Canada's agricultural negotiation position will thus be how the federal government will balance greater market access for export-competitive commodities while restricting significant access to the Canadian market in supply-managed commodities.

This chapter argues that one should expect a significant measure of continuity in Canada's agricultural trade policy. Historically, Canada has placed a high priority on a rules-based trading system; this objective will remain uppermost in the forthcoming agricultural negotiations. In addition, greater liberalization of markets will be a goal, but one conditioned by the political necessity to reconcile the disparate interests within Canada's agri-food sector. The Minister of Agriculture and Agri-Food has embarked on a bottom-up strategy of trade policy formulation, engaging the agri-food community in a wide consultation process. This process works towards a trade policy position that reinforces objectives on which the export-oriented and domestic-focused sectors can agree: the need to eliminate export subsidies and to promulgate new and clear trade rules to prevent countries from using non-tariff barriers to restrict trade. At the same time, Canada will need to concede greater market exposure through lower tariffs on supply-managed commodities.

CANADIAN AGRICULTURE AND THE WORLD TRADING SYSTEM

Trade policy has always been a vital component of Canadian agricultural policy. Canada's most important agricultural commodities are highly dependent on external markets, even while constituting too small a share of world markets—currently 3 per cent—to be effective price-setters. Given Canada's political economy, the government has always placed a high priority on a stable and open trading system. Multilateral and, more recently, bilateral trade agreements have been the preferred vehicle to arrest trade protectionism and open other countries' markets to Canadian foodstuffs. Thus, Canada supported the General Agreement on Tariffs and Trade (GATT) from its inception in 1948, endorsing its founding principle 'that a rules-based system would serve the long-run interests of the member-countries better than a power-based system' (McKinney, 1994: 467).

Agriculture was effectively excluded from the GATT liberalizing framework until the successful conclusion of the Uruguay Round. Once the United States obtained a waiver in 1955 from most of its GATT obligations concerning agriculture, other countries followed suit. Subsequent rounds, most notably the Kennedy (1963–7) and Tokyo (1973–9) rounds, failed to bring agriculture within the GATT ambit.

The Uruguay Round marked an end to treating agriculture as an exceptional sector. With the implementation of the Agreement on Agriculture, the Agreement on Sanitary and Phytosanitary Measures (SPS Agreement), and the dispute settlement mechanism, the agricultural policies of the approximately 100 GATT members became constrained to an unprecedented degree by international rules and dispute settlement procedures.

The Agreement on Agriculture sought to place agriculture on a more market-oriented path by requiring countries to make specific, binding commitments on market access, domestic support, and export competition, to be implemented over the period 1995–2000. To enable greater access to their domestic markets, countries were required to replace their non-tariff border measures (such as import controls and licences) with bound tariffs. Developed countries were subsequently to reduce these new tariffs by 36 per cent. In addition, minimum access requirements meant that countries had to allow imports (at minimal tariffs) equal to 3 per cent and rising to 5 per cent of domestic consumption over the six-year period. Members further agreed to reduce their aggregate domestic support by 20 per cent from their 1986–8 base. Producer payments not tied to production decisions or market prices (green box programs) were exempt from this discipline, as were producer payments not related to market prices but designed to limit production (blue box programs). Export subsidies were to be reduced 36 per cent by expenditures and 21 per cent by volume from their 1986–90 base, and new export subsidies are prohibited.

The direct effects of the Agreement on Agriculture on Canadian agriculture and agricultural policy were modest. The tariffs imposed on dairy, poultry, and egg imports were set at such high levels that they resulted in higher average rates of protection than the import quotas they replaced. Canada had already reduced its domestic aggregate support by the amounts stipulated. The process of re-designing agricultural income safety nets for the grains sector to meet the exempt criteria of non- or minimally trade-distorting measures was already under way and continued. The Agreement on Agriculture *did* dictate domestic policy reforms with respect to the commitment to reduce export subsidies on grain and dairy products.

Driven by the goal of reducing fiscal deficits, the government of Canada went well beyond the requirements of the Agreement on Agriculture. The 1995 federal budget completely eliminated export grain subsidies, rather than simply reducing them by the stipulated 36 per cent. Since the implementation of the Agreement on Agriculture, domestic aggregate support has dropped from $5 billion to around $2 billion, far in excess of the mandated 20 per cent cut. Canada has met and in some cases surpassed the WTO market access commitments for supply-managed products.[2] As a result, transfers to Canadian agriculture as a percentage of the total value of production are lower in Canada than in the European Union or the United States and well below the Organization for Economic Co-operation and Development (OECD) average (OECD, 1997: 31). The differences are especially stark with respect to government transfers to wheat pro-ducers. In 1997, European farmers received $116 per tonne of wheat in government subsidies; American farmers, $72; Canadian farmers, $15 (Wilson, 1998: 19).

UNFINISHED AND NEW BUSINESS:
THE NEED FOR FURTHER REFORM

While path-breaking in its effort to define 'clear, workable and oper-ationally effective rules' for agricultural trade (Tangerman, 1994: 149), the Agreement on Agriculture was less revolutionary in constraining the agricultural policies of industrialized countries and in opening markets. The immediate improvement in market access for grain and grain products, a high priority for the Canadian government and Canadian grain farmers, was relatively limited. Not only were the reductions in grain export subsidies modest, the Agreement on Agriculture effectively locked in existing agricultural expenditure policies in the United States and the European Union. It exempted from expenditure cuts the EU's 1993 Common Agricultural Policy (CAP) reforms, aimed at replacing price supports with less trade-distorting deficiency payments, as well as the US grain deficiency payments. These green box payments have continued to represent significant transfers to European farmers and American grain growers.

A major gain for Canada flowing from the Uruguay Round has been the heightened efficacy of the WTO dispute settlement mechanism (as compared to the predecessor GATT system). Trading relations based on rules and effective enforcement procedures, rather than on economic and market power, are obviously a high priority for Canada. The WTO trade dispute settlement procedures (in conjunction with those in NAFTA) have provided Canada with an important bargaining lever, helping to mitigate American threats to restrict Canadian access to the US market because Canada is trading 'unfairly'. Two examples are illustrative. The first occurred early in the implementation of the Agreement on Agriculture, when the United States challenged the high in-quota tariffs Canada placed on supply-managed products (milk, dairy products, eggs, egg products, poultry, and poultry products). A NAFTA panel agreed with Canada that the tariffs were legal within the terms of both NAFTA and the GATT/WTO. Moreover, the panel ruled that the GATT/WTO takes precedence over NAFTA (NAFTA Arbitral Panel, 1996).

The second example demonstrates the different bargaining power of Canadian agricultural officials before and after the Uruguay Round, and concerns American efforts to curtail Canadian agricultural exports, in particular grain, to the United States. In 1994, prior to the WTO Agreement on Agriculture, a surge in Canadian wheat and barley exports to the United States was met with American threats to restrict unilaterally Canadian wheat and barley shipments to the United States.[3] Canada negotiated concessionary quotas on its wheat sales to the United States to ward off the possibility that the United States would impose import controls, as it was then entitled to do under its domestic farm legislation. Had it done so, such import controls could have been converted to tariffs and tariff-rate quotas as part of US implementation of the Agreement on Agriculture. The

Agreement on Agriculture ended the US government's capacity to impose unilateral controls on wheat imports and, thereby, eliminated an important weapon in the American trade harassment artillery. The Agreement on Agriculture has *not* ruled out American harassment of Canadian agri-food products. Such harassment continues, affecting a range of commodities that includes beef, live cattle, and grains, but the WTO dispute settlement mechanism requires the United States to play more by the international trading rules and undermines its capacity to use its sheer economic weight to effect terms of trade in its favour. Thus, Canadian governments are better able to rebuff American pressure for curbs on legally traded Canadian grain and other exports without fear of American unilateral retaliation.[4]

The various provisions of the Uruguay Round, however, have fallen short in promoting market liberalism and eliminating non-tariff barriers and other trade-distorting agricultural policies. In 1998 Canadian grain producers continued to find themselves competing against the EU and US treasuries for export markets, without the export subsidies enjoyed by their European and American counterparts. In addition, new non-tariff barriers have arisen as effective border protection measures. Canadian cattle, pork, and grains continue to be stopped at the American border as US officials ensure that they meet American sanitary and phytosanitary standards. Food and safety measures have emerged as important technical barriers to trade. In short, the Canadian experience since the Uruguay Round reiterates the need to strengthen rules regarding non-tariff barriers in the form of environmental and health measures, and for further reforms regarding market access, export subsidies, and domestic support.[5]

WTO signatories have recognized the need to address technical barriers to trade in the next round on agriculture. The terms of the Agreement on Agriculture stipulated new negotiations, to begin in the fifth year of implementation, to continue the reform process. At the same time, members agreed to review the SPS Agreement and the dispute settlement mechanism. The commitment to new agricultural negotiations was renewed at the WTO ministerial meeting in Singapore in December 1996. At that time, the WTO Committee on Agriculture, created to oversee the implementation of the Agreement, began a work program assessing compliance with existing commitments and a process of analysis and information exchange in preparation for the 1999 round. Its work is intended to clarify specific issues related to market access, export subsidies, and domestic support.

DEVELOPING A CANADIAN NEGOTIATING POSITION

The Minister of Agriculture and Agri-Food Canada (AAFC), Lyle Vanclief, has defined Canada's priorities in the forthcoming WTO negotiations to be 'a more open, rules-based international trading environment' (Agriculture and Agri-Food Canada, 1998a). His senior official responsible for international trade has been more specific, reiterating that growth in Canada's agri-food sector is contingent not only on the 'rule of law', but also on phasing out export subsidies and implementing 'a system where more and more domestic support policies are less trade distorting and more production neutral'.[6]

A rules-based trading system without export subsidies is a goal on which all of Canada's agri-food sector and federal and provincial governments can unite. More problematic will be finding a consensus on issues related to market access. In recognition of the diversity of interests that comprise Canada's agri-food policy community, the minister has embarked on a consultative strategy with the agri-food sector designed to arrive at a negotiation position that is 'strong, unified and credible' (Vanclief, 1998).

A central element of the consultative strategy with the agri-food sector is the 'Take Note' hearings of the House of Commons Standing Committee on Agriculture and Agri-Food.[7] Designed to enable agri-food interests to air their interests and concerns, these hearings are being supplemented with bilateral meetings between the federal Minister of Agriculture and Agri-Food and farm groups. An industry-wide conference in April 1999 to bring the sector together with federal and provincial ministers of agriculture is the latest step in forging a consensual negotiating position to be taken to the federal cabinet.

This bottom-up approach to devising a negotiating position is consistent with the approach adopted during the Uruguay Round when the Agriculture, Food, and Beverage Sectoral Advisory Group on International Trade (SAGIT) provided a two-way consultation and information mechanism between the agricultural sector and international trade officials. The SAGIT mechanism and the significant advisory role for the farm community in formulating Canada's multilateral trade position paid off for Canada. Not only were farmers pleased with their input, but the government was able to formulate a 'balanced approach' that enabled a united Canadian position before external negotiators and a minimum of internal discord.[8]

The consultation with the farm community is paralleled by intergovernmental consultations and co-ordination among federal and provincial governments through the federal-provincial Agricultural Trade Policy Committee. Federal and provincial ministers of agriculture are in accord on the importance of further liberalization of international agricultural markets. They can be expected to disagree as to the respective emphasis to be placed on each of market access, export competition, and domestic support measures, depending on the relative importance to their provincial economies of export-oriented foodstuffs (grains, oilseeds, pork, and cattle), the food-processing sector, and supply-managed commodities (dairy, poultry, and eggs). On the whole, provincial governments have enjoyed extensive input into federal agricultural trade policy and have worked closely with Ottawa on trade disputes of significance to their farm sectors.[9]

The political economy within which Canada's farm community enters the 1999 WTO agricultural negotiations has changed in some important respects from that in effect throughout the Uruguay Round. First, as a result of domestic government policies and regional and multilateral trade agreements, Canadian farmers are now more exposed to market forces and more reliant on external markets for farm incomes. This dependence on market returns is clearly greater in the grains and oilseeds sectors than in the supply-managed sectors. However, even in the latter, changes have been implemented and future changes are anticipated to make the supply-managed sectors more competitive.[10] Since 1993, the value of Canadian agricultural and agri-food exports has increased by 50 per cent, owing to increases in both the volume and prices of exports (Canadian Agricultural Marketing Council, 1998: 2). The largest growth in exports has been in the higher-value processed foods and beverages, which have witnessed a doubling from 8 to 16 per cent in the past eight years. Second, the bulk of this trade growth has been with the United States, with the result that the Canadian and American agri-food sectors have become highly integrated. The United States supplies over 60 per cent of Canada's agricultural imports (American Farm Bureau, 1998: Table 7) and absorbs 57 per cent of Canadian agri-food exports (OMAFRA, 1997: Table 4). Third, a process of restructuring, consolidation, and concentration in the food- and beverage-processing sector has resulted in multinational enterprises (MNEs) now accounting for about one-half of food-sector exports. The emergence of such MNEs heightens the priority of competitiveness concerns and brings to the fore pressure to eliminate domestic regulations and policies—such as supply management—that impede the access of MNEs to low-cost inputs.

In short, as Canada prepares for the next agricultural negotiations, the ascendant interests of both governments and private agri-food interests lie with agricultural trade liberalization and the removal of domestic regulatory barriers to international competitiveness.

THE NEXT WTO AGRICULTURAL AGENDA

The WTO Agreement mandates further reform discussions on market access, export competition and subsidies, and domestic support measures. Other issues that will receive attention are technical and non-tariff barriers to trade and state-trading enterprises. Some issues, notably market access, will prove more problematic for Canada than others, such as eliminating export subsidies. Canada is likely to find itself on different sides of the world's two agricultural superpowers— the United States and the European Union—depending on the issue: with the United States on the need to eliminate export subsidies, but opposed to it on enhanced market access for sensitive products.

Market Access[11]
During the Uruguay Round negotiations, Canada attempted to defend its right to limit access to the Canadian market for commodities subject to domestic supply management. It sought to retain Article XI.2.c, which authorized import controls in such circumstances, and to expand its scope to include processed products for which supply-managed commodities are a major component. The availability of Article XI as a policy instrument allowed Canada to adopt a negotiating stance that defended the trade interests of the poultry and dairy sectors, dominant in Quebec and Ontario, without abdicating the trade-liberalizing interests of export-oriented western grains and oilseed sectors.

As noted earlier, the Agreement on Agriculture eliminated access to the import control mechanisms provided by Article XI.2.c, requiring import controls (quotas and licences) to be converted to tariff-rate quotas. The same policy instruments—tariffs and minimum-access commitments—are now of interest to both the export and import-sensitive industries, but in diametrically opposed manners. Accordingly, minus Article XI, Canada faces a major challenge as it enters the 1999 round: how to defend the current prohibitively high tariffs and low minimum-access commitments (on imports at much lower tariff rates) on supply-managed commodities, even while seeking maximum reductions in tariffs and further increases in minimum-access commitments for the export sectors (principally grains and oilseeds).

The absence of a consensus on how to reconcile the divergent interests of the import-sensitive and export-oriented sectors on the issue of market access is readily apparent. Organizations like the newly formed Canadian Alliance of Agri-Food Exporters[12] representing export-oriented agri-food interests, the Saskatchewan Wheat Pool, and Manitoba's Agricore, for example, are pressing the federal government to take a strong stand in favour of large increases in minimum-access commitments, maximum reductions in tariffs, with high tariffs subject to greater cuts and elimination of all in-quota duties. On the other hand, poultry and egg producers argue that tariff-rate quotas must be maintained and foreign product limited in its access to the Canadian market. Canadian negotiators, they argue, should pursue fairer trade rules, not freer trade rules or increased trade liberalization, and focus on non-tariff barriers such as food safety regulations.[13] The supply-managed sectors argue that they have more than met their commitments with respect to minimum-access requirements, and until other countries do the same they should not be required to grant more access. By contrast, those for whom poultry products are an input cost, the poultry processors, are urging that the tariffs that protect supply-managed commodities be gradually phased out.[14]

The position of AAFC is, first, to reaffirm its commitment to supply management as 'a sensitive area that is important' (Vanclief, 1998) and, second, to reiterate that supply-managed sectors should not be required to make concessions beyond those demanded of any other country. All countries, it observes, have the right to insist that sensitive sectors not be required to make abrupt changes overnight; rather, they need time to adjust to more open markets.[15] AAFC's position, it should be noted, is congruent with that of the national umbrella farm organization, the Canadian Federation of Agriculture, which advocates 'a balanced position' that achieves gains for exporters but without sacrificing the needs of import-sensitive sectors.[16]

Since the implementation of the Agreement on Agriculture, the United States has focused on Canada's high tariff-rate quotas for chicken, dairy, and egg products. Unsuccessful in its 1995–6 NAFTA challenge of these tariffs, the United States will certainly target them during the next WTO round. However, its own commitment to expanded market access will be tempered by domestic pressure to continue to protect its sugar, peanut, cotton, citrus, and other sensitive sectors.

Domestic Support Measures

Given its comparatively low level of government support relative to its international competitors, Canada's farm community is seeking reforms to both the level and type of allowable government support for agriculture. Canadian farm groups do not want government support eliminated; they are keen to keep the 'green' decoupled programs (those divorced from production decisions and market prices), deeming them vital to keep producers in business during a depressed price cycle. But Canadian farmers are seeking significant reductions in the high government transfers to agriculture in the European Union and the United States, including elimination of the EU 'blue box' production-limiting programs, which are currently exempt from WTO expenditure reductions. While trade-distorting support is the priority, Canadian farmers are likely to support disciplines on all agricultural expenditure programs.

In targeting blue box programs, Canada can expect to find an ally in the United States. Changes in the form of producer payments in the 1996 US Federal Agriculture Improvement and Reform (FAIR) Act have left the EU alone in the blue box. The FAIR Act has positioned US farmers on a trajectory of increasing reliance on markets and exports for producer income. Nevertheless, strong evidence remains, as witnessed by a $6 billion payment to American farmers in late 1998, of US government readiness to support American farmers when prices turn down. In short, the United States will support lower domestic subsidies, but not the termination of its domestic farm programs.

While the EU will support the principle that domestic support must be decoupled (divorced from output), it will not abandon its right to subsidize its agricultural sector. Under pressures of enlargement with the possible accession of ten Central and East European countries and the continuing high cost of the Common Agricultural

Policy (CAP), the EU is pursuing further market-oriented reforms to its CAP. It remains adamant about not abandoning its European model for agriculture (Fischler, 1998a). Its Agenda 2000 proposals confirm the high priority placed on maintaining a rural population and an environmentally sustainable agriculture. The proposals also retain blue box support: agricultural support payments in the form of direct aid to producers, rather than market price supports.

Export Competition and State-Trading Enterprises

A high and unanimous priority of the Canadian farm community is an end to export subsidies. As world grain prices plummeted in 1998, Canadian grain farmers were significantly harmed since the EU and the United States continued to subsidize their exports within WTO-allowable limits. Despite its continuing use of export subsidies, the Americans appear ready to reduce their levels in the next WTO round. The EU Agenda 2000 agricultural reform proposals currently being considered would move EU cereal and livestock prices to world levels, and can thus augur well for further disciplines on export subsidies.

The American willingness to forgo export subsidies is, however, likely to be linked to other countries' willingness to abandon other export competition instruments. A prime American target is state-trading enterprises, in particular the Canadian and Australian wheat marketing boards. State-trading enterprises, which include export and import monopoly marketing agencies, are not covered by the Agreement on Agriculture, but rather by GATT Article XVII. The United States has signalled its intention to place state-trading enterprises on the agenda; whether it will succeed will only be decided at the WTO ministerial meeting of 30 November–3 December 1999, on the eve of the commencement of the next WTO round. The Americans' long-standing complaint with state-trading agencies is that agencies like the Canadian Wheat Board are not sufficiently transparent in their pricing and marketing transactions.[17] Representatives of the prairie wheat pools will press Canada to resist any concessions on the operation of state-trading enterprises in exchange for elimination of export subsidies. Canada's chief trade negotiator, Mike Gifford, has stated that Canada is not prepared to discuss its different marketing philosophy. In arguing that the Canadian Wheat Board is not an unfair trading instrument, Canada can expect support from Australia and the EU (*Western Producer*, 1998a).

Technical and Non-Tariff Barriers

The dispute over hormone-fed beef between the United States and Canada, on the one hand, and the European Union, on the other, has highlighted the emerging importance of food safety and health measures as technical barriers to trade. Since 1989, hormone-fed beef has been denied entry to the European Union. The entry into force in 1995 of the WTO SPS Agreement provided a legal basis for Canada and the United States (whose animals are fed the hormones in question) to challenge the ban. Although the WTO has upheld the SPS Agreement's requirement that food safety measures affecting trade be justified on scientific grounds, the EU has been reluctant to abide by the WTO ruling, securing additional time within which to demonstrate the scientific validity of its hormone ban.

The meat hormone dispute demonstrates the wide gap dividing North Americans and Europeans on their willingness to rely exclusively on scientific criteria in determining the safety of agri-food products. The gap extends to European scepticism about the safety of genetically modified products, a scepticism unmatched in North America.

Canadian farm groups, like their American counterparts, are urging the federal government to take a strong stand in defence of the existing science-based SPS Agreement and against the use of sanitary or phytosanitary measures to block market access. Canadian and American agriculture has a competitive advantage *vis-à-vis* European farmers in using biotechnologies such as genetically modified canola and corn. Canada will push for developing an international framework to allow trade in genetically enhanced products, even while maintaining mechanisms to ensure human health and safety and environmental safety.[18] The EU, by contrast, will adopt a go-slow approach to approval of genetically modified organisms, demanding long-term tests to ensure their safety.

As Canada formulates its trade strategy over the next year, it is conscious that it is a relatively minor player in multilateral agricultural negotiations. Its influence will be enhanced through its membership in the Cairns Group[19] but, as during the Uruguay Round, it is unlikely to agree fully with the Cairns Group's market liberalization agenda. In the final analysis, therefore, Canada's capacity to secure its trade policy objectives will depend on how closely its goals parallel those of the two players who will decisively shape the next round of agricultural negotiations: the United States and the European Union.

LOOKING AHEAD: THE LIKELY RESULTS AND SUCCESS

A number of as yet unanswered questions will affect the outcome of the next round of agricultural negotiations. A first question is whether the round will expand beyond the WTO's built-in agenda: agriculture, services,[20] and trade-related aspects of intellectual property rights. Whether the agricultural round will remain a 'mini' round or will be expanded to a broader negotiation that includes tariffs on industrial goods and anti-dumping rules, for example, will not likely be determined until much closer to the commencement of the round. Canada would like a broader negotiation since, like the United States, it is looking to achieve more in trade negotiations than it has available to give up in terms of access to its own market. Countries like Japan and Korea are unlikely to accept politically difficult concessions in opening their agricultural markets without the possibility of obtaining concessionary market-access benefits for their industrial sectors. There is evidence that both the EU (*Western Producer*, 1998b: 63) and the United States are interested in a multilateral negotiation that includes all sectors of trade.

A second unknown that will affect the pace of the negotiations is whether the US administration will obtain fast-track authority for the WTO negotiations. If the view of an American trade policy expert is correct—that fast-track authority will be delayed until at least 2001— the round will proceed slowly without the necessary ingredient of American leadership.[21]

A third, and final question mark, arises over whether there is a sufficient perception of the need for agricultural reform to lend momentum to the 1999 round. On the one hand, there appears no urgency to reach agreement on new market-liberalizing reforms. There is nothing—yet—akin to the grain trade wars that underwrote the Uruguay Round. The most significant agricultural trading nations have reformed their agricultural policies to remove some of their trade-distorting effects. Most WTO members have met their commitments and some have exceeded them; the exception is a number of administrative issues related to tariff-rate quotas (OECD, 1997: 25). In addition, a number of countries that would be looked to for market-access opportunities—including those in Asia—have been hit by currency instability and an overall economic crisis. They can be expected to be leery of further opening their economies. There is also the question of the EU's interest in pushing forward a multilateral round while it is in the throes of reforming its own CAP: should it reform in advance of the negotiations or while they are under way?

If there are reasons to be pessimistic about a full-scale and expeditious agricultural round, there are none the less reasons to believe that the environment is propitious for further multilateral trade liberalization. First, agricultural communities in Western industrialized countries are now more 'conditioned' to trade liberalization than they were in the mid-1980s and may, therefore, mount less resistance to it. Even in the European Union there is recognition of the need for European agriculture to be more internationally competitive and to rely on exports for expansion (Miner, 1998: 20). The Agenda 2000 reform proposals position European agriculture in a more market-oriented direction. Second, an infrastructure is in place, in the form of the WTO Committee on Agriculture, to expedite the ongoing dialogue and information exchanges that enhance trust and make policy reform possible. Third, the agricultural negotiations will acquire some urgency when the 'peace clause' expires in 2002. It immunized countries from retaliatory measures if they observed their obligations to reduce subsidies and trade barriers. Finally, there is a growing sense that the use of environmental and health and safety measures as barriers to trade must be curbed.

In summary, the most likely outcome of the forthcoming agricultural negotiations will be further opening of agricultural markets, with leeway left for countries to practise different marketing philosophies. Modest expectations and limited reforms would appear to be the catchwords, as captured by the EU Agriculture Commissioner, Franz Fischer (1998b): 'This is not the time of ideological crusades, but of pragmatic approaches to promote a "rapprochement" of our respective agricultural policies while preserving a healthy dose of realism as to what is advisable and achievable.'

NOTES

1. The specific terms of reference for the negotiations will be set by the WTO ministers of agriculture when they meet, 30 Nov.–3 Dec. 1999.
2. Standing Committee on Agriculture and Agri-Food (29 Oct.1998). Imports of chicken constitute roughly 7 per cent of total domestic consumption; broiler hatching eggs, 21.1 per cent of total domestic requirements.
3. Later, American trade negotiators offered concessions on Canadian wheat export ceilings in exchange for Canada withdrawing protection for supply-managed products. For a full discussion of the dispute, see Skogstad (1995).

4. Under pressure from domestic interests, the US government undertook fact-finding investigations in 1987, 1993, and 1997 into whether Canadian cattle shipments were detrimental to the US market. There were calls for yet another inquiry in October 1998. In late 1998, North Dakota farmers mounted a blockade of Canadian grain and livestock. US trade officials came to the negotiating table when Canada said it was prepared to challenge the North Dakota action before the WTO and NAFTA.

5. These themes were reiterated by the farm groups appearing before the House of Commons Standing Committee on Agriculture and Agri-Food, beginning 22 Oct. 1998.

6. Testimony of Mike Gifford, Director-General of the International Trade Policy Directorate of AAFC, to the Standing Committee on Agriculture and Agri-Food, 22 Oct. 1998.

7. The three questions posed to groups that appear before the 'Take Note' hearings are: What are your long-term economic goals? What role can the next WTO round play in helping to realize these long-term goals? And what priorities should Canada pursue in these negotiations?

8. See testimony of Jack Wilkinson, President of the CFA, to the House of Commons Standing Committee on Agriculture and Agri-Food, 3 Nov. 1998.

9. The Canadian government has consulted closely with the governments of Quebec and Ontario, as well as other concerned provinces and the dairy industry, in preparing its submission to the current WTO panel examining the legality of Canada's dairy export-pricing system. The United States is challenging the milk-pricing and pooling system the Canadian dairy industry established in 1995, which enables milk for use in other dairy products and products containing dairy ingredients to be purchased at a lower price than that established by the milk-pricing formula. The scheme is designed to enable dairy processors and further processors to be competitive in domestic and global markets.

10. These changes include export marketing initiatives and giving Canadian processors access to supply-managed inputs at prices competitive with American counterparts. In July 1998, provincial and federal governments ordered more changes to provide national marketing agencies with greater flexibility to adapt to an altered marketing environment. See Wilson (1998a: 3).

11. Several technical issues related to market access implementation, highlighted by the WTO Committee on Agriculture (OECD, 1997: 25) and by farm groups appearing before the 'Take Note' hearings, are not considered here. These matters include the allocation of access under tariff quotas and limits on imports of particular products under broadly defined tariff-quota commitments.

12. The Canadian Alliance of Agri-Food Exporters includes the Canadian Cattlemen's Association, Canadian Meat Council, Canadian Oilseed Processors Association, Canadian Pork Council, Canadian Sugar Institute, Malting Industry Association of Canada, Ontario Soybean Growers Marketing Board, Ontario Wheat Producers Marketing Board, Prairie Pools Inc., and XCAN Grain Pool Ltd.

13. See testimony of Chicken Farmers of Canada and the Canadian Egg Marketing Agency to the Standing Committee on Agriculture and Agri-Food, 29 Oct. 1998.

14. Ibid. See testimony of the Further Poultry Processors Association of Canada to the House of Commons Standing Committee on Agriculture and Agri-Food, 29 Oct. 1998.
15. See the testimony of Mike Gifford to the Standing Committee on Agriculture and Agri-Food, 22 Oct. 1998: 'All countries have sensitive sectors, or high support levels in certain sectors, and they're not prepared to make abrupt changes to long-standing farm programs. When change comes it tends to come over reduction commitments of five or ten years.'
16. Testimony of Jack Wilkinson, President of the Canadian Federation of Agriculture, to the Standing Committee on Agriculture and Agri-Food, 3 Nov. 1998.
17. The Canadian Wheat Board has been subject to no less than seven investigations by American government officials since 1990, none of which has found evidence of unfair trading.
18. Testimony of Mike Gifford, Standing Committee on Agriculture and Agri-Food Canada, 22 Oct. 1998.
19. The Cairns Group of 15 agricultural trading nations was formed in 1986 to promote agricultural trade liberalization. It played an active role in the Uruguay Round and intends to do the same during the next agricultural round. It endorsed a Vision Statement in April 1998 calling for the elimination of all export subsidies and any domestic subsidies with trade-distorting impacts, as well as deep cuts to tariffs and disciplines on the use of export credits.
20. Negotiations on services are slated to begin in the year 2000.
21. Such is the view Charles Roh, a former Assistant US Trade Representative, presented at a seminar sponsored by the Ontario Ministry of Agriculture, Food and Rural Affairs (OMAFRA), 11 June 1998.

REFERENCES

Agriculture and Agri-Food Canada. 1998. News Release: 'Canada Achieves Objectives at Cairns Group Meeting', 3 Apr. Available at:
<http://www.agr.ca/cb/news/n80403ae.html>
American Farm Bureau. 1998. Analysis: 'U.S. Agricultural Export Experience with NAFTA Partners'. Available at:
<http://www.fb.corn/issues/analysis/nafta/NAFTA-index.html>
Canadian Agricultural Marketing Council. 1998. Appendix A: 'Prospects for Agri-Food Trade Growth'. Available at:
<http://www.agr.ca/policy/epad/english/pubs/adhoc/camc/appa.html>
Fischler, Franz. 1998a. 'Intervention. Session I: "Agricultural Policy Reform: Stock-taking of Achievements"'. OECD meeting of the Committee for Agriculture at ministerial level, Paris, 5–6 Mar.
———. 1998b. 'Speaking Notes. Session II: "The Need for Further Reform"', OECD meeting of the Committee for Agriculture at ministerial level, Paris, 5–6 Mar.
McKinney, Joseph A. 1994. 'The world trade regime: past successes and future challenges', *International Journal* 49 (Summer): 445–71.

Miner, William M. 1998. *The International Policy Environment for Agricultural Trade Negotiations*. Ottawa: Economic and Policy Analysis Directorate, Policy Branch, Agriculture and Agri-Food Canada.

NAFTA Arbitral Panel Established Pursuant to Article 2008. 1996. *In the Matter of Tariffs Applied by Canada to Certain U.S.-Origin Agricultural Products. Final Report of the Panel*. 2 Dec.

OECD (Organization for Economic Co-operation and Development). 1997. *Agricultural Policies in OECD Countries: Monitoring and Evaluation 1997*. Paris.

OMAFRA (Ontario Ministry of Agriculture, Food, and Rural Affairs). 1997. *Agri-Food Trade Update* No. 82, 27 May.

Skogstad, Grace. 1995. 'Warring over Wheat: Managing Bilateral Trading Tensions', in Susan D. Phillips, ed., *How Ottawa Spends 1995–96: Mid-life Crisis*. Ottawa: Carleton University Press, 323–47.

Standing Committee on Agriculture and Agri-Food. 1998. *Evidence*. Ottawa: House of Commons. Available at: <http://www.parl.gc.ca/InfoComDoc/AGRI/Meetings/Evidence/AGRIEV50-E.HTM> (22 Oct.); AGRIEV52-E.HTM (29 Oct.); AGRIEV53-E.HTM (3 Nov.).

Tangermann, Stefan. 1994. 'An Assessment of the Agreement on Agriculture', in OECD, *The New World Trading System: Readings*. Paris.

Vanclief, Lyle. 1998. Address to the House of Commons Standing Committee on Agriculture and Agri-Food, 22 Oct. Ottawa.

Western Producer. 1998a. 'EU backs Canada's wheat board', 18 June, 23.

———. 1998b. 'Non-ag issues wanted in WTO talks', 8 Oct., 63.

Wilson, Barry. 1998a. 'Ministers order sweeping change for dairy, egg, poultry industries', *Western Producer*, 23 July.

———. 1998b. '"Blood bath" in grain markets due to international subsidies', *Western Producer*, 3 Dec., 19.

5

Towards Internationally Contestable Markets: Trade Policy's Efficiency-Enhancing Response to Globalization?

PIERRE SAUVÉ AND J. CHRISTOPHER THOMAS

With the success of the Uruguay Round and earlier multilateral negotiations in reducing levels of import protection at national borders, attention has shifted to other impediments to trade arising from government policy or the conduct of private firms. The label 'new dimensions of market access' has been given to public policy measures such as competition law enforcement, government procurement practices, product certification and technical standards, research and development (R&D) policies, and investment incentives, as well as to private actions such as cartels, abuse of dominant position, and vertical foreclosure (see OECD, 1995). While such new dimensions have received considerable analytical scrutiny in academic, business, and government circles and in various international forums (e.g., the OECD, APEC, and the WTO) since the completion of the Uruguay Round, discussions have most recently centred on the incipient notion of 'international market contestability'. Developed initially within the OECD Trade Committee, the concept refers to the maintenance of a business environment in which competitive conditions are not unduly distorted or impeded by anti-competitive governmental *or* private action. The concept of contestability has already found its place in economic theory, particularly industrial organization theory, and has exerted significant influence on antitrust practice (see Box 1). This paper aims to show that it may also usefully be employed in a trade policy setting.

Considering trade, investment, and competition policies in a coherent and integrated manner, international market contestability represents an important qualitative deepening in the nature and degree of liberalization that can be sought in future rounds of multilateral trade negotiations. Securing the greater openness of markets to global competition is likely to entail some rewriting of the multilateral trading system's rules. The object of this paper is to explore some of the forces that underpin the 'contestability' issue, highlight the possible architectural or rule-design implications of anchoring competition values and principles more firmly within the multilateral trading system, and reflect on a number of political economy considerations that pursuing a competition-oriented trade agenda might generate.

TRADE POLICY IN A CHANGING ECONOMIC LANDSCAPE

More than a dozen years have elapsed since the 1986 launch of the Uruguay Round. During this time, political and economic changes, most remarkably in a large number of transition and developing economies but also within the OECD area, have led to an increased emphasis on the values of market-based competition. In developed and developing countries alike, the domestic policy framework has focused on structural adjustment initiatives directed at enhancing market forces by redefining the boundaries of government intervention, through regulatory reform that promotes structural change in major sectors, privatization, tax and social security reform, increasing labour market flexibility, and other related policies (see OECD, 1994a).

This period has also seen a significant global push towards trade and investment regime liberalization and, through the adoption of outward-oriented strategies, efforts towards greater integration into the world economy on the part of transition and developing

Box 1

The theory of contestable markets can be traced to the work of three American economists, William Baumol, John Panzar, and Robert Willig (1982), who posited that the scope for potential entry by new firms or products was an important consideration in determining a market's competitive condition or 'contestability'.

Baumol et al. argued that a market was perfectly contestable if three conditions were satisfied. First, new firms must face no disadvantage *vis-à-vis* existing firms. This means that new firms have access to the same production technology, input prices, products, and information about demand. Second, there are zero sunk costs; all costs associated with entry are fully recoverable. A new firm can then exit the industry costlessly: if entry requires construction of a production facility or the establishment of a physical presence in a market at cost K, then sunk costs are zero if, on exiting the industry, a firm can sell its facilities or commercial presence for K (less any amount due to physical depreciation). The third condition is that the entry lag (which equals the time between when a firm's entry into the industry is known by existing firms and when the new firm is able to supply the market) is less than the price adjustment lag for existing firms (the time between when it desires to change prices and when it can change prices). The inventors of the concept of contestability thus characterize a perfectly contestable market as one that is vulnerable to costless 'hit-and-run' entry and exit. Contestability is thus a theory for which potential competition plays the dominant role in generating competitive behaviour.

A central result of contestability analysis is that if a market is perfectly contestable, then an equilibrium must entail a socially efficient outcome. Of course, no real market is perfectly contestable and perfect contestability is a theoretical construct. Nevertheless, many markets requiring only a small entry and/or exit cost may come to approximate a perfectly contestable market. As with most theoretical constructs in economics or science, that the theoretical ideal is not realized does not diminish its importance.

A significant contribution of contestability analysis has been to focus attention on the importance of sunk costs in determining whether or not a market is a natural monopoly. While the relevance of contestability theory may be put into question to the extent that most industries have considerable sunk costs, it has none the less been instrumental in causing antitrust analysis to reduce its emphasis on market concentration and take proper account of potential competition.

Such a policy focus can be transposed to the trade policy field, insofar as the central purpose of promoting greater international market contestability is to reduce the incidence of transaction costs and more generally barriers to doing business generated by public and private anticompetitive practices that reduce overall economic efficiency (and impair conditions of effective access and presence in markets) by restricting the cross-border movement of goods, services, ideas, investments/investors, and business people.

economies (Thomas et al., 1991). Many of the latter have also signalled their commitment to reform by enacting and applying competition laws and policies (Sell, 1995). By choosing market-based
policies, these economies increasingly share with developed countries a stake in ensuring the functioning of competitive markets outside of their national territories. Without discounting differing views
among states as to the notions of efficiency and competition, and the
increasingly obvious need in a globalizing environment to temper
efficiency considerations with adequate doses of distributive justice,
the motivating principle of this converging policy framework has
been the promotion of greater efficiency through competition, both
domestically and internationally, with a view to providing a sounder
basis for sustainable and employment-creating economic growth (see
OECD, 1994b).

THE IMPACT OF GLOBALIZATION

A defining feature of the world economy is the increasing globalization of business operations. Linking production, technology, and
marketing along value-added chains, globalization of business has
sharply heightened competition in product and factor markets
throughout the world, fuelling improvements in productivity and
growth. The sheer force of globalization has made policies directed
at protecting and supporting 'domestic' firms and products more difficult to implement, not least because of the difficulty of meaning-
fully identifying national 'domestic origin' in a globalizing world.

A fundamental characteristic of globalization is the growing and
mutually reinforcing linkages between trade and investment as
modes of doing business. This has altered the scope and meaning of
market access, which, in the post-Uruguay Round period, is increasingly viewed as defining the conditions governing the access, presence, and protection for goods, services, investments, intellectual
property, and business people alike.

Before the World Trade Organization agreements entered into
force, the GATT was concerned almost solely with governmental measures affecting trade in goods. In addition to clarifying and amplify-
ing certain rules regarding trade in goods, the Uruguay Round
agreements dramatically extended long-standing GATT rules and principles to cover trade in services and national laws governing intellectual property rights. This went some way towards establishing a

more comprehensive form of market access. However, it did not go all the way. The WTO Agreement on Trade-Related Investment Measures (TRIMs), for example, merely confirmed the scope of GATT Articles III and XI and provided an illustrative list of covered measures. It did not deal with the much more substantial issue of investment protection *per se* such as is found in bilateral investment protection treaties and Chapter 11 of the North American Free Trade Agreement (NAFTA) or that had been envisaged under the OECD's Multilateral Agreement on Investment (MAI) (see Sauvé, 1994).

That being said, the Uruguay Round marked an important shift towards a much more comprehensive approach to the notion of effective market access, one that will undoubtedly be further elaborated in the next round of multilateral trade negotiations.

THE IMPACT OF CHANGING MODES OF PRODUCTION ON TRADE RULES

Trade negotiations can be likened to the process of peeling an onion. Removing one layer of barriers and distortions reveals another, and so on. The issues become more complex in each succeeding round (contrast, for example, the length and detail of the WTO agreements with their predecessors, the 1979 Tokyo Round Codes and Arrangements, and those agreements with GATT 1947). The most recent agreements are far more complex. Moreover, given the rapid changes in the way goods and services are conceived, produced, and delivered internationally, to some extent multilateral trade negotiators find themselves playing 'catch up' to changes being wrought by commercial actors.

The current dispute between the United States and Canada over the latter's measures in support of Canadian periodical publishers is a case in point. For many years, Canada maintained a ban on the importation of foreign magazines containing more than a limited amount of advertising aimed at the sale of Canadian goods and services. This prohibition was intended to prevent the possibility of advertising revenues being directed to reconstituted 'split run' magazines (those that essentially recycled US editorial content, mixed in a little Canadian content together with Canadian advertisements, and were then sold to the Canadian market). The import ban was GATT-inconsistent, yet for reasons that are not clear, the United States never challenged it in the GATT. What precipitated the US challenge of

Canada's periodicals policy was a new measure responding to an ingenious circumvention of the import prohibition by *Sports Illustrated*. Time Warner Inc., the magazine's publisher, conceived of the idea of producing the bulk of the editorial content in the United States, transmitting it by satellite to Canada, and printing the finished product (replete with Canadian advertising) in Canada. The product was now of Canadian origin, albeit comprising foreign editorial content. Canada responded by imposing an excise tax that led the United States to commence its successful WTO challenge.

This case illustrates the contestability point rather well. Technology created a means of combining components of trade and investment. The ban on the importation of the physical medium was circumvented by the electronic transmission of its content and physical transformation within Canada.

ADDRESSING REGULATORY IMPEDIMENTS TO MARKET ACCESS

An important challenge arising from the new dimensions of market access consists of developing a more coherent, seamless, and internally consistent set of non-discriminatory trade and investment disciplines to underpin the activities of globally active firms. The promotion of such 'modal neutrality' between the trade and investment modes of doing business marks the realization that trade and investment—access and presence—are complementary means for contesting markets (Lawrence, 1996). Coming in the wake of the last decade's surge in cross-border investment activities, such a recognition played a fundamental role in prompting OECD member states to launch negotiations intended to result in a 'high-standard' MAI. It was believed that a successful MAI would also, through positive demonstration effects, help to pave the way for the eventual and much needed incorporation of a comprehensive set of investment disciplines within the multilateral trading system itself (see Brittan, 1995; Graham, 1996).

As is discussed by Dymond in Chapter 2, the MAI negotiations turned out to be highly controversial and attracted substantial public criticism. The October 1998 decision by the government of France to withdraw from the negotiations marked the de facto demise of the MAI, prompting some questions on the likelihood of—and the forms in which—comprehensive negotiations on investment could in future be undertaken at the WTO.

Another feature of the new global economy is the growing market access implications of a set of issues previously considered to belong mainly or entirely in the domestic policy domain. This has already arisen in a number of public policy fields, including industrial, taxation, labour, and environmental policies. In particular, governmental regulation of telecommunications networks and services, support for regional development or R&D, the design and/or enforcement of health, safety, and environmental standards, and the application of licensing requirements to service providers may strongly influence the conditions of market access and, hence, the presence of foreign firms in national markets. Many states, particularly in the OECD area, have pursued efficiency-enhancing policies through domestic regulatory reform efforts. Yet the market access implications of such efforts, that is, the degree to which domestic regulatory behaviour promotes or inhibits trade and investment opportunities, as well as the economy-wide implications of regulatory heterogeneity, have only recently begun to elicit closer international scrutiny.[1]

The legal and policy issues at stake are complex. Trade and investment agreements tend to be drafted in general terms and lack the specificity of domestic legislation and regulations. As a matter of general principle, international law imposes the obligation upon states to take only such action as is necessary to ensure that effect is given to the international obligations that they have undertaken. Substantial differences in national legal systems, legislative practices, administrative law, and constitutional frameworks, let alone political, socio-economic, developmental, and other factors, inevitably lead to differences in the way in which broadly drafted international agreements are implemented in national laws.[2]

The WTO Agreement on Trade-Related Aspects of Intellectual Property Rights (TRIPs) illustrates the point. The Agreement represented a shift in GATT lawmaking designed to counter some of the effects of regulatory heterogeneity. It established in some detail what the substantive content of each WTO member's intellectual property framework must be. Member states are required to accede to certain international conventions, ensure that civil remedies are available to afford rights-holders certain basic protections, and prescribe criminal sanctions for serious offences. The TRIPs Agreement establishes a lowest common denominator of substantive and procedural legal obligations. Even so, the Agreement confirms that 'Members shall be free to determine the appropriate method of implementing the

provisions of the Agreement within their own legal system and practices' (Article 1: 1).

Thus, inevitably, there will be divergences in the substantive content and effectiveness of national regimes purporting to implement
common international obligations, and these will continue to affect
the conditions of market access.[3] Even the most precisely drawn
international agreements will be reshaped when implemented in different national legal systems.

THE GROWING IMPORTANCE OF COMPETITION POLICY

Another set of issues arises from the impact that private anti-competitive behaviour—conducted with or without government involvement, support, or control—can exert in the global economy (see
Hay, 1996; Janow, 1996). Such behaviour includes, *inter alia*, exclu-
sionary practices, predation, foreclosure effects, and strategic conduct, all of which can affect the international competitive process and
impair market access and presence opportunities. Various market
structures, such as strategic alliances and joint ventures in high-
technology sectors, as well as interactions between private and
governmental action, including the operation of public monopolies,
standard-setting procedures, statutory or de facto exceptions to application of competition law, and state aids, may exert similar effects.
Furthermore, the effectiveness of disciplines in all of the above-listed
areas is undermined if corruption is tolerated by governmental
authorities. Thus, corrupt practices and their impact on global business have also become prominent in international discussions, most
notably the OECD but also the WTO, and are certain to loom larger in
future multilateral negotiations.

Fostering competition is ultimately in the interest of the domestic
community. This objective has typically fallen within the purview of
domestic public policy, in particular, competition law and policy, and
should represent a unifying theme for policy-making as a whole.
Although there has been a recent trend towards convergence in
domestic competition regimes and in their coverage, especially
within the OECD area, differences between such regimes (in both substantive and enforcement terms) continue to affect competition and
market access opportunities.

This suggests that it is timely to consider whether a measure
of governance at the international level is feasible and desirable

(Jacquemin, 1995; Scherer, 1994). One reason for doing so is the desirability of promoting as much coherence as possible between domestic and multilateral policy objectives. Indeed, the increasing emphasis on market-based approaches and competition values at the domestic level would appear to be equally desirable at the international level. Moreover, the lack of—or constraints on—market competition has the potential to create significant international friction, and national competition law may not always effectively reach transnational anti-competitive practices, or may consider some of the market access issues in a different light, emphasizing domestic over global welfare considerations. The objective of preserving competition in the global marketplace may not be achievable with reliance solely on the operation of national competition policy regimes. It may need to be more firmly rooted in, and permeate the operation of, the multilateral trading system (Zampetti and Sauvé, 1996).

KEY POLICY CHALLENGES

The common element linking the above set of issues is their potential for affecting the nature and patterns of international trade and investment flows, and hence the quality or effectiveness of market access and market presence. The evolving economic landscape depicted above is exerting a strong influence on much of what has been termed the 'new trade agenda' emerging after the conclusion of the Uruguay Round. This agenda gives rise to a series of discrete, albeit interrelated, policy challenges:

- how to raise the prominence of competition values and principles in the design and operation of the multilateral trading system;
- how to strengthen the multilateral trading system through the development of a comprehensive set of investment disciplines;
- how to address public policies and government actions that affect or distort the conduct of international business and, in particular, those competition-restricting measures that arise from the domestic regulatory conduct of nations;
- how to deal with private practices and market structures having the same effect; and
- how best to strengthen public support for—and enhance confidence in the economy-wide (hence distributional) benefits

from—an open, competition-oriented, and rules-based trading system.

Widespread unilateral and regional trade and investment regime liberalization and the significant widening and deepening of the multilateral trading system have both contributed greatly to increasing efficiency and welfare in the world economy. In fact, the central objectives of the international trading regime, those of eliminating discriminatory treatment in international commerce and of progressively dismantling impediments to trade and investment, aim at promoting global welfare through increased trade and growth opportunities. By striving, albeit with still too many exceptions, towards progressively freer conditions of doing business globally, the multilateral trading system furthers competition and a more internationally efficient allocation of resources. At the same time, a number of other societal preferences and policy objectives, ranging from environmental protection to the promotion of employment, social development, or technology diffusion, are typically present in domestic policy-making and need to be mediated by and reflected in the objectives, design, and operation of the trading system. For the contestability vision to be politically palatable, efficiency considerations must go hand in hand with attempts to spread the benefits of liberalization more widely, both within and between countries.

For all the progress achieved during the course of the Uruguay and preceding GATT rounds, the multilateral trading system continues to be confronted with new and potentially conflicting demands. Beyond the WTO's built-in agenda, much remains to be done to equip the multilateral trading system with the range of instruments and institutional flexibility required both to mediate the tensions, new and old, that may arise or be intensified in a rapidly globalizing environment and to promote successfully the system's efficiency-enhancing liberalization objectives.

Recent years have revealed a widening gulf between the scope of issues prospectively appearing on the trading system's agenda— market access asymmetries stemming from differences in regulatory philosophies or practices, the right to contest a market through an established presence, private anti-competitive behaviour, the potentially competing logics of trade liberalization and environmental stewardship—and the still limited range of instruments with which to tackle them in a multilateral setting. Stated differently, one of the central tasks assigned to the trading system—that of rolling back impediments to market access and market presence—may prove increasingly difficult in the absence of a more balanced and comprehensive architecture of multilateral disciplines. The Dutch economist Jan Tinbergen was awarded the first Nobel Prize in economics for pointing out, among many other seminal contributions, a simple truism in economic policy-making: the need for a rough measure of equivalence between policy objectives and instruments (Tinbergen, 1952).

The potential 'assignment problems' resulting from the discrepancy between policy objectives and instruments represent one of the central policy challenges now confronting the multilateral trading system. Overcoming this challenge is key to preserving support in the system. Indeed, in the absence of a more complete and coherent set of rules with which to maintain and enhance the system's credibility and relevance in a globalizing environment, countries may be tempted to eschew multilateralism and favour regional or plurilateral routes to liberalization.[4] They may also be attracted by unilateral or bilateral approaches out of a belief that the multilateral system cannot deliver on its promises (see Sauvé, 1996).

TOWARDS A COMPETITION-ORIENTED TRADE AGENDA: THE INTERNATIONAL CONTESTABILITY OF MARKETS

One way of tackling the challenges noted above is to consider how to adapt the multilateral trading system to the evolving reality of deep integration (see Ostry, 1995). Policy-makers need to focus on a broader approach to market access, one that embraces the continuum of trade, investment, and competition policies with a view to better identifying and progressively dismantling public and private impediments to the international contestability of markets. From the perspective of the new dimensions of market access, the term 'internationally contestable markets' would describe, in the ideal case, market conditions in which the competitive process—the rivalrous relationship between firms—is unimpeded by restrictive or distortive public or private conduct. The competitive conditions prevailing in an internationally contestable market should secure effective access for foreign goods, services, ideas, investments, and business people, so that they are able to compete on terms equal or comparable to those enjoyed by local competitors.

Given that the focus on international market contestability is intended to allow for a more targeted and comprehensive approach to the removal of barriers and distortions that impede and impair market access and presence, the question of definition is not something to be approached in an abstract way. It implies, rather, a series of more practical questions concerning how best to ensure that conditions of market access and market presence and, more generally, of competition, are not *unduly* impaired or distorted—and become progressively less so—by the totality of potential public or private barriers to contestability.

This includes, of course, more traditional tariff and non-tariff border barriers about which much of the pre-Uruguay Round trading system was chiefly concerned. For some countries (particularly developing ones) or products (e.g., agriculture and textiles), these barriers remain of considerable importance despite the significant progress made in the Uruguay Round. In today's world of deep integration, barriers to contestability also relate to investment conditions, domestic regulatory conduct (ranging from standards-related issues to the licensing of services or service providers and merger review procedures), structural differences in the functioning of markets, and private anti-competitive practices.

Preserving the international competitive process would mean not only preventing anti-competitive governmental or private actions that impair access to the domestic market but also preventing similar action from being used to confer 'artificial' competitive advantages to domestic firms (including in foreign markets). For instance, the strategic or discriminatory use of government assistance may provide a competitive edge to domestic firms, effectively excluding or impairing the ability of new competitors (domestic or foreign) to gain access to or a presence in a national market. At the same time, to preserve competition from private anti-competitive behaviour, it may prove necessary to explore the need for and the modalities of introducing international disciplines that directly affect such behaviour. Consideration could thus be given to exploring the scope for internationalizing competition policy, an objective that a WTO Working Group on Trade and Competition was explicitly set up to explore at the December 1996 ministerial meeting in Singapore (as was done for trade and investment).

By helping officials take a balanced and comprehensive approach to the broad range of potential public or private impediments to effective access to—and presence in—markets, the focus on market contestability seeks to ensure that the removal of impediments in any one area is informed by, co-ordinated with, and complementary to efforts in other areas. Indeed, one key advantage of a competition-oriented focus is that it confronts negotiators with the need to ask how a proposed discipline or negotiated commitment will affect international competition and the operation of international markets, not merely to assume that the removal of a particular barrier or the adoption of an associated rule or remedy will automatically improve overall economic efficiency. Stated somewhat figuratively, the focus on market contestability seeks to achieve general, and not partial, equilibrium.

For example, meaningful liberalization of cross-border trade in consulting engineering services under the General Agreement on Trade in Services (GATS) would require that complementary commitments be envisaged in the areas of investment, government procurement, duty-free (temporary) entry of professional 'tools' of the trade, mutual recognition of professional licensing regimes, as well as the temporary entry of service suppliers. It would also imply that WTO members agree to subject professional services to national competition laws (which is often not the case) and, where such coverage applies, that such laws be enforced effectively.

More generally, by seeking to better balance and reconcile producer, user, and consumer interests within the trading system, such an approach could help to define the parameters of the international competitive process that governments find collectively acceptable. Dumping is one obvious example of a private practice that has elicited recurring friction within the trading system. The time may come when countries finally seek agreement on the kind of pricing behaviour they find acceptable in international trade. The aim of achieving internationally contestable markets could thus be used to set benchmarks for domestic public policy actions as well as international regulatory initiatives with a view to assessing the degree to which such measures exert pro- or anti-competitive effects.[5]

Just as conditions of perfect market contestability are unlikely to hold in reality (as is the case for 'free' trade), it is equally unrealistic to expect the conduct of business across borders to be fully immune from barriers to entry or presence and, thus, for domestic markets to be fully contestable by international firms and products. Indeed, a number of obstacles to market contestability may not be amenable to policy action or cannot simply be legislated out of existence—differences in culture or tastes, for example, and advantages of scale deriving from being first in a market (so-called 'first-mover advantages') (Graham and Lawrence, 1996). This suggests that contestability will always be a matter of degree. Yet the distinction between what does and does not unduly restrict conditions of entry, access, presence in, or exit from a market has to be defined more clearly and consistently than it has been to date in multilateral forums.

NEW RULES FOR A NEW WORLD? THE ARCHITECTURAL
IMPLICATIONS OF CONTESTABILITY

An important question that arises in considering the scope for securing the greater openness of markets to global competition is whether the multilateral trading system's current architecture of rules is adequate. This is a controversial issue, reflected in vastly differing levels of ambition that WTO members harbour *vis-à-vis* the system's desired post-Uruguay Round evolution. While the Uruguay Round performed what by any measure was a radical, and much needed, institutional face-lift, the fact remains that the changes that took place in the world economy during and after the Uruguay Round were even more radical. As a result, the multilateral trading system is confronted today with a potentially credibility-impairing assignment problem. Overcoming this problem by pursuing a widening array of complex policy objectives with first-best and pro-competitive policy instruments suggests the need for some degree of architectural reform. The core elements of any such efficiency-enhancing reform agenda include:

- broadening the scope and coverage of existing WTO disciplines;
- interpreting existing rules in a competition-oriented fashion (i.e., achieving a better balance between the notions of injury to competition and to competitors);
- exploring the need to integrate new or expanded disciplines on investment and on competition standards of regulatory behaviour within the multilateral trading system; and
- reflecting on the consequences of such possible integration for the design and operation of existing norms and institutions (e.g., ensuring coherence between rules on competition policy and trade remedies; or the interface between a comprehensive body of investment rules and GATS, TRIMs, or TRIPs).

WHAT CAN BE ACHIEVED?

Addressing competition policy in the WTO would be challenging. First, states—even those with comparatively similar competition laws and policies—do not always agree on the merits of an enforcement action. One state's efficiency gain can be viewed by another as a dangerous step towards market dominance. The US-EU dispute over Boeing's acquisition of the McDonnell-Douglas Aircraft Company illustrates the point. The proposed acquisition met with little resistance in the United States but encountered strong opposition from the European Commission due to its concern over the merged company's potential dominance of certain aspects of the aerospace sector (and its possibly adverse impact on the Airbus consortium). This dispute, which was finally resolved after weeks of threats of trade sanctions, illustrates the potential even for states with substantially similar antitrust standards to disagree over the impact of a proposed merger.

Second, there are—particularly among the developed states—a number of bilateral agreements on antitrust law enforcement and cooperation. They are administered by the competition law authorities, not trade policy authorities, and the convergence of trade and competition negotiations (and the prospect of new international rules) inevitably raises domestic, intragovernmental jurisdictional issues and disputes, i.e., turf tensions. The United States government (but not Congress), for example, which 50 years ago supported the inclusion of a chapter on restrictive business practices in the ill-fated Havana Charter to Establish an International Trade Organization, now resists the inclusion of competition policy in the agenda of the next WTO round. Much of the US resistance is rooted in the Justice Department's unwillingness to countenance multilateral negotiations that might require it to cede jurisdiction to another agency or see its present freedom of action subjected to multilateral disciplines.

Third, effective competition law enforcement requires the use of subpoena power and other domestic evidence-gathering techniques. Large volumes of confidential business proprietary information are routinely obtained and protected from unlawful disclosure to competitors. The ability to coerce the provision of evidence, the use of search warrants, and the protection of confidentiality are all governed by national law with extensive court supervision.

The WTO presently lacks the institutional powers and safeguards to deal with the evidence obtained in a normal antitrust investigation. It is unlikely to gain such attributes in the foreseeable future. The key questions, therefore, when considering the issue of addressing competition policy at the WTO are: what precisely *should* the WTO address by way of market access-impairing private anti-competitive conduct? and what *can* it do, given its present institutional powers and attributes? Addressing the second question first, even the most cursory of comparisons reveals that WTO dispute settlement, for example, pales by comparison to the sophistication of the domestic court procedures of the developed countries. WTO panels still do not have detailed rules of procedure; its standard rules are rudimentary. Although the Dispute Settlement Understanding (DSU) confers the power on a panel to gather evidence relevant to the matter before it, such power has to date been exercised sparingly and hesitantly. Procedures for the use of expert evidence are similarly undeveloped (although they have recently gained stronger currency in cases involving disputes under the Technical Barriers to Trade Agreement) and there are no effective means of protecting the disclosure of confidential information.[6]

Given the WTO's current powers, perhaps the most that can be achieved is the negotiation of a TRIPs-like agreement on trade-related competition law. Such an agreement would specify, in multilateral terms, commonly acceptable denominators for national competition laws. Some latitude might be given to members to define what matters should be civil offences. Members might agree to criminalize a small number of particularly egregious offences (such as price-fixing or bid-rigging). Certain basic legal protections for persons injured by anti-competitive behaviour could be considered. Finally, like the TRIPs Agreement, members' compliance with the multilaterally agreed rules would be disputable under the WTO's procedures, but would continue to operate in a subsidiary manner on the basis of significant deference to national laws and administrative procedures. Moreover, it bears recalling that the next round of multilateral negotiations, particularly under the aegis of the GATS, will likely lead to the continued, if narrowly sectoral, multilateralization of some aspects of competition policy, as was done in the regulatory Principles paper appended to the 1997 Agreement on Basic Telecommunications in the area of abuse of dominance.

POLITICAL ECONOMY CONSIDERATIONS

While attempts at reforming the WTO's architecture are likely to encounter strong bureaucratic resistance from many quarters, it is important to reflect, if somewhat counterfactually, on the systemic consequences for global trade and investment that could flow from the trading system's inability to adapt to a globalizing environment. Seen in this light, the central question appears not so much to be *whether* new or enhanced rules of the game are needed but rather *how* to make a competition-oriented trade agenda operational in negotiating terms.

There is thus a need to convince the trading system's key stakeholders—governments of developed and developing countries alike, internationally active firms, and consumers—that some measure of architectural reform is desirable both to maintain the multilateral trading system's overall relevance and credibility and to allow all WTO members to realize more fully the efficiency gains deriving from further trade and investment regime liberalization.

In reflecting on the possible need for architectural reform, a number of considerations of a political economy nature need to be brought to mind. One relates to what has been called *economies of scale in rule-making*, which may be achieved when the geographical coverage of rules extends to the largest number of countries. To preserve and build on the precious single undertaking of the Uruguay Round, it is essential that the future evolution of the trading system not result in a multi-tiered regime, with some issues confined to the regional level or pursued in a segmented manner in other institutional settings. Indeed, one of the salient characteristics of the globalization process is that it gives rise to broadly similar, and increasingly convergent, policy challenges for both developed and developing countries. The onus should thus be on WTO members to seek wherever possible to find multilateral solutions to what are already global challenges.

That being said, the scope for securing truly multilateral outcomes may not be the same across all policy domains. For instance, with fewer than 60 countries having adopted competition regimes, and with many such regimes being of a fairly recent vintage (particularly in developing and transition economies), it may well be that 'going multilateral' on competition policy may not be as straightforward as in the case of investment (which is the most inherently global of all policy domains, and where the direction of change in policy regimes worldwide has been strongly liberalizing) or of domestic regulatory conduct (in light of existing regional and multilateral disciplines affecting goods, services, and intellectual property rights (IPRs).

Hence, institutional flexibility and the need to accommodate variable geometries within the multilateral trading system (i.e., the possible need for plurilateral configurations in new areas subject to WTO disciplines) are key to realizing economies of scale in rule-making through the progressively wider geographical coverage of disciplines.

A second and closely related consideration pertains to what has been called *economies of scope* in rule-making. This relates to the advantages of developing more comprehensive, coherent, and integrated rules than those currently in existence and with which to underpin and discipline the conduct of business in a globalizing environment. *Comprehensiveness* refers to the need to address both governmental and private anti-competitive practices affecting trade and investment; *coherence* to the desirability of addressing trade and investment—in essence, flip sides of the same market access coin—simultaneously; while *integration* should be understood in terms of the development of a more generic (i.e., non issue- or sector-specific) body of rules applicable to goods, services, ideas, capital, and people in a less segmented way than is currently the case.

The case for such a 'one-stop shopping' approach to rule-design includes clear gains in transparency; greater responsiveness to business needs; lowered search, transaction, and negotiating costs (allowing WTO members to better gauge the costs and benefits of signing on—or not—to disciplines in new areas in instances where plurilateral outcomes may arise); lessened scope for institutional and regulatory segmentation and duplication; and a broader scope for achieving an overall balance of benefits.

Another key political economy consideration concerns the attitude that developing countries might adopt. Despite the OECD's strong and continuous efforts to maintain a dialogue with non-member economies, including on matters at the core of the contestability analysis, the fact that the concept bears the origin of the Paris-based organization has naturally fed some degree of suspicion on the part of developing countries, including the emerging economies of Southeast Asia (but less so among Southern Cone countries in Latin America). These concerns were compounded by the MAI process.

While concerns have been raised that the notion of contestability could appear as somewhat OECD-centric and not sufficiently attuned to the negotiating priorities or political sensitivities of developing countries, it is interesting to note that the policy dialogue conducted to date within the OECD has revealed much the same concerns, whether over the 'imperial' designs of trade policy or over the sovereignty concerns that flow from trade policy's increasing intrusiveness in domestic regulatory affairs. As noted earlier, in many instances this may be ascribed to the bureaucratic resistance that the move towards policy integration and one-stop shopping quite naturally elicits. Similarly, while the private sector typically voices strong support for efforts aimed at repealing investment and other regulatory barriers to doing business (indeed, for anything that restricts governmental action), support for rules aimed at disciplining private anti-competitive conduct is less forthcoming.[7]

Given the strong commitment to structural reform shown by developing countries during the last decade, reflected in a determined and mostly unilateral push towards trade and investment regime liberalization, it would not be surprising to see the latter champion the cause of a competition-oriented trade agenda. This is so for a number of reasons, not least of which is the fact that the focus on contestability helps to build a bridge between the so-called 'old' and 'new' trade agendas. While many developing country exports continue to face traditional barriers to market access (e.g., prohibitive or escalating tariffs in agriculture and other primary commodities, quotas on textiles and clothing, anti-dumping suits against manufactured exports, unduly burdensome procedures for product testing), multilateral progress on elements of the new trade agenda could actually help to better reveal the welfare losses arising from the maintenance of various anti-competitive measures in importing markets.

What's more, the integrated approach to trade, investment, and competition that is implicit in the contestability analysis may be particularly germane in smaller developing economies. Indeed, empirical analysis casts doubt on the ability of any one policy instrument to establish competitive market conditions, with domestic entry, open international trade and investment, and vigorous enforcement of domestic competition policy all essential in securing pro-competitive results. This is especially true in a small market with room for only a limited number of domestic firms operating at efficient scale, the typical setting for a developing economy. While each influence exerts some pro-competitive effect, they need to work together to maximize economy-wide welfare gains.

CONCLUDING REMARKS

This chapter has argued that one of the central policy challenges arising from the globalization of markets has been to confront governments with the need to promote competition values and principles—both domestically and internationally—and to develop a much broader understanding of the concept of market access than that which applied even as recently as in the Uruguay Round. This approach needs to embrace the continuum of trade, investment, and competition policy domains, its chief focus being the need to stem anti-competitive practices that unduly impede and distort the openness of markets to international competition, whether such conduct is public or private in origin.

The notion of 'international market contestability' that flows from policy analysis initiated within the OECD Trade Committee signifies an important qualitative deepening in the nature and degree of openness that could be sought for international competition. Indeed, even when most border barriers are removed (which has clearly not yet been accomplished despite the marked progress achieved in the Uruguay Round), genuine market openness, let alone market integration, is still far from being achieved. A wide range of 'behind the border obstacles' may continue to impede or distort the international flow of goods, services, ideas, capital, and business people.

The focus on international market contestability provides a standard to evaluate negotiations on a broad range of impediments to effective access and presence in markets, so that the removal of impediments in any one policy area is informed by, co-ordinated with, and complementary to efforts in other areas. An important feature of such a broader approach to market access lies in its advocacy of a more 'competition-friendly' trading system. By stressing the relative importance of the efficiency objectives pursued by the multilateral trading system, the deepening integration of the world economy raises the crucial question of the extent to which—and the manner in which—the international community is prepared to see competition values and principles assume greater prominence in policy- and rule-making and have such values permeate the operation and design of an evolving architecture of rules for doing business globally. This challenge is one to which all WTO members will need to devote consensus-building efforts in the coming years. In so doing, they can take solace from the fact that work undertaken over the last few years within the OECD and in various other forums points to a broadened understanding of the 'new' dimensions of market access within the policy-making community.

NOTES

The authors are grateful to Americo Beviglia Zampetti, Tom Brewer, Hugh Corbet, Crawford Falconer, Geza Feketekuty, Edward M. Graham, Michael Hart, and Robert Z. Lawrence for helpful comments and discussions.

1. The OECD in recent years has embarked on an interdisciplinary effort aimed at investigating the economy-wide implications—on growth, employment, innovation, market access, consumer welfare, and government effectiveness—of domestic regulatory conduct. The core objective of such work is to ensure that efforts at regulatory reform lead to lasting improvements in countries' economic performance while retaining the public benefits of regulatory programs. See OECD (1996).

2. In unitary legal systems, Mexico being an example, international treaties, upon ratification, have direct effect in domestic law; the very terms of the treaty form a source of domestic law equivalent in effect to legislation. In dualist states such as Canada and the United States, legislation is normally required to give effect to the treaty. This, of course, gives the legislature the opportunity to interpret the treaty when setting the terms of the domestic legislation.

3. Disputes over these kinds of differences in the implementation of the TRIPs Agreement and a similarly prescriptive agreement, the WTO Agreement on Basic Telecommunications, can be expected as members test the extent to which WTO dispute settlement will govern regulatory heterogeneity.

4. A case in point was the decision to initiate negotiations on a comprehensive investment agreement within the OECD, rather than the WTO, despite the fact that investment is perhaps the most inherently global of policy domains, that the clear trend over the last decade has been towards worldwide investment regime liberalization, and that (not uncoincidently) non-OECD countries account for an important and fast-growing share of annual flows of foreign direct investment.

5. For a discussion of possible criteria to assess in a trade policy setting the 'competition-friendliness of governmental conduct', see Feketekuty (1996).

6. With respect to confidential information it is instructive to contrast the DSU with the detailed obligations of NAFTA's Chapter 19, which requires each party to enact legislation to safeguard confidential information provided by firms in anti-dumping and countervailing duty investigations that are then reviewed by binational panels.

7. This problem is compounded by the strong degree of scepticism shown by large segments of the antitrust community *vis-à-vis* the prospects for internationalizing competition policy, and even greater turf resistance to the notion that a means of doing so could involve the multilateral trading system.

REFERENCES

Baumol, William, John Panzar, and Robert Willig. 1982. *Contestable Markets and the Theory of Industry Structure*. New York: Harcourt Brace Jovanovich.

Beviglia Zampetti, A., and P. Sauvé. 1996. 'Onwards to Singapore: The International Contestability of Markets and the New Trade Agenda', *World Economy* 19, 3 (May): 333–43.

Brittan, Sir Leon. 1995. 'Investment Liberalization: The Next Great Boost to the World Economy', *Transnational Corporations* 4: 1–10.

Feketekuty, G. 1996. *The Scope, Implication and Economic Rationale of a Competition-Oriented Approach to Future Multilateral Trade Negotiations*. Paris: OECD Trade Directorate, TD/TC(96) 6, Jan., derestricted.

Graham, E.M. 1996. *Direct Investment and the Future Agenda of the World Trade Organization*. Washington: Institute for International Economics, June.

——— and R.Z. Lawrence. 1996. *Measuring the International Contestability of Markets: A Conceptual Approach*. Paris: OECD Trade Committee, TD/TC(96) 7, Jan.

Hay, Donald A. 1996. 'Anti-Competitive Practices, Market Access and Competition Policy in a Global Economy', in OECD, *Market Access After the Uruguay Round: Investment, Competition and Technology Perspectives*. Paris: OECD.

Jacquemin, A. 1995. 'Towards an Internationalisation of Competition Policy', *World Economy* 18: 781–9.

Janow, Merit E. 1996. 'Public and Private Restraints That Limit Access to Markets', in OECD, *Market Access After the Uruguay Round: Investment, Competition and Technology Perspectives*. Paris: OECD.

Lawrence, Robert Z. 1996. 'Towards Globally Contestable Markets', in OECD, *Market Access After the Uruguay Round: Investment, Competition and Technology Perspectives*. Paris: OECD, 25–33.

OECD. 1994a. *Assessing Structural Reform: Lessons for the Future*. Paris: OECD.

———. 1994b. *The OECD Jobs Study—Facts, Analysis, Strategies*. Paris: OECD.

———. 1995. *New Dimensions of Market Access in a Globalising World Economy*. Paris: OECD.

———.1996. *Regulatory Reform and International Market Openness*. Paris: OECD.

Ostry, Sylvia. 1995. *New Dimensions of Market Access*. Occasional Paper No. 49. Washington: Group of Thirty.

Sauvé, Pierre. 1994. 'A First Look at Investment in the Final Act of the Uruguay Round', *Journal of World Trade* 28 (Oct.): 5–16.

———. 1996. 'Services and the International Contestability of Markets', *Transnational Corporations* 5 (Apr.): 37–56.

Scherer, F.M. 1994. *Competition Policies for an Integrated World Economy*. Washington: Brookings Institution.

Sell, S.K. 1995. 'Intellectual Property Protection and Anti-Trust in the Developing World: Crisis, Coercion and Choice', *International Organization* 49, 2: 315–49.

Thomas, V., et al. 1991. *Best Practices in Trade Policy Reform*. Oxford: Oxford University Press (for the World Bank).

Tinbergen, Jan. 1952. *On the Theory of Economic Policy*. Amsterdam.

6

High Finance and Low Politics:
Canada and the Asian Financial Crisis

DANE ROWLANDS

In the early half of 1997 Canadians may have been forgiven for thinking that the Pacific Ocean had shrunk. Political pronouncement and policy ritual proclaimed Canada to be a 'Pacific nation', complete with Team Canada trade missions to Asia. While the rhetoric far out-paced the reality of Canada's actual ties to the region (see Hampson, Molot, and Rudner, 1997), the hosting of that year's APEC summit in Vancouver was a clear symbol of Canada's apparent intention to insert itself into the region. Instead of a diplomatic triumph, however, the summit was eclipsed by the financial turmoil that by then was rapidly engulfing several of the East Asian economies. In the months that followed, the turmoil became a crisis that had also surfaced in Russia by August 1998—more than a year after it first appeared in Asia—and was threatening to spread to Latin America. The Canadian economy, too, was shaken, although perhaps not as irreparably as the faith that many people had put in financial liberalization. For this crisis, more than any preceding one, has been inextricably associated with the emergence of a more open market for international capital.

The purpose of this chapter is not to argue about the correctness of these perceptions, but rather the implications the crisis has for Canada and the policy responses it has provoked. The Asian financial crisis poses a challenge for Canadian policy-makers on three fronts. Domestically, the slump in resource exports to Asia and the fall in the value of the Canadian dollar require the Bank of Canada to walk a fine line between avoiding recession and supporting the currency. Internationally, there appear to be growing contradictions between the multilaterally managed international financial regime the Canadian government has traditionally supported and the increasingly liberalized international capital market the regime has itself promoted. Finally, the requirements of the domestic economy have to be reconciled with those of the international system upon which Canadians are reliant. These fundamental dimensions of policy, in turn, shape the ability of the Canadian government to provide leadership in a more closely integrated international economy.

The next section reviews the effects of the financial crisis on Canada's economy. This discussion is followed by an exploration of the domestic policy response, focusing primarily on the Bank of Canada. Canada's response at the international level is then reviewed. A final, concluding section reviews the themes that emerge in the initial parts of the essay.

THE EFFECTS OF FINANCIAL TURMOIL

The Mexican peso crisis of 1994–5 was not the first episode of currency instability in the 1990s, having been preceded by two separate incidents in Europe.[1] However, it was the first to involve a large, liberalizing emerging market and a group of countries beginning to attract the attention of resurgent private capital flows. It was perhaps for this reason that Michel Camdessus, managing director of the International Monetary Fund (IMF), described the Mexican debacle as the first financial crisis of the twenty-first century.

Although its immediate implications for Canada were not as prolonged or visible as the current crisis appears to be, it did alert Canadian policy-makers to the implications of increased international capital volatility. Indeed, as severe as the peso crisis was for

Mexicans, some of its manifestations in Canada were quite limited. For example, since the Mexican economy recovered fairly quickly, Canada's exports to Mexico were actually about 5 per cent higher in 1995 compared to the pre-crisis year of 1994, although this was admittedly less than a third of the growth rate for Canadian exports as a whole. In any case, less than 1 per cent of Canadian exports was destined for Mexico in 1994, and only a little over 1 per cent was destined for Argentina, Brazil, and Mexico combined. A slowdown in the big economies of Latin America was not going to result in a major decline in the demand for Canadian products.

Canada's currency, however, was more severely affected. From November 1994 to May 1995, Canada's currency depreciated by just under 8 per cent against the IMF's accounting currency, the Special Drawing Rights (SDR), and it also fell precipitously against the G–9 and G–10 currency baskets as computed by the Bank of Canada. However, the dollar did retain its value against its American counterpart, a much more visible comparison for most Canadians. Furthermore, there did not appear to be any extensive currency market intervention by Canadian authorities. Foreign reserves seemed reasonably stable and actually increased for much of the early part of 1995, ending the year 22 per cent higher than they had started. From some perspectives, therefore, and despite the many Canadian investors and exporters hurt by the peso crisis, the visible international effects on Canada appear to have been temporary and relatively mild.

Where the crisis did bite visibly was on the domestic side. Attributing changes in the Canadian economy to the peso crisis alone, however, is somewhat problematic. Interest rates had already been fluctuating, the bank rate having moved up and down between 6 and 7 per cent during the course of 1994. Nevertheless, the reaction to the crisis is clear: the bank rate rose dramatically from 6 per cent in the third quarter of 1994 to just under 8.5 per cent in the first quarter of 1995. The decline in real gross domestic product (GDP) growth rates that had occurred throughout most of 1994 continued precipitously after Mexico's crisis, becoming negative in the second quarter of 1995 and remaining low until the second half of 1996. Thus, the main effect of the peso crisis emerged in domestic output, clearly illustrating for Canadian policy-makers both the vulnerability of the Canadian economy to foreign financial problems and the risks of countering such shocks with interest rate changes.

The impact of the Mexican crisis contrasts somewhat with what occurred after the commencement of the Asian crisis, which appeared to hit Canada's economy surprisingly hard. The most visible manifestation of the crisis for Canada was the depreciation of the dollar. Between October 1997 and October 1998, the Canadian dollar lost 10 per cent of its value against its American counterpart. At one point in late August, after Russia's economic turmoil resulted in a devaluation of the rouble, the Canadian dollar dipped to a record low of just over 63 cents US, a 14 per cent decline in value from the third quarter of 1997.

The importance of the export markets involved in the crisis provides part of the explanation of its severe impact on the Canadian currency. While slightly under 2 per cent of Canada's exports were destined for the five developing Asian economies most severely affected by the crisis, just over 8 per cent go to East and South Asia as a whole. So the relative difference in the export markets involved in the two crises is substantial, especially if this whole Asian region is included. And the Asian region outside the key crisis countries has indeed been affected severely. Exports to the area fell by nearly $6 billion in the first three quarters of 1998, a drop of nearly one-third from the same period in the previous year. For individual countries, the fall in Canadian exports was even more dramatic. Exports to the Philippines fell over 60 per cent, while exports to South Korea fell nearly one-half. Of the larger markets in East Asia, only China (and Vietnam) experienced more modest drops of around 6.5 per cent.

Of equal significance is the decline in commodity prices. The economic collapse in the Asian economies—as major importers—led to a reduced demand and lower prices for a range of commodities. As key producers, their declining currency values made for tough price competition in some international commodity markets. The subsequent turmoil in Russia reinforced these pressures, especially since Russia and Canada are direct competitors in a number of primary commodities. These events contributed to the long-term decline in commodity prices that began well before the onset of the Asian crisis. In May 1998 the unit value index of Canada's exports had declined by over 4.5 per cent from the third quarter of 1997 and was almost 7 per cent lower than in 1996. As the decline in import unit values fell more slowly, Canada's overall terms of trade deteriorated. While Canada's reliance on commodities for exports has fallen from 60 per cent in 1980 to 40 per cent in 1996 (as reported by the

Department of Finance, 1998), the Canadian dollar remains heavily tied to commodities in the eyes of the financial market. While some may view this association as careless labelling by currency traders, the decline in commodity prices was none the less taken as a signal to sell off assets denominated in Canadian dollars.

In addition, perceptions of Canada's economic vulnerability and relatively large government debt, and concern over the security of investments, generated a so-called 'flight to safety' (Stinson, 1998). Stinson cites evidence from Statistics Canada showing how both foreign and Canadian investors abandoned Canadian-dollar-denominated assets for safer US investments, particularly US Treasury Bills. Too much should not be read into such events, however, and the analysts themselves debate the importance of such swings. While foreigners sold over $6 billion in Canadian stocks and bonds in September, they had purchased over $9 billion in such assets the month before. Canada's financial account is characterized by fairly large swings on a monthly and quarterly basis. For example, a surplus in the last quarter of 1994 was followed by three successive quarters of deficit, and the financial account moved from just under a $10 billion surplus in the first quarter of 1998 to a $6 billion deficit in the second quarter. Such reversals may indeed be related to the onset of foreign financial crises. It is also true, however, that larger deficits were recorded in the middle of 1996 and the beginning of 1997, when no such crises were unfolding. Perhaps the most important lesson to draw from these observations is that financial flows are volatile and very responsive to investor perceptions, and that even the quarterly net flows often dwarf the annual receipts from exports to the crisis countries.

There was, therefore, considerable downward pressure on the value of the Canadian dollar. In comparison to the Mexican crisis, however, the bank rate changes appeared somewhat more subdued. In what appeared to be a more dramatic crisis, the bank rate initially moved up only 1.5 per cent from the third quarter in 1997 to the first quarter of 1998. The equivalent change during the Mexican crisis was 2.5 per cent. On the other hand, the government appeared to use its foreign reserves more aggressively during the Asian crisis. The initial fall in the Canadian dollar's value was partly buffered by a decline in reserves of over $6 billion. Later in the year reserves were again sold to support the dollar. In August this policy led to a loss of over $4 billion US in reserves, a one-month decline of roughly 20 per cent. At this point, the bank rate was raised another 1 per cent.

In contrast to the Mexican crisis, however, real GDP growth remained fairly high in 1998. The dip in growth to an annual rate of just under 3 per cent in the last quarter of 1997 (compared to over 4 per cent in the previous quarter) was reversed in the first quarter of 1998. The early evidence suggests that overall economic growth for 1998 fell from just under 4 per cent in 1997 to just under 3 per cent, with predictions for 1999 at around 2 per cent (Little et al., 1999). Some of the decline is attributable to factors other than the Asian crisis, however, such as the strike at a key General Motors plant in the United States that led to lay-offs in both countries. While the slowdown in growth is significant, it seems mild in comparison to what happened during the shorter and less severe Mexican crisis. Furthermore, although the effects of the interest rate increase in the late summer of 1998 remain to be seen, employment growth in 1998 appears to have remained strong and the unemployment rate continued its longer-term decline.[2]

Therefore, the effects of the two crises on Canada's economy were manifested in fundamentally different ways. The most visible measure of Canada's international position is the exchange rate, which depreciated only mildly after Mexico's payments crisis. This depreciation has been far more dramatic since 1997. The international dimension of the Asian crisis, therefore, was emphasized as a consequence of the policy choices within the Canadian government, particularly those of the Bank of Canada.

THE DOMESTIC RESPONSE

In determining their response to the Asian crisis, Canadian policy-makers had to balance two objectives. These decisions were essentially within the purview of officials at the Bank of Canada. On the one hand, the severity of the crisis inevitably led to downward pressure on the value of the Canadian dollar, a boon to some exporters, but a burden on consumers and those who either need to import foreign inputs or have other foreign currency-denominated liabilities. A lower-valued currency can also contribute to inflationary pressure, both through the passing on of higher import prices and through any diminution of the gap between actual and potential output that may result from higher exports.

At the same time, trying to ameliorate the worst effects of a currency depreciation presents its own risks for the economy. Given the general inadequacy of foreign reserves in a prolonged contest with currency markets, the weapon of choice for central banks trying to restrain currency depreciation is the interest rate. Raising interest rates through the adoption of more restrictive monetary policies makes Canadian financial assets more desirable, leading to capital inflows that bid up the value of the currency. In addition, higher interest rates tend to reduce expectations of future inflation and exchange rate depreciation. Unfortunately, of course, these effects are accompanied by, and partly a direct consequence of, reduced demand. If taken too far, such a policy could tip an economy into recession.

In fact, the higher interest rates in Canada that followed Mexico's peso crisis have been identified as a factor in slowing down (and temporarily reversing) Canada's economic expansion in 1995 and 1996. Although growth eventually improved by the second half of 1996, the slowdown was a very visible reminder of the fragility of Canada's economic recovery. It is a lesson the Bank of Canada appears to have paid some heed to, although not without equivocation.

It is worth noting here that the reaction of the Canadian authorities during the first crisis is consistent with the basic policy prescriptions derived from economic theory. The Mexican crisis had its origins in the market for financial assets, affecting Canada not so much through the demand for goods and services as through the demand for assets denominated in Canadian dollars. The standard policy response in such a situation is to make these assets more attractive by raising their rate of return, a task that many argue was made more difficult by the lack of confidence in Canada's relatively weak fiscal position at the time. The lessons that the Bank of Canada and Department of Finance took away from the Mexican crisis were probably twofold: responding to crises with aggressive interest rate increases has serious repercussions for Canadian output, and the adverse consequences of such a policy are exacerbated when the government's fiscal situation is perceived to be weak.

The initial response to currency pressure arising from the Asian crisis also came in the form of an increase in interest rates at the end of January 1998. The rate increase was a response to the falling dollar and initially met with some success in propping up the currency's value. However, the policy attracted considerable controversy. Little (1998) reports that even supporters of the rate increase, such as Sherry Cooper of Nesbitt Burns, were critical of the Bank's mixed signals; officials at the Bank of Canada had indicated earlier that month that monetary conditions were acceptable. It is unclear whether this apparent reversal of opinion reflected the speed of financial market developments, miscommunication, indecision, or a deliberate attempt to keep markets guessing. William Robson of the C.D. Howe Institute was quoted by Little as bemoaning the Bank's 'inability to steer a steady course' or provide a 'coherent philosophy' for monetary and exchange rate policy. Critics of the interest rate rise were more severe in their comments. Little quotes a report by Peter Dungan and Steve Murphy of the University of Toronto in which they warn of 'serious consequences' if the interest rate increase were not 'quickly reversed'. The proponents of lower interest rates were clearly concerned about putting the brakes on a hesitant recovery, as had happened in 1994 and 1995.

These criticisms appear to have had some effect. Interest rates remained reasonably stable over the ensuing months, with the bank rate maintained at 5 per cent. The dollar continued to decline throughout the first half of 1998, although in a gradual fashion. However, when the Russian rouble was devalued in the summer, it renewed pressure on the Canadian dollar. In an apparent attempt to avoid further interest rate changes, the Bank played a cat-and-mouse game with foreign exchange markets, selling off foreign reserves to assist the dollar at unexpected times in order to deter speculators. When the Canadian dollar reached record lows, however, the Bank responded with a substantial increase in the bank rate, pushing it up to 6 per cent. As the dollar recovered strength and interest rates in the United States fell, the Bank of Canada began to reduce its own rate each month, reaching 5.25 per cent by mid-November.

To some extent, then, the events surrounding Mexico's problems probably helped to prepare Canadian policy-makers to face the Asian crisis. Economic shocks are felt either through price changes or out-put changes. By raising interest rates and defending the currency, the Bank of Canada arguably allowed the worst effects of the Mexican peso crisis to be absorbed by domestic producers. With the Asian cri-sis the Bank of Canada tolerated a substantial depreciation of the Canadian dollar. This apparent difference in reaction by the Bank, however, should not be interpreted as a fundamental policy shift. The Mexican crisis in 1994–5 and the devaluation of the rouble in the summer of 1998 were asset market crises, and the Bank of Canada's response to both was an increase in the bank rate. The Bank's will-ingness to accept a lower-valued currency was an acknowledgement of the worsening terms of trade being experienced by Canada; the depreciation of a currency arising out of a goods market shock should be accommodated by monetary authorities. Being slightly less aggressive with interest rates and somewhat more tolerant of currency depreciation, however, is at most a modest change in Bank of Canada behaviour. The presence of crises has not fundamentally altered the Bank's judgement about appropriate monetary policy.

While the Asian crisis has cast the Bank of Canada in a leading role on the Canadian stage, it has arguably affected fiscal policy as well. Or, perhaps more accurately, it may have helped the Department of Finance to *resist* changes to fiscal policy. At the height of Canada's fiscal crisis, the Department of Finance was able credibly to excuse itself from additional spending commitments. This considerable influence over policy elevated the status of Finance in Ottawa. As the deficit moved into surplus and as disagreements arose over the disposition of the federal government's growing resources, the emphasis on fiscal restraint became increasingly challenged.

To some extent the international financial crisis has again strengthened the position of the deficit-cutters in Finance. Both crises demonstrate the vulnerability of the Canadian economy. The very real danger that the Canadian economy would slide into recession and drag down government revenues has allowed the department to justify greater prudence in its budget process. More specifically, the 1998 budget stated that 'given the unusual degree of uncertainty in the outlook resulting from the recent development in Asia and abroad, the prudence factors used for 1999 are both set 100 basis points higher than the private sector consensus' (Department of Finance, 1998). The prudence factors adjust the short-term and long-term interest rates faced by the government, and are normally set at 80 and 50 points, respectively, above the private forecast consensus. Consequently, the department's official forecast of borrowing costs and interest payment outlays exceeds that predicted by the private-sector consensus by a significant margin.

Furthermore, the selling of Canadian dollar assets during the Mexican crisis was linked to Canada's high fiscal deficit and debt. Even with a relatively stronger fiscal and economic position Canada has been seriously affected by the Asian crisis. One of the effects of these crises has been to convince more policy-makers about the necessity of putting the country and the government on a firmer financial footing. Restoring confidence in an economy and its assets requires a more substantial interest rate increase (and associated reduction in demand and output) when a government has a large debt and deficit than when it is perceived as fiscally strong. It can be argued that this effect is even more pronounced in a world of more closely integrated financial markets.

What conclusions can we draw from this episode? First, foreign balance-of-payments crises clearly have an impact on Canada. As a small open economy heavily dependent on international trade and investment, and becoming more dependent over time, greater instability in international finance will increasingly challenge Canada's ability to manage its economy. While tying ourselves more tightly to the American economy through the FTA and NAFTA may have provided some shelter, it was clearly insufficient in this case. Furthermore, the differential sectoral and regional impacts of such crises will pose additional economic and political challenges for policy-makers trying to reconcile the conflicting needs of Canadians in terms of fiscal policy, monetary policy, and redistribution.

Second, as the size and influence of financial markets grow, there will be much greater potential for the perceptions of investors to induce destabilizing currency movements. This additional volatility will exacerbate the tendency for exchange rate adjustments to be exaggerated, and will increase the pressure on monetary authorities to intervene in defence of their currencies. In a sense, the stakes are being raised for central banks as they try to manage the effects of foreign events on the domestic economy.

Finally, recent financial crises have highlighted the importance of government finances. While Canada's relatively stronger economic and fiscal position in the second crisis did not prevent currency traders from dumping the dollar, weaker fundamentals would very likely have made the effects of the crisis more severe. Indeed, the argument of those in favour of international financial liberalization and integration has often been that it will induce governments to exercise greater fiscal probity. According to this argument, financial markets will swiftly punish those governments that permit high deficits or high inflation.

In this regard, both supporters and detractors of this argument will point to the Asian crisis as a portent of things to come. The lessons they draw from the experience, however, are very different. For some, the lesson to government will be to reform itself. For others, the lesson is to reform the international financial system. These two views are not necessarily mutually exclusive.

CANADA AND THE MULTILATERAL RESPONSE

Between 1982 and 1995, discussions about reforming the international financial architecture were limited to dealing with the fallout from the debt crisis or refining the regulatory structures involved in a series of isolated financial scandals that, although spectacular, did not seriously threaten the international system. The Mexican peso crisis changed this dynamic, catapulting the issue of financial crisis to the top of the reform agenda. One of the earliest and clearest indications of how the crisis affected Canada's policy on international financial reform emerged in the preparations for the G–7 meeting in Halifax.

First of all, however, there was a need to deal with the immediate fallout from the crisis. In this regard, Canada's involvement in the Mexican 'bail-out' was rather modest. Led by an exceptionally engaged administration in the United States, a substantial sum of money was pledged to the Mexican government to assist in the reconstruction of its economy, particularly the financial sector. As its part of the assistance package, the US government came up with $20 billion from its Exchange Stabilization Fund, with the Federal Reserve supplying a $6 billion bridging loan. The IMF, under intense pressure from the Americans, eventually put up $17.8 billion US. Aside from its responsibilities as an IMF member, Canada's participation was limited to the currency swap arrangement of $1 billion negotiated in conjunction with NAFTA, with the money borrowed being quickly repaid by the Mexican authorities.

As the immediate crisis subsided, policy-makers turned to the task of preventing further turmoil, or at least establishing procedures for a more effective response. While not a formal statement of government policy, the Report of the House of Commons Standing Committee on Foreign Affairs and International Trade, *From Bretton Woods to Halifax and Beyond: Towards a 21st Summit for the 21st Century Challenge,* is probably indicative of the concerns Canada brought to the international arena in this regard. Here, amidst concerns over institutional governance and the tenets of development policy, was a clear identification of the threat to the world economy associated with international financial instability. The Committee recommended the following areas for consideration at the G–7 summit: improved macroeconomic co-operation, enhanced resources and surveillance duties for the IMF, measures such as timely information disclosure to stabilize financial markets, the investigation of means to secure financial resources for development purposes (the Tobin tax being given some prominence in the Report), and improved institutional co-ordination to supervise and oversee financial markets.

These themes were echoed in the 1995 *Report on Operations Under the Bretton Woods and Related Agreements Act*, in which Canadian officials identified as policy challenges the issues of early warning, increased IMF resources, and IMF procedural changes to permit quicker intervention in crisis situations. In the period between the Mexican and Asian crises, therefore, the Canadian government seemed to support fully most of the key policy initiatives emerging within the IMF. Three initiatives to increase IMF resources were consistent with Canada's position: an increase in member quotas at the IMF, a special issue of the SDR, and an enlarged borrowing capacity embedded in the New Arrangements to Borrow (NAB). In addition, procedural reforms were enacted to speed up the Fund's response to financial crises. Finally, greater emphasis was placed on the IMF's surveillance duties, although the only obvious manifestation of this policy was the emergence of a new data reporting system to which members were encouraged to adhere. The Fund's consultations with member states under the provisions of Article IV did not appear to take on any additional importance, and did not provide any forewarning of the impending crisis in Asia in its public reports.

In fact, by 1996 many of Canada's concerns regarding IMF reform had seemed to be satisfied, and while the resource enlargement issue had not yet been resolved (and, due to American congressional intransigence, would not receive final approval until well after the Asian crisis was in full swing), other concerns crept onto the Canadian agenda. The 1996 and 1997 versions of the *Report* both included references to debt relief strategies for highly indebted poor countries (the HIPC initiative) as a key 'challenge' for the international financial system, reflecting Canada's long-standing humanitarian concerns.

One major issue emerged in the inter-crisis period, however, that proved to be both more prophetic and more contentious, eventually leading to a divergence of opinion between Canada and the IMF. For some time the Fund had been encouraging members to liberalize their capital accounts, which to some seemed to be a natural extension of its earlier efforts with regard to the current account. As most developed market economies had already removed such restrictions, most of the Fund's exhortations were directed to its developing country members. One of the initiatives taking form at the Fund was a proposal to alter its mandate to include capital account liberalization as a goal of its operations. Such a policy change, of course, would be in sharp contrast to the original Bretton Woods agreement in which capital controls were seen as valuable, perhaps even necessary, instruments for the maintenance of the pegged exchange rate system. With the demise of that system, and with the increased emphasis on market mechanisms, the promotion of capital account liberalization seemed to some to be a logical next step in international financial reform.

While the consensus basis with which the IMF, G–7, and other international monetary discussions operate is not conducive to outright statements of disagreement, Canada's hesitation over the liberalization initiative is evident in its call for a critical examination of the Fund's role in encouraging capital account liberalization. Canada's concerns were either allayed or overruled in subsequent discussions, as the IMF Interim Committee meeting in the spring of 1997 agreed that the Fund was 'uniquely placed to promote capital account liberalization', and that further work on the issue was to be pursued at the fateful September meetings in Hong Kong. By this time Canada had revised its position somewhat and instead emphasized that attention had to be paid to the process and sequence of reform, and that 'appropriate safeguards, transitional arrangements and approval policies will be required to ensure orderly progress toward capital account liberalization' (Canada, 1997: 15). While not inconsistent with IMF policy, the language appears to contrast somewhat with the Fund's apparent eagerness to get on with the job of dismantling controls.

Stanley Fischer, the IMF's first deputy managing director, in addressing the fifty-second annual meeting of the IMF and World Bank in the fall of 1997 in Hong Kong, emphasized the importance of capital account liberalization and the role of the IMF in securing open financial markets. Unfortunately, as Fischer made his presentation, Asian financial markets were collapsing at an alarming rate. The IMF quickly found itself taking the lead on bail-out packages to Asian states that went well beyond $100 billion US and threatened to overwhelm the Fund's resources. As part of the immediate crisis management process, Canada participated with a $1 billion US commitment to South Korea and a $500 million US pledge for Thailand, both contingent on compliance with IMF programs.

Of course, it should be recognized that the financial cost to Canada of participating in these sorts of bailout packages is generally minimal, and may on occasion even turn a profit. When the country in question actually draws on the funds, it constitutes a loan that is repaid with interest. The same is also generally true of any money channelled through the IMF itself, where the risk of default is even lower since Fund credit is generally recognized as being senior to other debt in the order of repayment. Therefore, aside from the exposure to certain risks, the inconvenience of ensuring that funds are available when needed, and the occasional use of concessional (below market) interest rates, providing financial assistance within the context of a bailout package does not constitute a burden on Canadian taxpayers, especially when the IMF is involved.

In announcing the contribution to the Korean package, Finance Minister Paul Martin stated his support of APEC proposals that recognized 'the central role of the IMF in ensuring the stability of the international monetary system' (Department of Finance, Press Release 97–111). While Canada was in apparent agreement with the Fund's handling of the crisis,[3] there are indications that Canadian officials disagreed with some interpretations of the events. The onset of a second major financial crisis in three years was seen by some as a disturbing trend. The emphasis on early warning and surveillance that emerged after 1994 was shown to be insufficient, as the financial problems in Asia seemed to catch many key players unawares. While it may have been too early, and with too inexperienced a system, to forecast these difficulties accurately—many of the basic statistical reporting guidelines were still far from being universally applied—it is also possible that such events are simply too difficult to predict with any degree of confidence. The implications of each interpretation are clearly different. Adherents to the first view would counsel refinement of the present system while maintaining the basic commitment to liberalization. The latter interpretation suggests that crisis avoidance needs additional emphasis, including the possibility of restraining capital markets or even reversing the drive for complete liberalization.

The statements emanating out of the Department of Finance indicate that the Canadian government's position, as usual, lay somewhere in between. More precisely, the government appeared to agree with the basic goal of liberalization, but disagreed about some of the operational details. This cautious approach included very public contributions to the debate about improving the current system of safeguards. In April 1998 the department released a proposal to improve international supervision and surveillance. The proposal suggested the creation of an 'international supervisory surveillance secretariat' within the current Bretton Woods institutional framework, with a mandate to review the financial-sector supervisory structures of member states. The emphasis on supervision, transparency, and disclosure was taken up again in the Finance Minister's 'Statement for the Interim Committee of the International Monetary Fund'. Consensus within the IMF and its membership for improvements in financial supervision seems quite strong, and so this statement simply emphasized Canada's continued support for the process. On some points, however, Finance Minister Martin identified some differences with IMF policy. The IMF was urged to 'enhance the transparency of its own operations and communicate its advice to its members and the public clearly and with more candour'. The issue of transparency at the IMF has been a long-standing concern of some members, including Canada.

More crucially, the statement hinted at divisions over the capital account liberalization issue. On the one hand, the minister indicated that he continued to 'strongly support making the promotion of orderly capital account liberalization as an "explicit purpose" of the Fund'. On the other hand, he questioned whether there was sufficient understanding of 'the complexities of the liberalization process to confidently identify the best approach in every situation' and said that he remained 'unconvinced that assigning the Fund formal jurisdiction over capital account transactions is necessary to effectively promote capital account liberalization.' The concerns over giving the IMF jurisdiction over liberalization for the Canadian government was at least partly motivated by legal issues. If assigning jurisdiction to the IMF implied exclusivity, then there was the problem of how to handle the issues already emerging in other fora such as the World Trade Organization, the Bank for International Settlements, and the Organization for Economic Co-operation and Development, all of which had hosted some discussions of relevance to the capital control issue. Second, the interpretation of capital account rules could give rise to disputes between different countries, which the Fund is ill-equipped to resolve in its present form. Finally, jurisdiction could be interpreted by some as giving the IMF *carte blanche* to use its influence and resources to 'coerce' countries into liberalizing.

The legal interpretation of jurisdiction was not the Canadian government's only concern. Perhaps more striking was the minister's emphasis on the 'importance of possible prudential considerations . . . that may include some limitations on short-term capital flows for a transitional period'. While the remarks were clearly in reference to a transition period, the suggestion that some controls could be beneficial in some circumstances could be interpreted as a challenge to the proponents of liberalization.

By the fall of 1998 the Canadian government took up suggestions for more specific—and more controversial—reforms. In a speech to the Commonwealth Business Forum in September (Department of Finance, Press Release 98–093), the Finance Minister reiterated the standard policies on transparency and cautious liberalization, but then went on to discuss proposals for ensuring that private-sector investors take on more of the burden of crisis management. Concerns over private-sector behaviour had by then become a hot topic. Several commentators had highlighted the potential for 'moral hazard', with the private sector deliberately pursuing high-risk investment strategies on the assumption that any major crisis would be resolved at public expense. To mitigate this problem *ex ante* and to ensure 'burden-sharing' *ex post,* an 'Emergency Standstill Clause' was suggested by the minister. Such a clause, according to the proposal, would temporarily prevent creditors from removing their investments in a crisis-stricken country. The countries to whom the funds were being repatriated would be the enforcers, preventing their institutions from selling off assets denominated in the afflicted currency if the IMF's Executive Board so agreed. These suggestions were repeated in Canada's statement to the Interim Committee of the IMF a few days later.

The Canadian government's announced position on international monetary reform generally, and crisis management specifically, came very close to the 'Declaration of G7 Finance Ministers and Central Bank Governors'. Essentially all of the points taken up by the previous Canadian press releases—transparency, supervision, carefully sequenced liberalization—were all present in the joint communiqué. There was also a reference to the need to foster 'greater participation by the private sector in crisis containment and crisis resolution, including through the use of innovative financing techniques'. The language is similar to that used by Canada's Department of Finance, although any specific reference to the Emergency Standstill Clause was notably absent.

The congruence between the Canadian policy statements and that released by the G–7 finance ministers and central bank governors should not be interpreted as Canada having forged a consensus around its position. The same concerns, and several of the same solutions, emerged worldwide. Scoffield (1998) quotes Sidney Weintraub at Washington's Center for Strategic and International Studies as saying that the idea of controls on international capital markets are 'being talked about all over'. And if the recent consensus reflects a less-than-pure commitment to unrestrained international finance, surely part of the explanation lies in the emergence of centre-left governments in the four European members of the G–7. It is also important to bear in mind that the Canadian government and the G–7 joint statement do not question the long-term desirability of liberalized capital accounts. Nor has the IMF (or perhaps, more accurately, its more pro-liberalization members) ever indicated a desire to remove rapidly all capital account controls without reference to the need for safeguards or caution. Earlier IMF statements did identify the need for an appropriate sequencing of reforms and the presence of adequate financial supervision, although some have expressed doubts about whether such acknowledgements amounted to much in practice (Helleiner, 1997: 17). More recent statements by the IMF re-emphasize these precautions. The differences within the G–7, and probably among the IMF Executive Board members, seem to be ones of emphasis rather than of fundamental principles. The emergence of a consensus is not, therefore, particularly surprising.

None the less, Canada had probably gone further in its contemplation of international monetary reform than most of its G–7 partners. As Scoffield (1998) reported, 'the recent interest in controlling those flows of capital is in stark contrast to attitudes of a few years ago, when ideas such as the Tobin tax on international transactions were given short shrift.' While Canada's Department of Finance had also discounted the value of the Tobin tax, these discussions had been held several years before. Furthermore, the consensus has seemed to move away from the strict adherence to full capital market liberalization towards an acknowledgement that speculative capital flows—however these are defined—may need to be discouraged in some way. Such a position is one with which the current Minister of Finance has appeared reasonably comfortable when it comes to the 'emerging market' and other developing countries. Finally, Canada has continued to emphasize the need to address the serious human suffering that has accompanied the Asian crisis, stressing that the welfare of the poorest must be not be subordinated in the operations of the international monetary system.

Canada's relative sensitivity—at least among G–7 countries—is easy to understand. The European members of the club are larger and more geographically and economically distant from the crises in question. Traditionally, monetary policy in the United States has appeared at least as likely to exacerbate or induce a crisis than react to it, as in the 1982 debt crisis, and its economy appears largely impervious to overseas financial tribulations. More recently the American government has taken its leadership responsibilities in international finance more seriously, reducing interest rates in part to resuscitate the global economy. Furthermore, the American Congress approved legislation to enlarge the IMF's resource base, albeit somewhat tardily, and has sufficiently tempered its strong support for the goal of financial liberalization to facilitate the emerging consensus for greater caution on matters of implementation. Japan has been caught in the centre of the recent crisis, but has seemed preoccupied with its own internal financial problems. After an early attempt to seize the initiative with the doomed Asian Monetary Fund proposal, Japan has contented itself with providing financial support in the context of the IMF programs in the region. As the smallest economically and most internationally oriented of the G–7 countries, Canada is much more sensitive to these events, which may go some distance in explaining the Canadian government's relatively greater willingness to contemplate a more cautious approach to liberalization.

CONCLUSIONS

What themes emerge from this review? First of all, the process of economic liberalization and integration has left Canada even more reliant on international conditions than in the past. This interdependence has brought many benefits to Canada, even if it has been accompanied by certain policy challenges, including the fact that Canada can be seriously affected even when distant markets of limited importance to Canadian exporters become troubled. The transmission mechanism of these difficulties will increasingly be volatile capital markets. Because Canada's economy is small relative to those of the economic powers, a change in the sentiments of financial market players will easily overwhelm the capacity of the Canadian government to resist the effects of foreign crises. Having supported the creation of a liberalized international financial system, the Canadian government must now come to terms with some of its more awkward implications.

One of the first policy problems the government must handle is the extent to which the exchange rate should be used to insulate the domestic economy from these external shocks. Fundamental policy does not appear to have changed. During both the Mexican crisis and Asian crisis, the Bank of Canada used interest rate increases to slow down precipitous declines in the dollar's value that seemed to result from asset market disturbances. However, the events surrounding the Asian crisis have also shown the Bank to be comfortable with the use of the exchange rate as a buffer against external shocks, particularly those that reflect fundamental changes in the terms of trade. Therefore, while the Canadian dollar has been permitted to explore new territory against its American counterpart, and the phrase 'record low' became ubiquitous on nightly newscasts, the more severe Asian crisis has not yet had the severe impact on aggregate Canadian output that may have been expected given the experience of 1995. While recession continued to be a real possibility, especially when Brazil began exhibiting signs of succumbing to the crisis, much of the Canadian economy remained remarkably buoyant. Instead, the adverse production effects were sectoral and regional in nature, with British Columbia bearing much of the burden.

The second challenge is how to avoid being targeted by turbulent financial markets in the first place. In this regard the presence of financial crises have highlighted the role of government finances in a globalized economy. The confidence of investors and traders is much easier to maintain when the government is not struggling with its own fiscal situation. The fact that the interest rate increases needed to stabilize currency markets were smaller during the Asian crisis than the Mexican crisis may be attributable, at least in part, to the reduction in public deficits in Canada that occurred in the intervening years. As financial markets become increasingly internationalized, the pressure to maintain (or achieve) more sustainable government debt levels will remain. Some will view this externally imposed constraint as a challenge to Canadian political sovereignty, while others will celebrate it as a valuable balance against public extravagance. However one regards the discipline imposed by international markets, it is a reality that governments and citizens must recognize and accept as being one of the features of an integrated global economy.

Globalization is by no means omnipotent, however, and there is still a crucial role for states to play in shaping both their own economic destinies and that of the international system. If crises are indeed becoming a more permanent feature of the economic system, then states will have to learn how to deal with them at the multilateral level. On its own, Canada cannot possibly lead the international monetary system out of a financial crisis of the sort that emerged in Asia. As a relatively small economic player, Canada is not well suited to the role of lender of last resort in the classic sense. Our economy cannot absorb enough imports to lift many countries out of recession, even though by avoiding a serious slowdown in growth Canada has been able to continue its imports of goods from crisis countries. Of some concern is the fact that the Canadian government's efforts to stabilize the dollar and insulate producers from the shock have mirrored the policies adopted in the crisis countries themselves: higher interest rates and a decline in the value of currencies relative to the US dollar. These policies may have detracted somewhat from the need to boost the demand for Asian products and divert capital in their direction. Had Canada been in a stronger position fiscally and economically it may well have been able to choose policies that contributed more significantly to such efforts. Therefore, our capacity to contribute to the resolution of these crises depends partly on having a more robust economy ourselves.

Perhaps of greater importance, however, has been Canada's role in entertaining suggestions on how to modify the international system to make it less susceptible to crisis. Although the Canadian government has been a steadfast supporter of the multilateral system and agreed to make financial contributions to the Asian bail-out packages, it has not been content simply to fall in line behind the views of larger and more influential countries. This is not to suggest that the Canadian government has advocated throwing sand in the wheels of international finance, to paraphrase James Tobin. But Canada's relative vulnerability has appeared to make it more circumspect than some of its G–7 or IMF colleagues in terms of the push for global financial liberalization. The slightly more moderate position of the

Canadian government on this issue, its emphasis on the practical dimensions of liberalization, and its willingness to consider the possible need for short-term controls and greater protection during periods of transition have eventually emerged in the consensus position of the G–7. The Canadian government cannot claim to have engineered such a consensus through its diplomatic or financial influence, however. Instead, there was a convergence between our own caution in such matters and the unsettling events of the Asian crisis that forced all governments to place more emphasis on proper financial supervision and other precautionary policies as a prerequisite for financial liberalization.

Taking a critical—some would say sober—second look at capital market liberalization does not constitute a victory of low politics over high finance. The acceptance in theory of the possible need for temporary restrictions on international finance should not be interpreted as a trend. A willingness to contemplate precautionary policies is still a far cry from actually enacting them, and policy practice has not yet run up against market reality. Even if it were deemed advisable, Canada would have a difficult time reversing its own integration into international financial markets, let alone convincing others to do likewise.

Rather than discourage the process, therefore, Canada's most useful contribution to the international system may be to encourage a sounder process of integration. As the memory of the crisis fades, and as less intrusive reforms of the system continue apace, key countries may see the need to introduce additional regulatory procedures as less urgent, less important, and perhaps less desirable. There may indeed be attempts to return to the fast lane on the road to financial liberalization. As the G–7 country with the heaviest reliance on the international economy, Canada may have a critical role in reminding others of the need for caution in the pursuit of international financial integration. In addition to championing the need for sound regulatory and supervisory systems, Canada can also provide valuable expertise to countries seeking to implement such precautionary measures. Through these initiatives the Canadian government can help to ensure that premature financial liberalizations are avoided.

Finally, in the event that such precautionary measures are insufficient to prevent or mitigate international financial crises, Canada is still well placed diplomatically to bridge some of the gaps that may emerge between rich and poor countries. Should it become apparent that more intrusive financial market intervention or co-ordination is needed, Canada's reputation for moderation and its international connections make it possible to represent its less wealthy partners in the Francophonie and the Commonwealth to its colleagues at the OECD and the G–7, and vice versa. Membership in regional fora and the Cairns Group also enables the Canadian government to play a central role, perhaps even a leadership role, in international discussions on financial reform (Kirton, 1998: 4). Mediating a breach over the fundamentals of globalization, however, will also require sound ideas. The Canadian government has already brought many ideas to international discussions, and efforts to develop more will undoubtedly continue.

Some less-developed countries, nongovernmental organizations, and academics have questioned the wisdom of financial globalization. For the Canadian government, however, and for its counterparts in many other rich nations, the recent financial crises have not yet led to a serious reconsideration of the goal of liberalized international financial markets. Instead, the Asian crisis has served as a reminder of the need to be properly prepared before contemplating liberalization and the need to assess carefully the speed and sequence of any transition to a more liberal financial regime. If these precautionary measures do indeed prove insufficient, the emergence of future crises may well constitute a more serious challenge for Canada and its partners in the multilateral system.

NOTES

This paper has benefited tremendously from the comments of Paul Jenkins, Larry Schembri, Michael Hart, and the participants at the *Canada Among Nations* workshop held in December 1998. None of these persons should be held accountable for the views expressed in the paper, or the errors that may remain.

1. The data for this section are drawn primarily from the International Monetary Fund's *International Financial Statistics*, the Bank of Canada's *Bank of Canada Review*, and Statistics Canada's *Canadian Balance of Payments*, Catalogue 67–001–XPB, and *Canadian International Merchandise Trade*, Catalogue 65–001.
2. Caution should obviously be exercised in attributing developments in the Canadian economy exclusively to the presence or absence of foreign crises. Domestic factors, and those prevailing in the United States, are far more critical in this regard.

3. The conditions imposed by the IMF as part of the assistance packages were, however, quite controversial in other circles, having attracted considerable criticism from a surprisingly wide spectrum of commentators.

REFERENCES

Bank of Canada. 1998. *Bank of Canada Review*. Ottawa, Summer.

Bank of Canada. 1998. *Monetary Policy Report*. Ottawa, Nov.

Canada. 1994–7. *Report on Operations Under the Bretton Woods and Related Agreements Act*. Ottawa.

Department of Finance. 1997–8. Press Releases 97–111, 98–093, and Statements to the Interim Committee of the IMF. From Web site: <http://www.fin.gc.ca>.

Department of Finance. 1998. *The Budget Plan 1998: Building Canada for the 21st Century*. Ottawa.

Government of the United Kingdom. 1998. 'Declaration of G7 Finance Ministers and Central Bank Governors'. From Web site: <http://www.hm-treasury.gov.uk/pub/html/docs/g7dec.html>.

Hampson, Fen Osler, Maureen Appel Molot, and Martin Rudner, eds. 1997. *Canada Among Nations: Asia-Pacific Face-Off*. Ottawa: Carleton University Press.

Helleiner, Gerald. 1997. *Capital Account Regimes and the Developing Countries*, vol. 8 of *International Monetary and Financial Issues for the 1990s*. New York: United Nations.

House of Commons Standing Committee on Foreign Affairs and International Trade. 1995. *From Bretton Woods to Halifax: Towards a 21st Summit for the 21st Century Challenge*. Ottawa: Government of Canada.

International Monetary Fund. 1997. *International Financial Statistics Yearbook*. Washington: IMF.

Kirton, John. 1998. 'Canada and the Global Financial Crisis of 1997–8: G7 and APEC Diplomacy', mimeo.

Little, Bruce. 1998. 'Bank of Canada confounds critics', *Globe and Mail*, 9 Feb., B1, B9.

Little, Bruce, Ann Gibbon, Brent Jang, and Konrad Yakabuski. 1999. 'Economy gearing down', *Globe and Mail*, 5 Jan., B1, B4.

Scoffield, Heather. 1998. 'Capital flow controls winning support', *Globe and Mail*, 14 Sept., B1, B5.

Stinson, Marian. 1998. 'Foreigners unload $6.3-billion in Canadian equities', *Globe and Mail*, 25 Nov., B9.

7

Third Pillar or Fifth Wheel?
International Education
and Cultural Foreign Policy

JOHN GRAHAM

In the short term, the economic activity generated by cultural, scientific, and education related activities is extremely important for the Canadian economy. . . . In the medium and long term, a country that does not project a clearly defined image of what it is and what it represents is doomed to anonymity on the international scene.

Special Joint Committee Reviewing Canadian Foreign Policy, 1994

Cultural Affairs, in addition to politics and the economy, are one of the pillars of our foreign policy.

Canadian government response to the Special Joint Committee, 1995

Almost 50 years ago the Royal Commission on Arts and Letters (the Massey Commission) reported that 'cultural matters are becoming more and more an essential part of foreign policy.' But, the commission noted, 'our cultural relations are still in an elementary and almost non-existent stage.' Although a few scholars such as Harold Innes warned that the Canadian character would dissolve in an American sea unless we set about defending our cultural interests, not much was happening. Eighteen years later *The Times Literary Supplement* declared that 'Canada has done little, especially externally, to eradicate its traditional image of philistinism.' Strong stuff, but not wholly unfair. In 1976, the Ontario government's Commission on Canadian Studies observed:

> it is little wonder . . . that our image abroad is vague, when it is not a complete distortion. Canada is still rarely viewed abroad as a distinct country where our society, whole history, politics and literature merit serious intellectual examination. A few of the old ice and snow myths linger on and the epithet of the unknown country may have acquired new meaning.... Canada's cultural relations abroad have been severely neglected.

Transmitting the message of Canada's burgeoning cultural vitality has not been a strength of Canadian foreign policy. In 50 years most of the features of the architecture of government have changed dramatically. Cultural foreign policy has grown, but it is probably the part of the architecture that has changed the least. The purpose of this chapter is to plot these changes, consider the efforts to place cultural foreign policy among the objectives of Canadian foreign policy, and examine the impediments that have, with astonishing persistence, frustrated the realization of these efforts. While cultural diplomacy, described as the 'third pillar' of contemporary Canadian foreign policy, comprises an ever-widening spectrum of activities— from music, drama, dance, and the plastic arts and Canadian Studies to distance education and the marketing of Canadian university education abroad, to name a few—and while the condition of the pillar itself is a central theme, the focus of this chapter will be more specifically on the academic or international education dimension.

Change in the cultural and academic export policies of the Department of Foreign Affairs and International Trade (DFAIT) has come about slowly and piecemeal. The Cultural Affairs unit in the Information Division of the former Department of External Affairs was transformed to a full division in 1968. Academic Relations Services, subsequently a division, was established in 1971 with responsibility for the management of scholarship programs, the foreign service visitor program to Canadian universities, and a loose mandate to liaise with those parts of the academic community involved with Canadian foreign policy. Academic Relations initiated Canadian Studies abroad as a new dimension of cultural foreign policy in 1974. Since April 1975 this has been an established government program, with headquarters budget and personnel support. Canadian Studies was incorporated in the department's first five-year cultural plan, announced that year by Secretary of State for External Affairs Allen MacEachen on the occasion of the inauguration of the chair of Canadian Studies at the University of Edinburgh.

The mid-seventies saw signs of movement and effervescence—the result of a happy convergence of good leadership by Patrick Reid, Director-General of Public Affairs, the accommodating and far-sighted views of MacEachen, and the availability of money. The department's embrace of cultural and academic programs was advancing, but the centrality of cultural and academic programs within foreign policy was not established. An unexpected blow was struck in 1983 when the department introduced a radically new operational structure designed to give greater cohesiveness to policy through improved teamwork. In the new organization, almost all non-political activities (trade, immigration, culture, and academic relations) were removed from their functional homes and were redistributed by region and grouped with political affairs under the geographical bureaus. I became the Director-General of a Geographic Bureau at this time. I valued the new span of control (each sector brought with it financial resources from its former functional base), the teamwork, and policy cohesion, but I did not understand that this policy, by reducing the Cultural Bureau to a shell, had undermined its capacity to develop a professional cadre of officers experienced in international education and culture and had removed its ability to give a central coherent impulse, standards, and form to cultural foreign policy.

SAVED BY THE SENATE

> In the great scheme of things, the arts and culture are generally deemed to be of minor consequence, at least as far as governments . . . are concerned.
> (John Meisel, *Flora and Fauna on the Rideau:*
> *The Making of Cultural Policy*)

Apart from a brief forward surge between 1986 and 1989 when budgets doubled under Joe Clark, the situation grew steadily worse. As austerity began to bite in the early nineties, cultural and academic budgets were seen as easy targets by senior DFAIT management, who still regarded these as peripheral to Canadian foreign policy objectives. How peripheral was soon apparent. Senior management proposed to shift cultural and academic activities, including the remnants of the International Cultural and Academic Bureau, out of the department altogether and into the framework of a merged Canada Council and Social Sciences and Humanities Research Council (SSHRC). This was described by Reid Morden, the deputy minister, as 'back to basics'. The proposed change was incorporated by the government of the day in Bill C–93 (1993). Rescue came not as the result of some eleventh-hour reprieve by ministers or mandarins becoming aware that foreign policy was being amputated of one of its own vital limbs (C–93 passed the House of Commons with a large majority), but from the Senate—by a margin of a single vote. The unexpected rescue was the fruit of independent thinking by several senators, including opposition to the merger of the Canada Council with the SSHRC.[1]

Reprieved, the stewards of cultural foreign policy remained, but as an unwelcome presence in the department. This left the Cultural Bureau more demoralized and rudderless than before. Fortunately, the general election of October 1993 resulted in a new government and a new foreign minister. André Ouellet came with a very different view of the place of culture and international education in foreign policy. One of his first acts was to suspend implementation of the previous government's decision to close down most of Canada's cultural centres abroad. Soon afterward, in March 1994, he and the new International Trade Minister, Roy McLaren, set in motion the first comprehensive review of Canadian foreign policy since the end of the Cold War and the more visible onset of globalization. At the instigation of Ouellet, and encouraged by the Director-General of the International Cultural and Academic Bureau, Alain Dudoit, and by Emile Martel, a special emphasis was to be placed on cultural and academic diplomacy.

RISE AND SLUMP OF THE THIRD PILLAR

Culture is the face of Canada abroad. To the extent that foreign policy is dependent on foreign public recognition—an identifiable image and a sense at all levels of what we stand for, what kind of society we are, what we sell— that policy is dependent on our projection of our culture. What's more, we

> are more dependent on that cultural projection than the handful of larger countries who are our allies and our competitors and who have other ways of projecting their image. (John Ralston Saul, *Culture and Foreign Policy*)

The task of formulating a fresh design, making recommendations, and suggesting the principles and priorities to guide Canadian foreign policy was assigned to a Special Joint Committee of the House of Commons and Senate Reviewing Canadian Foreign Policy. It soon became clear that the committee, composed of seven Senators and 15 MPs, possessed a number of striking advantages. The Senate co-chair was former Foreign Minister and Deputy Prime Minister Allan MacEachen. Members included Senator Jacques Hebert (of the Applebaum/Hebert Commission) and MPs John English and Bill Graham. The inspired scribe who wrote most of the report was John Halstead, and the task of providing the committee with an in-depth position paper on 'Culture and Foreign Policy' was given to John Ralston Saul.

Ouellet was not satisfied that he had given the Special Joint Committee a strong enough signal about the importance he attached to cultural diplomacy, and the department had not mentioned culture in the guidance paper it had prepared for the committee (see Hay, 1995). Ouellet therefore approached former minister Serge Joyal to prepare a study on international cultural affairs, higher education, and scientific co-operation. In fact, Ouellet persuaded his friend Joyal to shelve temporarily a very similar project he had been contracted to undertake for the Department of Canadian Heritage. Joyal's report was submitted to Ouellet in September 1994 and made available to the committee (Joyal, 1994). The committee now became a venue for a vigorous discourse on international culture and education, which attracted more attention and testimony than other areas of foreign policy except international development assistance. Witnesses included representatives of the Association of Universities and Colleges (AUCC), the Association of Canadian Community Colleges (ACCC), the Canadian Bureau of International Education (CBIE), the Association for Canadian Studies in the US, and the British Association for Canadian Studies.

Ouellet and the committee had uncorked a storm of complaint, remarkable for the severity of the indictments about government neglect of cultural diplomacy. Joyal had assembled statistics demonstrating where Canada stood in relation to its principal competitors.

The differences between the expenditure, and therefore the value, that Canada assigned to cultural diplomacy, in contrast to other countries, were dramatic (Special Joint Committee, 1994: 62). Spending on cultural diplomacy and international education was calculated as:

France	$26.50 per capita
Germany	$18.49 " "
United Kingdom	$13.37 " "
Japan	$12.60 " "
Canada	$ 3.08 " "

Other statistics compared the percentage of public expenditure devoted to international culture, science, and education:

France	.23
Germany	.16
United Kingdom	.21
Japan	.18
Canada	.03

Expressed in other terms, per capita spending by Canada was 13 per cent that of France, 17 per cent that of Germany, and approximately 25 per cent that of the UK and Japan. It was instructive and disturbing to realize that annual German cultural expenditure in Canada, including the Goethe Institute, was almost equal to DFAIT's entire budget for international education relations with the developed world (approximately $4.5 million).

The European Union (EU) and the United States each spend approximately $1 billion per year on international education, research, and training. In the case of the EU the amounts are over and above the major investments made by individual governments on a bilateral basis—particularly by France, Germany, and the UK. For its part, the US spends five times per capita more than Canada on international education.

In his report Joyal complained that Canada's cultural foreign policy had been stagnating or even regressing since the Applebaum/Hebert recommendations of 1982. He noted that the limited engagement of the Canadian government is further weakened by 'fragmentation of resources as a whole and a multiplication of responsibility centres, accentuating the erosion of Canada's presence abroad'. Not only were these resources dispersed across perhaps a dozen departments and agencies, this disorder was mirrored in the Department of Foreign Affairs and International Trade. Seven different functional and geographic branches and bureaus shared responsibility for international education along with the Bureau of International Culture and Higher Education (as it is now called). This profusion is the result not of design but of random growth in the absence of a strong central focus, as geographic divisions have succeeded over the years in prizing away pieces of budget for purposes related to their function or region. A few of these programs should remain where they are to ensure they enjoy the necessary specialized management, but most should be knitted into a co-ordinated, mutually reinforcing system. In an internal review of cultural programming dated June 1994, the department acknowledged that the dispersion of resources both outside and inside DFAIT has 'led to policy incoherence, inefficiencies in delivering government programs and, it is reasonable to assume, excessive administrative costs.'

The EU confronted its own problems of project proliferation and duplication in higher education by rationalizing its various programs for international education within two frameworks: 'Socrates' for higher education and 'Leonardo' for vocational training. Consolidation began in 1995, and the seven-year budgetary projection for the period commencing in the year 2000 for 'Socrates' and 'Leonardo' is valued at approximately $4.8 billion.

The three-volume *Report of the Special Joint Committee*, including dissenting opinions by the Bloc Québécois and Reform Party, was submitted in November 1994. In a rapid response, the government of Canada tabled its Foreign Policy Statement on 7 February 1995. This statement encompassed the entire foreign policy spectrum. In their covering letter ministers Ouellet and MacLaren congratulated the committee for its 'ground breaking work concerning the projection of culture and learning abroad' and agreed with 'the stress placed on the importance of culture and learning'. The government endorsed Joyal's vision of cultural diplomacy as one of the three pillars of Canadian foreign policy. The projection of Canadian values and culture stood on equal footing beside 'promoting prosperity and employment' and 'protecting our security within a stable global environment' among the goals of Canada's new foreign policy framework. Specifically, the government proclaimed that it 'fully intended to pursue cultural, scientific and educational relations as key components of Canada's foreign relations' and noted that as knowledge becomes 'a key element in international competitiveness, education plays a critical role in prosperity.'

The government was careful to hedge its commitment to the third pillar with cautionary noises about the availability of funding, and there was nervousness about how far political will would follow political rhetoric. Nevertheless, this far-reaching undertaking, along with positive and specific responses to the recommendations of the Special Joint Committee, represented a change in direction and gave heart to academic and cultural communities and organizations. Ouellet confirmed his earlier undertaking that no cultural centres would close.

The rejoicing was to be short-lived, however. Within two years of the proclamation of the three pillars, more formally known as 'Principles and Priorities for the Future', most of the bright expectations had not moved off the drawing board, and even the existing flimsy structure was being eroded by cuts and reallocations of funds. Figure 1 demonstrates the scale of this erosion.

By the fall of 1996 the outlook was bleak indeed. Senior DFAIT management advised the International Culture and Academic Relations Bureau that funding allocation for the academic/international relations programs would sink from the level to which they had dropped in the 1996–7 fiscal year by a further 33 per cent for 1998–9 and onward. The modest budget of the Cultural Affairs Division was spared. However, the actual damage inflicted on the core programs was masked. The official development assistance (ODA) programs funded by CIDA, but managed by the Academic Relations Division, were to be cut by 28 per cent while the non-ODA programs (to G–7 countries, Spain, and Latin America) were scheduled to lose 59 per cent. Appalled by these figures, the Academic Relations Division concluded that any attempt to redistribute the remnants of its budget across its core programs would lethally undernourish all of them. It was therefore decided to cancel all programs, including the marketing of Canadian universities and colleges, distance education, Commonwealth awards, and the Fulbright scholarships, in order to leave the flagship program, Canadian Studies, with enough for survival.

What was happening? While the ongoing bite of austerity can account for sluggishness or inaction in procuring the financial and personnel resources necessary to give substance to the third pillar commitment, how was it that even the scaffolding around the base of the pillar was being dismantled? There was a cabinet shuffle.

Figure 1

International Cultural Affairs and Academic Relations

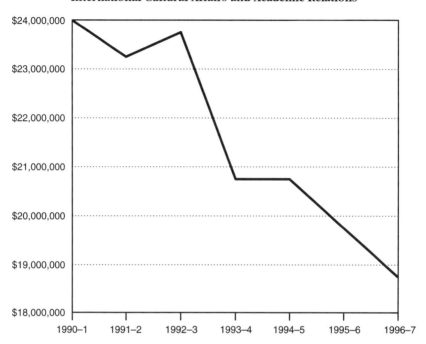

Sources: Joyal, 1994: Table 12; DFAIT.

Ouellet was replaced as Foreign Minister by Lloyd Axworthy, who was (and is) an enthusiastic supporter of the third pillar. Yet despite the formal inauguration of the third pillar and the explicit support of two foreign ministers in succession, significant erosion was taking place. This confounded the international community. Some two years after the strategy was introduced, a Japanese delegate at a bilateral meeting on cultural and educational exchanges expressed curiosity about Canadian cultural policy. Noting that Japan also has a three-pillared foreign policy (although in their case culture is the second pillar), the Japanese official pointed out that since the announcement of the third pillar there were only reductions in Canadian program-ming for Japan: 'What', he inquired, 'does your third pillar mean?'

In the late fall of 1997 a small group of persons outside the depart-ment, concerned about the increasingly visible wreckage of cultural diplomacy, began to lobby Axworthy's office. Thwarted by his own senior management in his efforts to sustain the third pillar, Axworthy welcomed outside support. In January 1998 he formed the Academic Relations Advisory Committee as a subcommittee of his Foreign Policy Advisory Committee and a sister to the Cultural Affairs sub-committee established about two years previously.[2] The Academic Relations subcommittee was chaired by Lorna Marsden, president of York University. It met over conference calls and in person in Ottawa in March and submitted a number of recommendations to Axworthy:

- a stop to the hemorrhaging of funding support and a commit-ment to restore to previous levels;
- a clearly enunciated policy that brings cultural and academic diplomacy into the main career path of the department;
- an equally clear directive to departmental senior management and to heads of missions (in those countries where there is a program) confirming the priority that DFAIT attaches to these programs;
- effective co-ordination with CIDA expenditures on education that presently have no adequate linkage with the DFAIT cul-tural/academic strategy;
- strengthening the department's capacity to support the mar-keting of Canadian universities and colleges abroad;
- recognition that universities are not only central to public pol-icy, but increasingly instruments of public policy.

In April 1998, the new budget restored $2 million to the Academic Relations program. The intervention of the subcommittee proved timely, as were pressures from other parts of the international edu-cational constituency: the AUCC, ACCC, CBIE, and others. However, the process was not straightforward and DFAIT stubbornly resisted the necessary reallocation of funds. The key factor was the minister's belief in the value of these programs and his determination not to allow the department to override him on this issue. Seeing once again on his desk departmental estimates that showed that the funds had not been restored, Axworthy is reported to have said that he would not allow the main estimates to go forward unless the alloca-tion for international education was reinstated.

Increased funding was accompanied by organizational and per-sonnel changes in the department. A new Assistant Deputy Minister, Hugh Stephens, was appointed, as were a new Director-General and a new Director of Academic Relations. All of these people demonstrated renewed enthusiasm for the mission of cultural and academic diplomacy. As an indication of this commitment, Hugh Stephens reinstated 'culture' to the title of his area of responsibility.

In October 1998, a consortium of non-governmental organizations launched an 'International Learning Strategy for Canada'. This initiative was the result of collaboration among the AUCC, the ACCC, the CBIE, the World University Service of Canada (WUSC), the International Council for Canadian Studies, and the Canada-US Fulbright Commission. The consortium expressed alarm that federal support for international education was 'fragmented and under-resourced' and falling behind that of our competitors 'in the race to position countries strategically in the global knowledge economy through programs that build a critical mass of human resources with international knowledge and skills'. Acknowledging the success and vision of the US Fulbright and the EU 'Socrates' programs, the consortium recommended establishing a flagship program in support of international education that would have 'a significant impact on Canada's human resources by doubling the number of students with first hand international experience and cultivating stronger involvement by faculty and teachers as agents of change in internationalization.'

More specifically, it was argued that the proposed flagship program would enable the federal government to implement the Memorandum of Understanding signed by Canada with Chile, Argentina, and Brazil in the course of the 1997 Team Canada missions to those countries. These Team Canada visits proved to be a useful vehicle in enabling the AUCC and others to market Canadian higher education more aggressively in South America. They were the means by which the Prime Minister and other senior mission members were sensitized to the enormous potential of international education as an exportable service. (CBIE estimated the global market for international education for 1996 at US $28 billion.) The visits also served to help educate policy-makers in DFAIT to the reality that international education has a higher multiplier effect than many other Canadian export sectors.

CANADIAN STUDIES

The experience of DFAIT's Canadian Studies Program is a case in point. The purpose of the program is to develop an informed awareness and a balanced understanding of Canada, its values, and its scholarship

(Graham, 1976: 39). With a very modest investment by the department over a period of 25 years, the Canadian Studies Program has grown into a network of more than 250 university centres and/or programs spread across 30 countries. It is estimated that there are now 7,000 academics teaching Canadian studies in these countries and close to 150,000 foreign students taking courses on Canadian topics. This network has created its own support system of a dozen journals with a Canadian focus. The restored annual budget for Canadian Studies is today only $4 million. Some years ago the Association for Canadian Studies in the US calculated that for every dollar invested by the Canadian government, American academic institutions contributed $13. The AUCC estimates that for every dollar invested in Canadian Studies, $4 are generated for spending in Canada.

Despite the globalization of communications and energetic information programs, knowledge about Canada is probably subject to more distortion than that of any other country of comparable political and economic significance. What can be done about narrowing the gap between image and reality? Clearly, it is by no means always true that knowledge of Canadian subjects will acquire its appropriate level of acclaim by a natural process of scholarly dissemination and academic enterprise, and it is even 'less likely that a discipline or multidisciplinary network of Canadian subjects will be accorded a respectable place in the calendar of discriminating universities by the same natural chemistry' (ibid., 40). It can be argued that the recognition of the quality of Canadian literature, particularly in Western Europe, was transmitted through a number of key Canadian Studies centres and that, consequently, the enormous commercial and image-shaping success of Canadian literature was significantly facilitated by that process. An excellent example of critical leverage by Canadian studies scholars, in this instance J.M. Lacroix, president of the Canadian Studies Association in France, is the recent decision by the French Ministry of Education to select the works of Margaret Atwood as required reading throughout France's secondary school system for a certificate in English.

There are other striking examples, but there are also deficiencies. Across the 30 countries where Canadian Studies programs are in place, many are so financially undernourished that their credibility is at risk. Obtaining the impressive cost-benefit ratios associated with Canadian Studies requires at least minimum investment in library resources, faculty study trips to Canadian universities, visiting scholars from Canada, translation of texts, and conference costs. At present the Canadian government is not adequately priming the pump of Canadian studies abroad and is falling behind competing countries in the projection of cultural resources abroad.

CANADIAN STUDENT MOBILITY AND MARKETING
CANADIAN UNIVERSITIES AND COLLEGES ABROAD

The Canadian position is also slipping in two important dimensions of international education. Our major competitors in the US and Europe have set a goal of having at least 10 per cent of their students experiencing a segment of their higher education in another country. Canada currently has seen just over 3 per cent of post-secondary students studying abroad, leaving us at a disadvantage in the accumulation of international experience and skills.[3] Canada's performance in the marketing abroad of our universities and colleges is little better. A study prepared for the CBIE in 1996 expressed alarm that 'Canada is the only major receiving country consistently reporting declines in international student numbers at its universities.'

The benefits of having foreign students in Canadian post-secondary institutions should be apparent. Diversity generates cross-fertilization and intellectual synergy. The linkages forged with Canada and its values, skills, resources, and people by foreign students return enormous dividends when the students go on to build their lives and professions in their own countries, and some of the most significant of these dividends are non-quantifiable. There are, furthermore, significant financial advantages to international student inflows. An Australian study estimated that by the year 2000 there will be approximately 1.8 million students engaged in studies outside their own countries (CBIE, 1996). On the assumption that each foreign student spends about $18,000 per year on tuition fees, living, and other costs, it is projected that the global market for international students will reach some $32 billion by the year 2000. The same study estimates that this flow of students would generate about 462,000 jobs internationally. The Canadian share was estimated at some 9,000 jobs.

One can imagine what the government's response would be if a market potential on this scale were identified for Canadian-made capital goods or manufactures. Yet, in the marketing of our post-secondary capabilities Canada is falling back due to neglect. Over the period 1985–95 Australia and the United Kingdom were able to more than triple the number of international students in their universities.

Australia, two-thirds the size of Canada, already hosts a larger number of international students. More recently, the British have embarked on an ambitious program promoting international student recruitment within a new and forward-looking strategy for cultural diplomacy. Today there are more international students studying for British university degrees outside the country than actually in the UK.

Spurred by criticisms from the Special Joint Committee, John Ralston Saul, and Serge Joyal, together with some push from the university community, DFAIT decided to establish a number of Canadian Education Centres in Asia, Latin America, and Eastern Europe to disseminate information about educational opportunities in this country. Management control of these centres was contracted out to the Asia-Pacific Foundation of Canada, resulting in a loss of program coherence. The problem has now been rectified and co-ordination of the relationships with these centres has been vested in the International Academic Relations Division of DFAIT. Nevertheless, Canada continues to lose its share of the international student market.

Although Canadian Education Centres were underfunded in relation to competing initiatives of other countries, it was hoped that this would be more than offset by the educational cost advantage conferred by the devaluation of the Canadian dollar. Indications are that this has not happened because, generally, cost is not a primary determinant for student selection of a university abroad. Canada suffers from a perception in some quarters that this country does not have first-class universities. Indeed, provincial underfunding of universities has had a deleterious impact on standards of excellence. The Ontario and Quebec governments have been the major villains in this regard. The consequences of financial deprivation extended beyond the universities themselves, as Martin Rudner (1997: 212) observed 'the weakening competitiveness of Canadian higher education can have far-reaching ramifications for the longer-run competitive disadvantage of Canada's knowledge-based industries.' This disadvantage is compounded by the distortions or opaqueness of Canada's image in overseas markets.

SERGIO MARCHI TO THE RESCUE

In a speech delivered to the Canadian Education Industry Summit in Toronto in October 1998 Sergio Marchi, the Minister for International Trade, declared that 'education is now an industry', thus adjusting nomenclature to fit his trade agenda. Marchi used the occasion to announce the formation of an Education Marketing Advisory Board, to be chaired by Sheldon Levy, president of Sheridan College, and composed mostly of the heads of the prominent NGOs in international education. Its mandate is to give 'informed and comprehensive advice to the Minister for International Trade on education marketing issues . . . on trends in the education industry . . . the current and anticipated capacities of the education export industry . . . on how . . . DFAIT and [other] relevant federal departments can assist the education industry in its marketing efforts abroad . . . [and] on extension and contraction of overseas marketing centres.' The minister indicated how impressed he was that the second largest group in the Team Canada mission to Latin America in 1997 came from the education sector and remarked that 'internationalizing Canadian education is also a top priority for me personally.' But the question is not just whether ministers and DFAIT are showing signs of renewed vitality in this area—they are; it is whether the government of Canada is actually prepared to commit commensurate resources and policy support to make this an operational priority.

The question will be answered, in part, by the fate of a proposal to double the budget for nearly the full range of programs in the DFAIT International Academic Relations Division: distance learning, scholarships, education marketing, and Canadian Studies. Many of Canada's major partners (the US, Western Europe, Japan, Australia, and New Zealand) have expressed interest in the expansion of scholarship exchange programs on the basis of reciprocity. The proposal to cabinet includes fresh funding that would enable Canada to take advantage of these opportunities. New funding is also being sought for the development of 'knowledge networks' to expand Canada's role as a broker, creator, and disseminator of knowledge. Foreign Minister Axworthy is supportive, the Assistant Deputy Minister has pushed it, and it is notable that the core of the department's senior management has accepted it. This could be a signal of change, or perhaps a recognition that there is little point in bureaucratic resistance to a proposal that anyway will have to compete for new money against more popular contenders such as health care.

WILL THE THIRD PILLAR GO THE WAY OF THE THIRD OPTION?

Although their focus is not identical, there is no mistaking the expressed will of both Foreign Minister Axworthy and Trade Minister

Marchi to support the third pillar. In both cases their commitment appears to be underpinned by an understanding of the degree to which successful cultural diplomacy reinforces the confidence and creativity from which that success springs. For the most active proponents of cultural diplomacy, this implies something beyond merely the export earnings generated by cultural enterprise or the education industry. The sector is no longer under attack from within and the mood, for the moment, is cautiously upbeat. The positive approach of ministers and the enthusiasm of the Assistant Deputy Minister and Director-General have permeated the Bureau of International Culture and Higher Education. But what happens when Axworthy leaves? His role, usefully complemented by Marchi on the education marketing side, has been indispensable. It was Axworthy's concern that influenced the selection of an Assistant Deputy Minister well disposed to the area. It was his intervention that restored funds to rescue most international education programs. The good fortune of having ministers who understand the value of a vibrant cultural foreign policy is never secure, and perhaps even less so under a Prime Minister who has no particular affinity for the area. Although there are, of course, senior officers with a benign approach to cultural diplomacy, the record indicates that these programs have not been safe in the corporate hands of the department's senior management.

The issue then becomes one of what can be done by the present ministerial leadership to embed these programs more firmly into DFAIT's corporate agenda. Through its neglect the department has signalled in effect that the academic/cultural field is a dead end for qualified and ambitious officers. Good officers working in the area are effectively penalized in career terms. As a result there are very few. About 75 per cent of the officers in the Bureau of International Culture are on secondment from other departments or agencies or have been hired on contract. Most have excellent credentials for their assignments, but because their contracts tend to be for the short term and exclude postings abroad, they cannot be expected to develop a strong sense of identity with the department or commitment to its long-term goals. John Ralston Saul made a related point in his presentation to the Special Joint Committee: 'Canadian diplomats should be given the incentives and the tools necessary to become effective cultural, scientific and educational sales persons for Canada. What this requires is more an attitudinal change in the Department of Foreign Affairs and International Trade than significant new resources.'

The cultural and international education area must be able to attract, sustain, and eventually reward highly qualified persons if the third pillar is to become the reality intended by its architects. It is unlikely that change for the cultural and academic side can take place within the present departmental environment. (The department as a whole is suffering from low pay scales, attrition, and few promotions.) Real change will probably not occur until officers in this sector can work within a reasonably secure and forward-looking institutional framework. Serge Joyal and others have recommended that a separate cultural agency be established that would report to the Foreign Minister and be modelled on the British Council or Goethe Institute. If the British Council model is followed, the new agency would be allowed to sell services (e.g., language teaching abroad). The British Council covers about a quarter of its budget through its own enterprise. Periodic secondments to and from the cultural/higher education community would expand internal dynamics and external outreach. Whatever the merits—and, in my view, they are considerable—it is unlikely to be saleable to cabinet in its present mood.

There is, however, another option—perhaps a halfway house to a cultural agency. Almost all other distinctive activities within DFAIT have their own career stream: economic/political, trade, and consular management. Why not create a cultural/academic stream? A change of this kind would be low-cost and provide the career structure necessary for continuity and recognition. To build these changes into the bureaucratic structure of DFAIT and to highlight the priority that departmental management attaches to these programs, it will be important to ensure that the future assessments of Canadian diplomatic missions (and of the heads of posts) also explicitly address their performance in the cultural/educational domain.

The Joyal and Special Joint Committee reports sparkle with solid, practical recommendations. Many of these recommendations were acknowledged in the government's response, but few have been implemented. One that merits urgent attention is the recommendation that programs focused on cultural export and international education, now dispersed across various federal departments and agencies, be centred within DFAIT, that the lead role of the department be reaffirmed. But more important is the need for governments at federal and provincial levels to recognize that Canada continues to fall behind our competition in the developed world at significant costs to our economy and to our creative vitality.

It is unlikely, and unnecessary, that the third pillar will stand as tall as *peace* and *trade* on the plinth of Canadian foreign policy, but it is plainly in the national interest to treat culture and education as a fundamental dimension of Canada's international relations. John Ralston Saul has noted: 'we can't afford not to.'

NOTES

1. It is improbable that the rescue by the Senate on this occasion would have been possible if this body had been elected.
2. The members of the Academic Relations Committee were: Lorna Marsden (chair), Jan D'Arcy, John English, Gwyneth Evans, Robin Farquhar, John Graham, Ann Medina, and Jean Pigott.
3. 'An International Learning Strategy for Canada', prepared by a consortium of the AUCC, ACCC, CBIE, WUSC, ICCS, and the Canadian-US Fulbright Commission.

REFERENCES

Canadian Bureau of International Education (CBIE). 1996. *Where the Students Are*. Ottawa: CBIE.

Graham, John. 1976. 'Recent Growth of Interest in Canadian Studies Abroad', *International Perspectives* (Sept.-Oct.).

Hay, John. 1995. 'Protecting Values and Culture: An Episode in the Making of Canadian Foreign Policy', *Canadian Foreign Policy* (Fall).

Joyal, Serge. 1994. 'Refocussing Canada's International Cultural Policy in the Nineties: Issues and Solution', unpublished report to the Minister of Foreign Affairs, Sept.

Rudner, Martin. 1997. 'Canada and International Education in the Asia-Pacific Region', in Fen Osler Hampson, Maureen Appel Molot, and Rudner, eds, *Canada Among Nations 1997: Asia-Pacific Face-Off*. Ottawa: Carleton University Press.

Special Joint Committee. 1994. *Report of the Special Joint Committee Reviewing Canadian Foreign Policy: Principles and Priorities for the Future*. Ottawa: Parliamentary Publications Directorate.

8

Battlefields and Birds:
New Directions for Cultural Policy

KEITH ACHESON AND CHRISTOPHER MAULE

The occasional skirmishes between Canada and the United States over cultural trade and investment are evolving into full-scale warfare. But just as bird-life miraculously survived the devastation of the French countryside during the Battle of the Somme, many of Canada's cultural industries are not just surviving but flourishing. In this chapter we examine why, despite current success, the cultural policies of the past not only contribute to these trade disputes but are counter-productive in terms of their stated objectives. The successes achieved in international markets are the result of the talent of Canadian artists and entrepreneurs, while the current policy framework, based on what we term 'the nationalist view', retards these initiatives. An alternative rationale for an open cultural policy, which we favour, is contrasted with the prevailing nationalist approach. This chapter examines the arguments put forward in support of the two positions, as well as a discussion of the policies and a listing of the disputes. In the conclusion, we suggest the direction for future policy initiatives.

THE NATIONALIST VIEW

Since the end of World War II, protectionist cultural policies have been promoted and sustained by Canadian governments of all political stripes. The nationalist approach uses the following set of facts to support its case (Rabinovitch, 1998: 30):

- 70 per cent of the music on Canadian radio stations is foreign content;
- 60 per cent of all English-language television programming available in Canada is non-Canadian, reflecting the importation of many American channels and programs;
- 33 per cent of all French-language television programming available in Canada is foreign;
- 70 per cent of the Canadian book market consists of imported books;
- 83 per cent of our newsstand market for magazines is made up of foreign magazines;
- 84 per cent of retail sales of sound recordings in Canada feature foreign content (including 69 per cent of French-language retail sales);
- 95 per cent of feature films screened in theatres in Canada are foreign (this percentage can be even higher in English-language markets);
- 86 per cent of prime-time English-language drama on Canadian television is foreign, mostly from the United States;
- 75 per cent of prime-time drama on French-language television in Canada originates outside Canada.

These and similar statistics can be found in numerous government and industry pronouncements arguing that protection is needed for the production and distribution of Canadian content in the different media. Limited market size in Canada and competition from imported content are seen as giving American productions an overwhelming advantage in the English-language market. A policy of import substitution is advocated in parallel with the continued but restricted availability of foreign-produced content. Providing shelf space for Canadian content is a frequently espoused objective. In the absence of Canadian content policies, it is argued that sovereignty and national unity will be undermined. What successes have been achieved in the cultural industries, nationalist advocates claim, are derived from discriminatory domestic policies and the exclusion of the cultural industries from the obligations of international agreements. This approach must be sustained and adapted to embrace new technologies such as the Internet. A pillar of the nationalist view is that culture is different from other economic activities and thus justifies special treatment.

THE OPEN VIEW

We question the assumptions underlying the nationalist view and the figures used to support it. Not only are the resulting policies often based on poor economic reasoning, they are iatrogenic in undermining the set of activities they seek to promote, which we believe deserve support. An alternative view is slowly emerging and the monolithic position of government is fragmenting. Those seeking an explanation from the government on domestic cultural and trade policy matters are likely to receive one view from Heritage Canada and differing perspectives from the Department of Foreign Affairs and International Trade (DFAIT) and Industry Canada. Heritage Canada holds to the nationalist view. DFAIT's responsibilities in handling trade disputes have led it to recognize the need for change. Successive Ministers of International Trade have noted the primacy given to cultural trade issues in dealings with their American counterparts. Industry Canada is increasingly aware of the dilemma of protectionism and the continued ability of Canadian producers to access emerging opportunities in foreign markets.

What is the rationale for the open view? It contends that a country with a small domestic market, further subdivided linguistically, has an interest in open markets in order to gain economies of scale. A small country stands to benefit from a rules-based approach for the settlement of trade and investment disputes.[1] The ability to compete in international markets is a sign of a successful domestic industry, one that generates the resources needed to promote local domestic content and to compete internationally. By way of contrast, industries built on subsidies sustained over a long period of time seldom emerge from their infant industry status. Instead, they develop a core of rent-seekers who argue for continuing protection. At some point governments must withdraw their financial support and force these activities to face the winds of competition.

The open view notes the bias of technology. Technological change is favouring smaller firms in terms of both production and distribution. For example, there are no longer shortages of distribution outlets for audiovisual material. An expansion of outlets has created an enormous demand for new content as well as opportunities for small innovative producers. If they cannot succeed in this environment without protection, then the problem may reflect on the quality and appeal of the content produced rather than on the circumstances of production. User-pay systems permit financing for the production and distribution of material for narrow audiences as opposed to financing from advertising and the public purse.

Larger revenues can be obtained by selling specialized content into internationally dispersed niche markets, for example, for English-language comedy or French-language classical drama. Both mass and niche markets are international. If Canadian producers are internationally successful, the figures will show them having a small share of the domestic market but a similar share of a much larger international market. Producers from the United States certainly have an advantage by being able to finance productions for their large domestic market, but that advantage is substantially mitigated if foreign firms can freely sell in the United States. Firms from small countries in other industries have demonstrated their international competitiveness. For example, the domestic market for Canadian (Nortel), Swiss (Nestlé), Dutch (Philips), and Swedish (Volvo) multinational firms is a small proportion of their global sales.

The argument that successes achieved to date would not have been possible without the existing domestic policies has been neither proved nor disproved. An analysis would depend on establishing a plausible set of counterfactual circumstances and speculating on what might have occurred in the absence of the measures taken. At best there has been some replacement of imports by domestic production, but these are expensive measures to sustain, and as the nationalists' figures show, import displacement has been limited.

What has happened, and has not been emphasized, is that a number of successes in Canadian cultural exports have occurred where the market opportunities for expansion do exist. This growing international competitiveness of Canada's cultural producers will be threatened by foreign retaliation against Canadian protectionist policies. Even if Canadian policies, introduced on the grounds of the need to protect an infant industry, have contributed to industry growth in the past, it is difficult to sustain this argument given the achievements obtained in international markets today.

All industries argue for their uniqueness, and they all have a certain point. T.S. Eliot perhaps said it best. To paraphrase a bit of dialogue in the *Cocktail Party*, 'everything is different and remarkably like everything else.' Financial services require attention for 'prudential reasons'—governments cannot allow unsafe financial institutions. Health and pharmaceutical products are unique in that they affect the physical and mental well-being of the population. Agriculture and food security, oil and energy security, national defence and personal security, court systems and legal security all offer unique goods or services of value to citizens. Culture, too, is different: it plays a vital role in securing a nation's history and character. But it is a mistake to adduce extraordinary circumstances for culture, claiming that it is not subject to economic forces and then lobbying the government for protection and resources. When we hear repeatedly that culture cannot be treated merely as a commodity or industry or in terms of economic analysis,[2] this is usually followed by claims for more resources from the state. At best this argument is naïve, at worst, hypocritical.

THE FACTS

In our view, arguments in favour of the open view are more persuasive and are supported by a close examination of the existing data, both those cited by the protectionists and other facts. The small percentage share of Canadian producers in the different media, *vis-à-vis* those from outside Canada, especially from the United States, is presented by the protectionist side without an indication of the percentage that would be appropriate for judging Canadian performance. If Canada represents about 7 per cent of the international market for English-language media, a competitive Canadian firm producing content with international appeal would have this share of all markets including Canada.[3] For product sold internationally, such as drama and children's programming, one would expect a low percentage share of the domestic market but a similar share of foreign markets. What needs to be reported is Canada's share of all markets and the revenue earned by Canadian works domestically and abroad.

Anne of Green Gables, an incontrovertibly Canadian program, has enormous appeal to audiences abroad, particularly in Japan, and Canadian animation programs sell well internationally. Most programs that are successful in Canada do well in the much larger international market. For the ones that do not succeed abroad, Canada has a public broadcaster, the Canadian Broadcasting Corporation (CBC), and a number of provincial public broadcasters that can be directed to fund and carry them. Some program genres, such as news and current affairs, are more specific to the domestic market and represent, as would be expected, a much higher than 7 per cent share of the domestic market and a much lower percentage of the international market.

Another deficiency of the market share figures quoted above is that they often confuse what is available with what is purchased or viewed. For example, while television broadcasters may be forced to program a given percentage of Canadian content (Cancon), actual viewership may be less. In fact, figures for Canadian viewing of Canadian drama and variety programming show that despite the years of enforced Cancon requirements for television broadcasters, the viewership of these programs remains low for English-language programming, although higher for French-language programs where language provides more of a natural barrier to imports.[4] Where viewers have a choice among the best programs from a number of sources, an improved quality of Canadian offerings will increase market share at home and, more importantly from a revenue perspective, from abroad. If numerical policy objectives are to be used, they should reflect the nature of the international market for the genre of program.

Other erroneous facts are frequently cited. Canada has been reported to be the second largest exporter of television programs, a claim that not only conflicts with the case for continued protection but is probably inaccurate and definitely cannot be substantiated by published information since there are no data for global television exports. We have traced the first appearance of this 'fact' to 5 June 1995, in 'Speaking notes on behalf of the Honourable Michel Dupuy (then Minister of Communications)', where it is reported that 'Canada is now positioned as the world's number two exporter of entertainment programming.' Since then, this fact has been repeated by industry representatives and the media on numerous occasions, even though Statistics Canada and Heritage Canada cannot confirm its veracity and have been unable to provide a source for this statement. An Organization for Economic Co-operation and Development (OECD) report on the available data on trade in film and television services for 14 countries shows Canada ranking behind the US, the UK, France, and Italy in each of the years from 1990 to 1993 (OECD, 1994: 109).

Seldom recognized in reporting cultural data is the difficulty of attaching nationality to programming. Increasingly, financing for cultural productions comes from multiple national sources using a mix of national inputs, sometimes the result of official co-production treaties but often due to pre-sales of programs in different national markets. Under a co-production treaty both countries may allow the program to be counted as national content in each country, thus leading to double counting. Unofficial co-productions create similar difficulties.[5]

Canada is not the only country where problems of interpretation arise. The United States claims an importance for exports of audio-visual programs that we have found difficult to reconcile with the facts. In Europe, production partners for *Baywatch,* an archetypical American program, include American, Italian, German, and Spanish firms. In the UK, this program is counted as 50 per cent European content while in the remaining member states of the European Community it is 100 per cent European content (Commission of the European Communities, 1998: 115).

What the data do not disclose is that those arguing for protection are often the same persons or firms benefiting from being approved conduits for the distribution of imported material. Sales of Canadian book publishers and film and television distributors are a mix of domestic works and foreign works for which the Canadian company acts as agent. In other media, foreign content is mixed with Canadian content in what are termed Canadian works. Canadian newspapers make extensive use of material collected by foreign news services. The *Globe and Mail* each day republishes two pages of news from the *Wall Street Journal,* and on a regular but not daily basis, content from *The Economist* and *Sports Illustrated.* Even the CBC distributes foreign programming as part of its schedule. Indeed, its level of Canadian content is not much higher than that of commercial broadcasters who resist the distribution of domestic content because it is less profitable than foreign content.

The nationalist discussion focuses on imports only. A more balanced approach would also consider Canadian cultural exports and outward investment. In the newspaper industry, while inward foreign investment is limited by provisions of the Investment Canada Act, there is considerable outward investment by firms such as Thomson, Hollinger, Quebecor, and Torstar. Thomson purchased American-owned West Publishing Company in June 1996 for $3.4 billion, the largest Canadian acquisition that year. In 1997, Thomson reported that 3 per cent of its assets were in Canada and 75 per cent in the United States. Some firms, such as Hollinger, have invested in foreign newspapers. Quebecor owns printing plants abroad and reports a significant printing contract for Time Warner in the United States.[6] Torstar owns and operates Harlequin Books, a highly successful subsidiary that generates most of its revenue from abroad, especially in the United States. Operating profit from book publishing exceeded that from newspapers from 1991 to 1997 (Torstar Annual Report, 1997: 34–5).

Aside from Harlequin, Canadian publishers and their authors actively promote their books in foreign markets. Canada's increasing number of successful authors would be hurt financially if their work was confined to domestic markets. Some, such as Mavis Gallant, also live and work abroad but write about Canadian themes. Both Gallant and Alice Munro publish their short stories in foreign periodicals like *New Yorker* and have done so throughout their careers. Canadian and foreign readers get access to these Canadian stories by reading foreign publications.

Periodical publishing is the one print area where Canada does not have extensive exports in terms of the copies sold. There are exceptions: *Hockey News* and the *Northern Miner* have a considerable percentage of their distribution in the United States, about 65 per cent and 20 per cent respectively, and at one time *Harrowsmith* was publishing a split-run edition in the US until this initiative was halted by Canadian excise tax legislation aimed at preventing foreign split-runs from being sold in Canada.[7] Many Canadian periodicals depend on export revenues from the sale of advertising space to foreigners. A recent edition of *Maclean's* was found to have over half of its advertising pages associated with foreign goods and services. Trade publications are often in receipt of foreign advertising expenditures.

In broadcasting and cablecasting, Canadian firms either have or have had foreign investment in Australia, Ireland, New Zealand, and the United States. CanWest Global properly bills itself as an international media company. In its 1998 fiscal year, 52.2 per cent of its broadcasting operating profit was generated in Canada, 40 per cent in Australia, and 7.8 per cent in New Zealand. CHUM has been successful in selling channel formats to a number of other countries, while the CBC delivers its programming on the Trio service and a version of Newsworld to DirecTV in the United States. Canadians can access Trio only if they have a 'grey market' subscription to DirecTV.

The most significant investment by a Canadian company in foreign media is Seagrams' acquisition of a major Hollywood studio, Universal Studios, and in a separate deal, Polygram, a leading European record producer. For years the complaint has been heard that Canada cannot compete against Hollywood. Now that it is part of Hollywood, one would have expected expressions of satisfaction from supporters of the nationalist viewpoint. None have been heard so far. Other Canadian film and television producers—Alliance Atlantis, Cinar, Coscient, and Nelvana—have grown rapidly to become publicly traded companies. Foreign licensing of current productions and of their libraries contributes significantly to their expansion. To illustrate, Cinar reported revenues of $19 million from the United States and $21.5 million from the rest of the world in fiscal 1997. The 1997 annual report of the company notes that these sources provide over 50 per cent of total production revenues. A significant part of the Canadian revenue attributed to Canadian sources of these companies comes directly from Telefilm and other grants.

In the popular music industry, Celine Dion, Alanis Morissette, Shania Twain, Bryan Adams, and Anne Murray enjoy considerable popularity throughout the world. They follow a number of Canadian artists and technicians, newscasters and directors who have received international recognition: Mary Pickford, Raymond Massey, Lorne Green, John Candy, Jim Carey, Peter Jennings, Robert McNeil, David Cronenberg, and Norman Jewison, to name but a few. Canada has also had notable success in training persons for employment in the animation industry at home and abroad, and in exporting its production services by providing attractive locations for productions by offshore producers, especially in British Columbia, Ontario, and Quebec. Meanwhile, all provinces and a number of cities are joining this bandwagon by establishing film commissions to promote their locations.

A review of the data for Canadian cultural imports and exports, including the extent of outward investment, suggests not only that

Canadian interests would be harmed if other countries retaliated against protectionist Canadian policies, but that Canada would benefit from open access to foreign markets and a rules-based regime to govern disputes. Divisions are likely to appear in those industries that depend on subsidies but where some firms are increasing their dependence on foreign markets.

THE POLICY ANOMALIES AND RELATED ISSUES

The policies that have led to the trade policy disputes between Canada and the United States and also with Europe have often been based on faulty economic reasoning and have given rise to a set of anomalies that harm the industries they seek to assist. Since the 1960s, successive Canadian governments have introduced policies aimed at directing advertising revenue to Canadian magazines and away from split-run or regional editions of foreign, especially American, consumer magazines. Yet, in the process of accommodating American interests, Canada has made special tax rulings and exempted certain publications from its policies. The most recent dispute arose in connection with a Canadian excise tax on advertising in split-runs, a prohibitive tariff on split-runs, and postal subsidies found to be contrary to Canada's World Trade Organization (WTO) obligations. Canada removed the policies in response to the WTO ruling but introduced new legislation, Bill C–55, The Foreign Publishers Advertising Services Act, which is viewed by the United States as equivalent to the excise tax in effect.

Canadian policy has resulted in the anomalous situation that *Reader's Digest* is the 'Canadian' consumer magazine with the largest circulation in Canada and *Time* among the largest. In defending Bill C–55, a government spokesperson (29 Oct. 1998) told the House of Commons: '*Time* has been in Canada for years. *Time* has Canadian content. *Time* is not a split-run edition. *Time* cares about Canadians. *Time* continues to tell Canadian stories.' Aside from the fact that it is incorrect to state that the Canadian edition of *Time* is not a split-run edition of the magazine, it appears that history is being rewritten.[8] Some Canadian legislators have forgotten who their original 'enemy' was. Time and now Time Warner, the 'bad guys' of Canadian periodical legislation when these policies were first introduced, are now presented as the 'good guys'.[9]

Bill C–55 and the predecessor excise tax have been justified as a response to foreign publishers exploiting a loophole in prior policy designed to curb split-runs. The claim is that *Sports Illustrated* was able to launch a split-run by circumventing the prohibitive tariff by transferring editorial content electronically. What is ignored in this account is that Time Canada, which had no exemption, has been doing the same thing for over 20 years and no Canadian government had chosen to challenge its actions. At first, Time imported the material on film, a physical item that could have been stopped at the border, and subsequently has used electronic means to deliver its editorial content to a printing plant in Canada.[10]

Foreign investments in the Canadian cultural businesses are reviewable under the Investment Canada Act. The 'Baie Comeau Policy' of 1985, as amended in 1992, was introduced with the objective of placing the control of book publishing and distribution in Canadian hands. Foreigners cannot start new businesses in these areas without yielding majority control to Canadian investors, and cannot exercise de facto control whatever their ownership. In cases of indirect acquisition of existing foreign-owned companies, the revised policy permits foreign control if the investor gives to Investment Canada satisfactory undertakings that are of net benefit to Canada and to the Canadian-controlled sector of the book industry. This policy is based on the cross-subsidization argument that Canadian-owned operations are more likely to promote and sell Canadian talent. The facts do not support this contention. When Cineplex-Odeon became Canadian-owned, there was no marked difference in the nationality of films shown in its theatres as opposed to those owned by foreign distributors. We expect no appreciable change now that the merger of Cineplex-Odeon with Sony Pictures will transfer majority ownership of that chain back to foreign hands. With minor variations, cinema owners exhibit those films that are likely to earn the highest returns. This is exactly how commercial broadcasters would behave if they were not subject to Cancon rules imposed by the Canadian Radio-television and Telecommunications Commission (CRTC), and is the reason why the rules were introduced.

Canadian-owned book publishers justify receiving subsidies on the grounds that they publish more Canadian-authored books than foreign-owned publishers in Canada. However, only Canadian publishers qualify for government grants to support Canadian authors.

As far as retail bookstores are concerned, we do not know whether they sell more Canadian-authored books because Investment Canada rules make it difficult for foreign bookstores to operate in Canada. Some have been allowed to operate as minority partners while others have been denied that right on the basis that the foreign interests still controlled the enterprise. We would expect any bookstore operating in Canada to distribute Canadian books if there was a reasonable chance of making a sale. Canadian-authored books are available on the foreign on-line Internet services such as Amazon.com presumably because there are requests for such items. In sum, the cross-subsidization argument is based on a false understanding of economic behaviour, but it serves certain domestic interests by sheltering them from foreign competition.

Investment Canada has had to adapt the rules to accommodate some foreign investments in book distribution and not others. Borders Books was prevented by Investment Canada from owning 49 per cent of a Canadian book distribution operation in Canada, while Barnes and Noble, with a lower percentage ownership, has an equity interest in Chapters. The distinction rested not on ownership, since both foreign investors had an allowed minority position, but because Borders was deemed to have de facto control as determined by Investment Canada in a closed process.[11] The next dispute in this area may arise over whether foreign companies with management contracts to run Canadian college and university bookstores have de facto control. A number of these contracts have now been signed. Meanwhile, the Internet is providing an ordering system for books that Investment Canada rules cannot touch.

Cancon rules for television broadcasting, specialty, and pay services are another strange policy animal. These rules apply to the broadcast and not the print media, a distinction that makes no logical sense since both distribute Cancon and increasingly the Internet is a conduit where both print and audiovisual materials are found. The historical reason is that the allocation of limited spectrum in the past permitted governments to attach conditions to broadcast licences regarding content, which they were unable to do with the print media. There would be a tremendous fuss nowadays if newspapers, periodicals, and bookstores, for instance, were required to carry a certain amount of Cancon. Consistency in policy-making suggests that all media should be treated equally. In practice this does not occur.

In applying these Cancon broadcast content rules peculiar circumstances can arise as a result of the administrative procedures used to rate films and programs. A film about the RCMP made by an Australian would not be considered Cancon; a film by a Canadian company and director about the Australian gold rush would. Content is measured by the nationality of the inputs used, not by the content of the story, so that the claim that these policies assist in telling Canadian stories to Canadians is at best only half true. The Canadians may be telling the stories but the stories may have nothing to do with Canada. Similar anomalies exist elsewhere. *Black Robe* is an Australian-Canadian co-production with an Australian director.[12] The story has no obvious connection with Australia, other than an Australian director, just as *Baywatch* has none with Europe.

Introducing new policies and providing exceptions (grandfathering) for existing foreign-owned firms has been a technique frequently used by Canadian policy-makers that results in anomalies in film distribution as well as periodical publishing. The major Hollywood studios are exempt from Canadian film distribution policy. One of these studios is Canadian-owned, and others are Japanese, Australian, and at one time French-owned. The Australian owner now has American citizenship. Each time grandfathering occurs, the potential exists for newcomers to protest that they are not receiving national treatment, as occurred recently in the case of Polygram prior to its acquisition by Seagrams.

Finally, as implied in some of our examples, technological change, especially the Internet, is circumventing many of these domestic policies. One round of the battle to determine how the Internet is to be regulated is being fought out before the CRTC. Many members of the cultural community want broadcasting-type regulations to apply so that content policies can be imposed. Opponents, including suppliers of hardware and distribution services, favour no content rules or only rules for controlling socially unacceptable material such as pornographic, violent, and hate content. In our view it would be a mistake to impose Cancon rules even if it is technically feasible. Any attempt to do so will almost undoubtedly lead to further international disputes.

One area that needs to be examined more closely is competition policy. Although there have been inquiries, a court case in the 1930s, and a set of undertakings in the 1980s regarding film distribution, and the Competition Bureau has just completed a three-year monitoring of the merger that created Chapters, much remains unexamined. Some countries, including Canada and the United States, permit the operation of export cartels—agreements between producers that apply to foreign markets only and would not be permitted to operate in domestic markets. The Motion Picture Association of America is registered under the enabling US legislation for export cartels. The mutual dismantling of legislation that permits firms to do abroad what is illegal at home would assuage fears that these powers are abused.

The difficulties experienced with administering domestic policies, combined with advances in technology, have led to the trade frictions to which we now briefly turn. At times it is suggested that our international obligations are different from our domestic policies and that somehow the two clash. This is misleading. Our international obligations are part of our domestic policies since governments have freely entered into these agreements. If there is a misunderstanding of what the obligations mean, that is a result of ignorance or poor advice at the time the agreements were signed. For example, it is clear that cultural goods have been subject to the trade obligations of the General Agreement on Tariffs and Trade (GATT) since 1948. The fact that it was not widely discussed until the 1997 WTO decision on Canada's periodical policy does not mean that it was an obligation that had been newly introduced. No one had challenged national policies affecting cultural goods prior to this event, but the potential for challenge had long existed.

TRADE AND INVESTMENT FRICTIONS

Many of the trade frictions in the cultural sector have been well publicized. Others have received less attention, in part because of their complexity. Some fall into the potential or imminent category. In a forthcoming book (Acheson and Maule, 1999) we examine each of these disputes in detail and draw implications for domestic policies and international agreements. The areas of dispute are listed below:

1. The series of Canadian periodical policies—corporate tax measures, prohibitive tariffs and an excise tax, postal subsidies, and criminal penalties on placing certain advertisements in split-run magazines—have attempted to divert advertising expenditures from foreign to Canadian consumer magazines.

2. The American-owned Country Music Television as an eligible cable service in Canada was delisted, and replaced by a Canadian alternative.

3. The attempt continues to deter direct satellite broadcasters from servicing both the Canadian and American markets jointly rather than separately.

4. Efforts continue to protect a separate Canadian book wholesale and retail system in Canada.

5. A patched-together film distribution policy has selectively restricted the distribution of non-proprietary film rights to Canadian distributors. The grandfathered exceptions and discretionary suspension of some aspects of this policy have resulted in a limited and uneven application of these policies. A side-effect has been the generation of a dispute with the European Community regarding the discrimination against the film distribution activities in Canada of Polygram before its takeover by Seagrams.

6. Neighbouring rights legislation rewards performers and record companies for the public performance of their recorded music material on a reciprocal basis rather than on a national treatment basis.

7. Domestic dubbing is required by the province of Quebec.

8. Increased subsidies and tax credits supporting national production and distribution of cultural products are sold or licensed internationally.

9. The implementation of program ratings systems and associated hardware designed to assist viewers in controlling television content have a trade-distorting potential.

10. The policy regime to be applied to the Internet, and whether it will contain nationalistic content restrictions, remains to be determined.

CONCLUSION

Based on these empirical observations, which we believe are more substantive than those of the proponents of nationalist policies, our view is that domestic cultural policies and the treatment of culture in international agreements require drastic re-evaluation. Even in the absence of international obligations and changing technology, domestic policies are poorly formulated to achieve their stated objectives.

Over the years, the policy framework has been captured by the industry or those parts that benefit from it. They have been ably supported by advisers to the industry and by Heritage Canada and its preferred consultants. However, the monolithic support of other government departments is crumbling. If change is to come about it will require a change of mind-set by proponents of the nationalist view that is similar to contemplating a Darwinian as opposed to a creationist interpretation of the origins of species.

What's to be done? First, a truce should be called and the hostilities ended. The opponents should refrain from repeating mindlessly, on one side, that culture is different and merits protection, and on the other that culture is merely entertainment and is no different from any other traded good or service. Instead, there should be an attempt to bring about some meeting of the minds on what facts accurately describe the situation and what conditions give rise to the frictions. At the same time, it can be recognized that Canadian concerns and the problems that occur with the United States are not unique to these two countries. Recently, Korean film producers, when faced with the possibility of losing their domestic film quotas, held a public funeral procession for the death of their industry; and the European Union has reported on the debilitating effect that the system of subsidies in Europe has had on audiovisual production and the declining theatrical attendance for European films.

The empirical facts should provide the background for understanding the economics of each of the cultural industries and the particular problems that arise. Hopefully, a consensus will emerge on what needs to be addressed in an international agreement. In the interests of initiating a debate, we suggest the following points for discussion.

(1) Focus cultural policy objectives on promoting creativity. This does not always equate with cultural industries. By switching the focus from industries to individuals, emphasis will be placed on understanding the process of creativity, which may mean giving more attention to nurturing it in the educational system, the participatory cultural sector, non-profit and co-operative cultural ventures, and the home, the earlier the better.

(2) If support is needed for certain activities, such as the breaking into the market of first-time authors, musicians, actors, directors, and publishers, provide subsidies targeted at these groups rather than at those that do not need support. Although subsidies can be

subjected to countervailing actions by other countries, there is considerably more leeway in using subsidies consistent with international trade obligations than is the case with some of the other cultural policy measures used to date.

(3) Encourage the cultural industries to seek foreign markets as a way of strengthening their domestic capabilities and avoiding the limitations of a restricted Canadian market.

(4) Recognize that Canada is not well served by taking a cultural exemption in international trade and investment agreements. Exemptions do not eliminate disputes. They push them into an arena of soft diplomacy where those with political power prevail. The alternative may be to consider a special WTO agreement on culture similar to that for financial services, telecommunications, and information technology.

If reason does not prevail in convincing proponents of existing policies that change is needed, continuing cultural trade wars and the onslaught of technology will likely force change anyway. While the birds of Canadian culture are still managing to sing, the escalation of trade disputes could have devastating effects in the future.

NOTES

The authors would like to thank Elizabet Filleul, Leslie Milton, Killaine Sharman, and Stephen Whitehead for comments on earlier drafts of their research, and the Social Sciences and Humanities Research Council of Canada for a grant in aid of research. The views expressed are those of the authors.

1. On 3 Dec. 1998 the Assistant Deputy Minister for Trade and Economic Policy, Department of Foreign Affairs and International Trade, testified before the House of Commons Standing Committee on Culture: 'Canada, as a middle power, must always be better served by more precise enforcement of a rules-based system. If you're left to softer diplomacy, you invite greater exercise of economic leverage and the size of the club carried by our larger trading partners may well be larger than ours. . . . I think overall we are better served by more precision and more breadth of the rules in the system.'

2. The alleged contradiction of the term 'cultural industries' is discussed in Dorland (1996: 349).

3. The estimate of 7 per cent is probably high. It is based on the populations of the US, the UK, Australia, New Zealand, and the English-speaking part of Canada. A comparable estimate for the French market, the proportion of the French-speaking Canadian market to the total French-speaking market, would be 11 per cent based on the French-speaking population of Canada, Belgium, and all of France.

4. In the fall of 1996, in the English-language drama/comedy program category, 23.9 per cent of the schedule was Canadian content and had 8.8 per cent of total viewership; for variety programs, 2.5 per cent was scheduled and 1 per cent viewed (Stanbury, 1998: 10).

5. A commentary on recent British films notes that the vagaries of multinational financing make the notion of ascribing a nationality to a firm a dated one: 'the best British film to open in United States theatres, "Velvet Goldmine," was actually an American film, or, at least, was directed by an American, Tom Haynes. The film . . . represents a good argument for no longer speaking of British film, or American film, or Irish film.' *New York Times*, 20 Dec. 1998, AR13.

6. Quebecor Inc. extended a contract to print US regional editions of *Time*, *Sports Illustrated*, and *People* magazines in excess of one million copies per week. Quebecor Annual Report, 1997: 17.

7. The excise tax legislation was the subject of a dispute panel ruling by the WTO that led to withdrawal of this legislation by Canada in 1998. The reference to *Harrowsmith*'s split-run in the United States appears in Canada's submission to the WTO (26 Sept. 1996).

8. In testimony before the Standing Committee on Canadian Heritage, 18 Nov. 1998, George Russell, editor of Time Canada, stated that his magazine was the major example of a split-run magazine in Canada.

9. In a 13 Nov. 1998 submission to the Standing Committee on Canadian Heritage, we have stated our views as to why the measures contained in Bill C–55 would not work and would almost certainly invite retaliation against either cultural or other industries in Canada.

10. The Canadian tariff measure prevented the importation of certain periodicals. Time Canada imported the editorial content of the magazine, which may not have been considered to be a periodical until it was combined with advertising and then printed in Canada. At the time of writing (April 1999), the future of Bill C–55 is unclear. Canada is stating its intention to pass the legislation, while US interests have threatened retaliation against Canadian exports of cultural and other goods and services. It is possible that a political compromise will be reached similar to that regarding the delisting of Country Music Television as an eligible cable television service in Canada.

11. Investment Canada rules for new and existing investment in the cultural industries are dealt with under Section 15 of the Investment Canada Act, which requires notification of investments above a threshold of $5 million for the cultural industries, a threshold lower than that for other industries. Within this general policy is a book-publishing policy dealing with indirect acquisitions of non-Canadian book companies and a film policy dealing with film distribution rights.

12. The Australian broadcasting authorities told us that, despite being made under the official co-production treaty between the two countries, *Black Robe* would not be counted as Australian content if and when broadcast in Australia. This would be contrary to the understanding reached in signing a co-production treaty.

REFERENCES

Acheson, Keith, and Christopher Maule. 1999. *Much Ado About Culture*. Ann Arbor: University of Michigan Press.

Commission of the European Communities. 1998. *Audio-Visual Services and Production 1998*. Single Market Review, Series II, Impact on Services. Brussels: European Commission.

Dorland, Michael. 1996. 'Cultural Industries and the Canadian Experience: Reflections on the Emergence of a Field', in Dorland, ed., *The Cultural Industries in Canada*. Toronto: James Lorimer.

OECD. 1994. *OECD Services 1994*. Paris: OECD.

Rabinovitch, Victor. 1998. 'The Social and Economic Rationales for Domestic Cultural Policies', in Dennis Browne, ed., *The Cultural/Trade Quandary: Canada's Policy Options*. Ottawa: Centre for Trade Policy and Law, Carleton University.

Stanbury, W.T. 1998. *Canadian Content Regulations: The Intrusive State at Work*. Vancouver: Fraser Institute, Aug.

9

Grand Strategy—or Merely a Geopolitical Free-for-all? Regionalism, Internationalism, and Defence Policy at the End of 'Canada's Century'

DAVID G. HAGLUND

In late 1997 Canada hosted, to much fanfare, the annual leaders' summit of the Asia-Pacific Economic Co-operation (APEC) forum. The site of this event was Vancouver, a city that gives expression to the dramatic transformations in Canadian demographics over the course of this century—a century that, at the outset, showed promise of becoming Canada's own century, as the Prime Minister of the day, Sir Wilfrid Laurier, so memorably phrased it. Now, with the twentieth century drawing to a close, talk is less of any particular country's claim to proprietorship over the future; instead, the discourse dwells upon which *region* of the globe is best able to stake its claim to temporal dominion. There was a growing feeling that Europe, its latest groping for union to the contrary notwithstanding, has already had its moment in the sun and that the dawn of a new era is at hand.

Once again, a Canadian Prime Minister has undertaken to depict the features of that new era. Speaking in Washington in April 1997,

Jean Chrétien waxed metaphoric about a 'bridge' to the future, a phrase reminiscent of the recent American presidential campaign, in reference to the next century that was but a half-decade ahead. 'I profoundly believe', said the Prime Minister, 'that the bridge which you heard so much about during your election campaign, is the bridge that will span the Pacific Ocean. . . . I believe the 21st century will be the Pacific Century. We share the good fortune of being Pacific countries as well' (DFAIT, 1997).

Only two years later, it was a rare optimist who could speak with such confidence about the coming 'Pacific Century' (Coker, 1988: 5–16). Indeed, barely twelve months after his 'bridge' speech, Prime Minister Chrétien was at it again, only this time it was another region whose glowing promise he was extolling. Together with other leaders of the Western hemisphere (minus Fidel Castro, upon whom he was shortly to drop in) the Prime Minister sang the praises of a much-heralded Free Trade Area of the Americas (FTAA) at a summit in the Chilean capital, Santiago, in April 1998. Observers of the Santiago meeting could be excused if they had the impression that Canada's future was henceforward going to be situated increasingly within its own hemisphere, and that the twenty-first century was going to be an 'American' one in the broadest sense of that adjective, and in the economic arena above all. The Liberal government's international goal, as explained that same month by the Trade Minister, was to realize 'nothing less than a free trade area stretching from the Arctic Circle to Argentina: one giant market' (DFAIT, 1998).

CANADIAN FOREIGN AND DEFENCE POLICY IN FLUX

If any evidence were required to support the claim that Canadian foreign and defence policy—the pair of which can be described as 'grand strategy', as explained below—has been 'destructured' by the ending of the Cold War, these musings by the Prime Minister and other ministers would be a good starting point. It really does appear that Canadian policy has been in search of new geographical bearings in this *fin de siècle*. Not all has been in flux, of course: Canadian grand strategy continues to provide an outsized place for the promotion of trade, an endeavour that Frank Scott rightly identified more than 65 years ago as one of the invariant facets of foreign policy (Scott, 1932).

If not all things have been changing, enough apparently are to give the impression that Canadian grand strategy has entered an era in which innovation is the catchword if not the impulse of policy-makers. Some of the latter even speak of a 'revolution in diplomatic affairs', suggestive not only of a new security agenda but also of a new set of challenges for foreign policy problem-solving. Trends in contemporary Canadian foreign policy reflect the shifting balance of locus and *level* of Canadian engagement with the world. So closely linked are the two themes that sometimes the level of engagement will be inferred from the site of engagement. This happened during the early Cold War when a relatively robust Canadian military presence in Europe was held to symbolize a strong commitment to 'internationalism', and it has happened in reverse since 1992, when the abandonment of the four-decades-long policy of stationing Canadian forces in Germany was heralded by some as the onset of a new age of isolationism.

It remains nearly impossible to consider the two themes of regionalism and internationalism except in reference to each other. Take, for instance, a much-discussed recent diplomatic catchword, 'niche diplomacy'. As originally employed by policy analysts a few years ago, this term implied that Canada would continue to be 'internationalist' in orientation, only it would perforce be so in a more selective manner. Canada would emphasize only those tasks that fit best with its resources and values, leaving for others those missions that were either too costly or too distasteful for Canadians to undertake. Usually, the latter missions were said to reside in the area of military security, and to the adherents of niche diplomacy Canada would be well advised to stick to those spheres in which it is thought (sometimes erroneously) to possess a comparative advantage: providing aid, providing advice and mediatory skills, and, if the military had to be used, providing support to conventional peacekeeping.

However, the niche concept soon began to have a regional dimension attached to it, giving the logic of selective internationalism not only functional but also geographic specification. In line with the Prime Minister's propensities for Asia and Latin America, itself reflecting a commercial thrust in grand strategy, niche diplomacy tended to be conceptualized in these regional terms. These regions, it was held, were the beckoning horizons in Canada's future, or so it looked to many of those who were making and studying foreign and security policy during the mid-1990s. To confess an interest both in Europe and in the venerable 'North Atlantic Triangle' was almost to admit to being intellectually *dépassé* if not downright perverse. To be sure, diplomats were and remain quick to assure their listeners that Canada would be engaged *everywhere* internationally, and they carefully eschewed even the pretence of choosing one region over another, preferring instead the wisdom contained in the homely aphorism that comparisons are invidious.

But it is the business of policy analysts, just as it is the obligation of government decision-makers, to compare, and in so doing sometimes to make the case for a particular, not universal, policy orientation. That case need not be made in a geographical context, but it very often is, in large measure because a traditional method of organizing the work of government happens to be through regionally specific bureaus and divisions of the Department of Foreign Affairs and International Trade (DFAIT).

WHAT IS GRAND STRATEGY, AND WHY CAN'T CANADA HAVE ONE?

A paper proposing to discuss Canadian 'grand strategy' within the context of regionalism and internationalism would appear to be more than a mild curiosity. After all, in a country like Canada where it is problematic for analysts and policy-makers alike openly to advocate a role for the 'national interest' in the crafting of foreign and defence policy, to dwell on grand strategy is practically to verge upon the otherworldly. Neither is it just Canadians who might be tempted to dismiss out of hand the relevance of this variant of strategizing. To some analysts, it is not only oxymoronic but preposterous for 'lesser' powers anywhere even to countenance having a 'grand' strategy, which must remain the *chasse gardée* of the great powers.

It is not that Canada never possessed, or was *seen* to possess, a set of distinctive foreign policy traditions and roles. Quite the contrary; whether it concerns the 'dominant ideas' about which Kim Nossal writes so sensibly, or certain 'internationalist' traditions that have constituted so much of the lore of Canadian diplomacy, scholars have been anything but hesitant to pin labels on Canadian policy dispensations (Nossal, 1997). Yet when it comes to strategy, the crowd thins appreciably, due in large measure to a fundamental confusion about the very meaning of strategy—grand or otherwise.

Strategy, it is often thought, must be about things military. Yet Canadians, it is often claimed, are an 'unmilitary' people. Add to this that what military the country does have is small and getting smaller still, it would seem to follow that any discussion of Canadian grand strategy must be a short one. The problem with this syllogism is that the major premise is incorrect. Thus, while strategy may be about things military, it need not be restricted to that category, nor is that category the most important component of the set. As for the minor premise, Desmond Morton has put it best in arguing that while some Canadians may be flattered to think themselves unmilitary, the reality is that wars 'not only made modern Canada possible; they helped shape the myths and memories of a divided national identity' (Morton, 1992: ix).

The notion that only the grand need bother to have a grand strategy would seem to be confuted by the very essence of strategy, as properly understood. Strategy would seem to be a more urgent imperative precisely for those states that are not bounteously endowed with the material attributes of power than it is for those acknowledged great powers, whatever their number in the post-Cold War world. How, then, should we properly conceive of strategy and grand strategy? We should start by recognizing that the term 'strategy' has a civilian military application, where it is applied to processes that link those things that organizations seek to accomplish with the resources they have available to accomplish the task(s). As such, it is not a difficult concept at all, for as John Lewis Gaddis explains, '[b]y "strategy," I mean quite simply the process by which ends are related to means, intentions to capabilities, objectives to resources' (Gaddis, 1982: viii).

Typically, when strategy takes on broader-than-military significance for policy, involving political and economic factors that contribute to a state's overall purposes, it can become endowed with the adjective 'grand'. At this stage the simplicity of the unmodified concept begins to disappear, and grand strategy becomes a murkier category, held in Barry Buzan's words to be 'precisely the art of comprehending a diverse but interacting set of factors sufficiently clearly so as to be able to identify lines of action that maximize benefits and minimize costs' (Buzan, 1991: 372–3).

Scholars and other analysts can and do disagree about the composition and relative importance of those factors, but it is important not to lose sight of the identifying content of grand strategy: (1) it must be at least as concerned with peace as with war, and ideally should be more concerned with the former than with the latter; (2) it must be inclusive in that it comprehends such considerations as diplomacy, national morale, and political culture; (3) it must attend to a consistent balancing of ends with means; and (4) it must be guided by, and responsive to, national interests. As enunciated by Paul Kennedy, the 'crux of grand strategy lies therefore in policy, that is, in the capacity of the nation's leaders to bring together all of the elements, both military and nonmilitary, for the preservation and enhancement of the nation's long-term (that is, in wartime *and* peacetime) best interests' (Kennedy, 1991: 5).

Attentive Canadians will have no difficulty linking the third point in the above paragraph with debates about the country's defence policy. Concern for the consistent balancing of ends with means was what inspired so much of the work of Rod Byers, who coined an expression—the 'commitment-capability gap'—that ranks as one of the most memorable contributions to the lexicon on that policy. To attain balance, of course, it helped to have some idea of what the ends of policy were supposed to be, and in this regard as well Byers's work was noteworthy in its concern that there be efficient pursuit of those ends through the most rational possible co-ordination of Canadian foreign with defence policy. This concern has continued to find an echo into the present, if only because co-ordinating the two spheres of policy has proven so frustrating. Nevertheless, it makes no sense to discuss defence policy independently of foreign policy, for the latter ostensibly provides the overarching framework of, and conceptual basis for, the former.

END OF THE ROAD FOR THE 'WILLY SUTTON'
APPROACH TO STRATEGY?

In defence policy as in foreign policy, Canada prefers to act abroad on a multilateral basis, as do most states, even if, from time to time, the lure of unilateralism proves irresistible. Whatever else the Cold War did for Canadians, it simplified matters. 'The Cold War', writes Robert Bothwell, 'gave Canada a place that was never a mystery, though it was occasionally in question. The end of the Cold War, by contrast, forced Canada and its citizens to conceive new roles in a different world. In the late 1990s they were still wondering what role, and in which world' (Bothwell, 1998: 109).

In the making of strategy, threat has been a great simplifier not only for Canadians. The legendary bank robber, Willy Sutton, was once asked why he robbed banks. 'Because', he responded, 'that's where the money is.' For policy-makers in North America after 1949, the question, 'Why are you so involved in Western Europe?' could partly have been answered by the geopolitical equivalent of Willy Sutton's retort: because the global balance of power, and North American security, required that the Eurasian land mass—potentially the greatest single source of power on earth—not be allowed to fall under the control of a hostile country. Europe was where the power was. It was also where the threat was.

Today, the Cold War is a thing of the past, and there appear to be no bids for supremacy over the Eurasian land mass being made by hostile anti-democratic powers. While 'risks' may abound, they pale in comparison to the threat posed by totalitarian or authoritarian states for more than 60 years—i.e., first by Nazi Germany, then by the Soviet Union. Moreover, power itself has become more diffused throughout the international system at the same time as its contents and meaning have been altering. This has rendered more difficult the task of assigning geostrategic weight to particular regions—a task at which geopoliticians and many international relations realists used to excel during the era of great-power threat.

It has become harder if not impossible to calculate, as some would have us do, which regions of the world are intrinsically significant (to Canada) in strategic terms. However much it may have been fair during the Cold War to criticize governments in Ottawa—most particularly, those presided over by Pierre Trudeau—for acting internationally as though they were unaware of political power realities, a similar criticism would ring hollower today. The compelling punch of geopolitical interest has been removed from the debate about which (if any) region should assume pre-eminence in Canadian grand strategy in the twenty-first century. As a result, a regional free-for-all has evidently supplanted the Eurocentrism of yore. Or has it?

THE GEOPOLITICAL JAMBOREE: WHICH REGION FOR CANADA?

In one of those quips almost everyone seems to recall Canada was dubbed (by Herman Kahn) a 'regional power without a region' (Dobell, 1972: 4). In fact, the opposite seems closer to the truth: Canada has never been a regional power, say on the scale of a Brazil or a Nigeria, nevertheless it has possessed a distinct region. Today, Canada might even be said to possess many regions. It has before it a rich menu of geographical choice, as proponents of an enhanced Canadian concentration on particular geographic focuses mix it up with each other in a lively geopolitical jamboree.

What Kahn, one of the pre-eminent American strategic gurus of the Cold War period, no doubt meant was that Canada was one of the world's ranking countries, and were it not for the fact that it lived in the overwhelming shadow of the United States its aggregate capabilities would have endowed it with the wherewithal (if not necessarily the will) to stake out a claim for regional pre-eminence. In some ways, the early postwar bid for middle-power status (as opposed to the later, more normatively based 'middlepowermanship' so ably lampooned by John Holmes) constituted an alternative means of reaping for Canada the influence that was thought its due, albeit influence within a broader region than North America (Holmes, 1992: 90-105). That region was, initially, the North Atlantic Triangle, adjusted so that its easternmost angle was, starting in the late 1940s, henceforth going to be portions of the Western European land mass and not merely the United Kingdom.

Over the years since the end of World War II, Canadian strategy has come to shift, haltingly at first, to embrace regions beyond that Triangle. As a result, many have argued that couching the discussion of strategy in a regional context is no longer relevant. Others maintain that thinking, talking, and acting regionally still are germane; it is just the North Atlantic Triangle that no longer makes any sense.

Officially and publicly the government of Canada, in both its 1994 defence White Paper and its 1995 foreign policy framework, eschewed a regionalized foreign and defence policy. Rather, government policy-makers adhere to a universalistic strategy, such that it becomes unnecessary and even counter-productive to attempt to appraise parts of the world on the basis of their particular importance to Canadian interests. It is as if Canadian grand strategy is being fashioned on the shores of Garrison Keillor's Lake Wobegon, a happy place where 'all the women are strong, all the men are good-looking, and all the children are above average'.

Yet, are all regions of the world equally pertinent for Canada, official statements to the contrary notwithstanding? Certainly, advocates of geographic focus have emphasized three regions of particular salience for Canadian foreign policy, notably the North Atlantic Triangle, the Asia-Pacific, and the Western hemisphere. The latter can in turn be divided into two subgroupings, the United States alone as the cynosure of Canadian strategy, and the wider hemisphere including the United States as the focal point of Canadian foreign and even defence policy in the coming century. Below, I discuss the trio of contending camps, starting with the atlanticists, who are the principal proponents of the North Atlantic Triangle.

ALSO PRESENT AT THE CREATION: CANADA AND THE ATLANTICIST VISION

Conventional wisdom about Canadian strategy suggests that the beginning of the post-1945 era constituted a marked break from what went before, so much so that the descriptor 'revolutionary' seems hardly out of place when applied to subsequent trends in foreign and defence policy. Against this view has come the recent reminder by Hector Mackenzie that although Canada's postwar policy would turn out to be much different from the pre-war, this change was more gradual than radical, and in the years immediately after 1945 it was not clear that there would even *be* a change of any significance. Indicative of this policy continuity in the early postwar years was the indifference of Prime Minister Mackenzie King to the United Nations (which he thought likely to be every bit as feckless as the League of Nations had been) and his persistence in guarding against 'entrapments' in Empire/Commonwealth security undertakings, which is what he thought the Berlin airlift of 1948 represented and in part was why he refused to authorize Canadian participation.

There was more continuity than sometimes imagined in postwar Canadian grand strategy, and in this respect Hector Mackenzie's reminder is an apt one. However, his treatment of the policy implications of the North Atlantic Triangle metaphor is less helpful. It is misleading to dismiss 'that Canadian conceit', the atlanticist impulse, as merely a 'geometric fabrication [that] helped Canadians to identify their interests and values with familiar influences and relationships, but . . . was fundamentally a restatement of the obvious setting for Canadian decision-making' (Mackenzie, 1997: 16).

There was much more to it than that, and it is undeniable that the Triangle 'conceit' did something beyond perpetuating the familiar. Canada's atlanticist engagement generated momentum for a novel policy dispensation that would feature a commingling of idealism and realism in Canada's postwar internationalism, and this within a North Atlantic regional context. One could even maintain, as does

Stéphane Roussel in a thought-provoking paper, that those years not only were revolutionary for Canadian statecraft, but also witnessed an attempt by Canadian foreign policy élites to build a breathtakingly different international order founded on the Kantian aspiration for peace through democracy and interdependence (what today would be called the democratic, or liberal, peace). Not merely was the Canadian diplomatic thrust intended, then, to enhance the country's role and responsibilities in the international system, it aimed at transforming that very system. This was Canada's 'Kantian moment', whose vehicle would become the North Atlantic 'community', otherwise known as atlanticism (Roussel, 1998: 5).

In the half-century since the signing of the North Atlantic Treaty memories have become clouded about the origins of the Atlantic alliance, not only in the United States. Many observers, including not a few in Canada, seem to regard the North Atlantic Treaty Organization (NATO) as an American-designed mechanism for the accomplishment of one aim only, the containment of Soviet expansionary communism. They are wrong on two counts. The alliance was something into which a reluctant US had to be drawn, and its purposes have from the outset transcended the goal of providing collective defence to Western Europe and North America.

In the words of the doyen of the new multilateralism, John Ruggie, what eventuated in the postwar Atlantic world—i.e., the elaboration and spread of a web of multilateral organizations at whose centre was the NATO alliance—was 'less the fact of American *hegemony* . . . than it was the fact of *American* hegemony'. Or, as two other scholars put the same self-centred thought, the 'overall political character of the West is really an extension of the political character of the United States' (Ruggie, 1992: 567–8; Deudney and Ikenberry, 1993/4: 20–1; Weber, 1992).

It would serve no purpose to seek to minimize or deny the outsized American contribution to the construction of postwar atlanticism. Nevertheless, others were present at the creation of that order. Canada was prominent among the small group of states that forged postwar atlanticism. Suffice it to recall that after the Czechoslovak coup of February 1948, London and Ottawa began to redouble their efforts to entice Washington into tripartite discussions that might lead to a multilateral, collective defence scheme intended to enhance Western security and promote Western values. Already in November 1947, the three countries had begun exploratory talks, in secret, about alternative security arrangements to the United Nations, by now seen to be entering a paralysis engendered by the rapidly emerging Cold War.

US attitudes, especially in Congress, towards a robust multilateral defence scheme were lukewarm, notwithstanding the later reconstruction of those attitudes by today's new multilateralists. Outside pressure from recent allies—and at the time Britain and Canada were America's chief and perhaps only security partners—was needed to convince Congress that if it authorized such a radical departure from America's historic policy of peacetime aloofness from the European balance of power, it would not be left doing all the work single-handedly.

Intergovernmental discussions among Canada, Britain, and the United States resumed in Washington on 22 March 1948 and would eventually involve France, the Benelux countries, and Norway. The result was the North Atlantic Treaty, signed on 4 April 1949, whose charter members included all the above countries plus Denmark, Iceland, Portugal, and Italy. In an address of 29 April 1948, Louis St Laurent, Secretary of State for External Affairs and soon to be Prime Minister, pledged that Canada would more than play its part to bring into being an 'overwhelming preponderance of moral, economic and military force. . . . In the circumstances of the present the organization of collective defence in this way is the most effective guarantee of peace' (House of Commons, 1948: 3438–50).

These themes were repeated throughout 1948 by St Laurent and other Canadian policy-makers crusading for an Atlantic community. Significantly, even though the explicit purpose of this community was to be collective defence, its furtherance would require a combination of political and economic as well as military means. The latter would eventually be realized through the architecture of the North Atlantic Treaty Organization and its attendant military commitments and institutional arrangements. The former were prefigured in Canada's successful attempt to endow the alliance with a charter obligation to work towards political and economic community-building—an obligation found primarily in the Washington Treaty's 'Canadian' article (Article 2), and also in Article 4, enjoining the members to consult on important matters.

Over the years it seemed that NATO concentrated almost exclusively on its military role, relegating to a decidedly lower order of priority those matters of a political and economic nature relating to the task of community-building. This may have been the case during the Cold War, for understandable reasons. But in the post-Cold War years we have witnessed the resurfacing of some of the concomitant ideas circulating at the time of the alliance's construction. NATO has begun increasingly to reflect much of the idealism associated with the vision its Canadian promoters had of atlanticism.

In the Canadian context, atlanticism has represented a balance of threat-based 'realism' and an 'idealism' derivative of identity and values. Not surprisingly, the diminishing role of the former has led to a renewal of interest in the latter. But even during the Cold War, the relationship between Canada and atlanticism had always had more than a military dimension, for atlanticism itself represented an aspiration towards something grander than a mere military alliance. In the words of the late John Halstead, atlanticism has been much more than a geographical construct; it constitutes a 'social phenomenon based on shared norms' and has served as the fountainhead for most of the world's contemporary international organizations (Halstead, 1993: 151).

The geographical thrust of atlanticism was bound to be affected, over time, by a reassessment of the relationship between Canada and a resurgent Europe. Atlanticism began to be confused with regionalism—or at least with the region known as Western Europe. As Canada's relations with Europe changed to reflect the latter's growing importance in world politics, so, too, did Canada's attachment to the ideal of atlanticism require revision. This was to mistake the part for the whole, and it has had ramifications for Canadian defence policy starting in the second postwar decade and extending into the current decade.

Indeed, it seemed as if Europe could hardly be less in vogue among sapient Canadians as the 1990s began. And with Euro-fatigue came a second impression, that atlanticism itself had become a spent force. Fortifying that impression was the chorus of voices advocating an alternative regional focus for Canadian foreign policy.

THE REGIONAL CONTENDERS:
ASIA-PACIFIC AND LATIN AMERICA

What is striking about the advocacies of an alternative regional focus for Canadian grand strategy is the degree to which they are predicated upon materialistic considerations, commercial ones in particular. To be sure, as Frank Scott pointed out early on, trade has been the leitmotif of Canadian grand strategy for several decades. It is not difficult to detect the presence of this commercial impulse in Canada's most recent foreign policy framework document, *Canada in the World*, in which promotion of prosperity (through the enhancement of trade) is listed as one of three priorities, and perhaps the top priority (DFAIT, 1995).

The economic determinism of much of the recent advocacy for an Asia-Pacific or Latin American focus does stand out in clear relief. In the Asia-Pacific case, it is sometimes said that Canada's changing demographic make-up should be reflected, all things being equal, in its grand strategy, giving the country a foreign and security policy that 'looks like Canada'. Yet, it is hard to escape the conclusion apropos the Asia-Pacific region that it has primarily been the colour of money, not of people, that has attracted the interest of policy-maker and policy wonk alike. To be sure, there is nothing wrong, and much right, with an approach that seeks to enhance Canadian economic interests, assuming that other Canadian values do not get traduced in the process. All governments, Canada's included, must try to promote the well-being of their people, and if the happiness and prosperity of others can be enhanced in the bargain, so much the better.

The problem with the Asia-Pacificists is not their stress on the economic content of the region. It is how they have sought to endow economics with broader meaning. Advocates of an Asia-Pacific focus have mishandled economic reality in two ways. The first has been to exaggerate the importance of the current level of trade between Canada and countries of the Asia-Pacific region (a point to which I return in the following section). Despite the hoopla associated with Team Canada missions to Asia over the past few years, Canada's economic ties with Asia remain limited, with only some 9 per cent of exports destined for that region. Moreover, even though the past decade has been one in which Asia-Pacific business has been increasingly coveted, the reality is that Canada was losing market share even when Asia's economies were growing so dynamically. Canada's current share of Asia-Pacific markets, about 1.6 per cent, lags behind that of other G–7 countries.

Even more problematic has been the tendency of many analysts to succumb to the fallacy of projection and assume that trends extant today will continue tomorrow. The dramatic collapse of the region's 'miracle' economies brought on by Thailand's currency crisis of summer 1997 invites the thought that insofar as projections about Asia's future are concerned, the most prudent response should be caution, tempered with humility in the face of the unknown.

Daryl Copeland, writing shortly before the onset of the Asian collapse, provided the best example of the fallacy of projection when, in advocating for greater Canadian involvement in the Asia-Pacific, he asserted without demur the following: that by 2000, the Asia-Pacific region '*will* account for 40 per cent of world trade, and 400 million Asians *will* have personal incomes at or above the averages of the member states of the Organization for Economic Cooperation and Development'; that during the course of the coming decade the Asia-Pacific '*will* generate 60 per cent of global economic expansion'; and that in little more than 20 years, 'the Asia-Pacific *will* be home to seven of the world's ten largest economies, and China *will* have overtaken Japan and the United States to become the world's largest national economy' (Copeland, 1997: 2–3; emphasis added).

Not all who advocate a greater focus on the Asia-Pacific do so for economic reasons, and the ending of the Asian boom can be expected to lead to a shuffling of rationales undergirding the case for growing attentiveness to the region. Renewed attention to that region may indeed be warranted, especially as the security implications of the Asian financial implosion become more fully comprehended. We should be clear on what it is that an Asia-Pacific in decline holds in store for Canada. If it promises to command more of our attention, as it could well do, it will also likely imply a growing claim on Canadian resources, which reverses the order of gain assumed to attach to a greater Asia-Pacific profile just a few years ago. We may find ourselves having to commit treasure, and possibly some blood, to the preservation of an Asia-Pacific security order whose overthrow could imperil Canada's own interests. That prospect, while real (though not to be exaggerated), is hardly what the aspirants for a greater Asia-Pacific focus had in mind when the vision of the coming Pacific Century aroused their interest a decade or so ago.

What of the case for a growing concentration on the Western hemisphere? In many ways it mirrors, or parrots, the Asia-Pacific advocacy. To the extent that hemispherists limit their focus to the Americas north of the Rio Grande, they might even be said to have carried the day, based solely on an analysis of economic factors, such as trade and investment flows. However, few hemispherists are prepared to stop at the Texas-Mexico border, and their advocacy has to be assessed in terms not of a Canada-US focus but of wider Canadian-American-Latin American relations.

Here, too, there is an assumption that economic regionalization is occurring, is deepening, and has enormous implications for Canada, whose region is said, more and more, to be 'the Americas'. Although trade and investment data do not support the contention that Latin America has emerged as a prominent area of Canadian commercial activity, recent political-economic arrangements—including the formation of NAFTA and the conclusion of a bilateral free trade agreement with Chile—hold out two hopes. The first is that the Americas will assume greater importance for Canadian economic interests, to the benefit of both Canada and Latin America. The second is that the precepts of a rules-based, multilateral, free trade regime might be invoked against the implicit fear of regionalized trade elsewhere in the world, and this through the promotion of a wider free trade arrangement in the Western hemisphere.

The advocates of a greater Latin American focus in Canadian grand strategy tend to regard the hemisphere as an alternative, not an extension, to atlanticism. In part, they base their arguments for a growing attentiveness towards Latin America on the assumption that Europe is of diminishing relevance to Canada. Now it is being maintained that it is Mexico and, by extension, other Latin countries that rank second (and third, etc.) in importance to Canadian interests, after the United States. Canadian core interests are held to be engaged in Latin America at three levels: trade policy, market access, and regional governance. Moreover, the case for an Americas focus is buttressed on the assumption of a 'common culture and shared values' between Canadians and Latin Americans, which implicitly slights the Asia-Pacificist contention for a non-European alternative (Daudelin and Dosman, 1995: 1–11; Klepak, 1996).

Since the current intensity of Canadian-Latin American economic linkages is not as impressive as that between Canada and the Asia-Pacific (though there are exceptions, as evidenced by the importance of Chile to the Canadian, and especially British Columbian, mining industry), advocates make recourse to the promise of the future of hemispheric economic interdependence. To a large extent, that promise is based on the construction of the mooted Free Trade Area of the Americas (FTAA), expected to be accomplished by 2005. If it is realized, it will, according to its boosters, constitute a positive development not only for the hemisphere, but for the entire global trading order. Whatever the ultimate demonstration effect of hemi-spheric free trade upon the rest of the world, the FTAA, to its pro-moters, will likely endow Canada's trade policy with an even deeper 'Latin American colouring' than it hitherto possessed (Christie, 1995).

As with the Asia-Pacific claimants, the advocates of a greater focus on the Western hemisphere do not limit their arguments to economic factors, even if these seem to be uppermost in their thinking. Security, as well, is invoked as an issue-area likely to demand a greater share of Canadian attention and resources than at present. This is especially the case as 'new' problems surface as objects of worry in the post-Cold War era. Certainly international criminal activity has attracted increasing attention on the part of Canada and its G–7 partners. In this regard, the criminal activity most likely to involve a Latin American connection is, of course, drug trafficking, an activity that threatens hemispheric security because of its impact on democratic development prospects in the region.

THE TRIUMPH OF *INNENPOLITIK*?
ASSESSING THE REGIONAL ALTERNATIVES

What is most significant about the geopolitical jamboree is the extent to which it is inspired by a conviction that domestic political vari-ables have become the primary factors shaping grand strategy. It may very well be that *Innenpolitik* is now uppermost in determining grand strategy; for that matter, perhaps it always was. However, it should not be imagined that domestic factors necessarily are forcing a reorientation of Canadian grand strategy away from the North Atlantic Triangle. If anything, it could be said that they are doing the opposite.

Let us revisit the discussion of the previous section and examine some apparently 'objective' economic data. Consider the claim made during Canada's Year of Asia Pacific (CYAP), 1997, namely that Canada does nearly 90 per cent [!] of its exporting within the 18-member APEC. Some $248.5 billion worth of exports in 1996 going to APEC members has meant, it is argued, that the Pacific Rim has emerged as a 'priority' of Canadian policy. How could anyone gainsay such argumentation, when the data reveal that in 1995 a mere 6.8 per cent of Canada's merchandise exports were destined to markets in Western Europe, compared with the overwhelming share headed to APEC members? Moreover, a similar discrepancy appears on the import side, where only 11.5 per cent of Canada's merchandise imports (again, based on 1995 figures) originated in Western Europe, as compared with 83 per cent from APEC (Senate, 1996: 23–33; Hettmann, 1996: 303–23).

What should be made of these figures? Not too much. While the data are correct, they are also deceptive. This is because of the overwhelming presence of one APEC member, the United States, in Canadian economic life. Taking account of Canada's trade with the United States greatly reduces the discrepancy between Asia-Pacific and European trade profiles. While Canada's trade across the Pacific exceeds its trade across the Atlantic, the regionalist case is somewhat less compelling. Were trade with the United States to be considered within a wider North Atlantic framework, then that area would represent some 87 per cent [!] of Canada's merchandise exports and 79 per cent of its merchandise imports.

Furthermore, when one examines investment flows, it emerges that Western Europe ranks second only to the United States both as a source of capital and as a destination for Canadian investment. In fact, quite unlike the situation in trade, for Canadian investors the EU is becoming relatively more, not less, important. In 1985, slightly less than 13 per cent of Canadian direct investment abroad was in the European Community; a decade later, that share had risen to nearly 20 per cent. The same trend applies to Canadians' portfolio investments. Similarly, Europe now accounts for 21.5 per cent of all foreign direct investment in Canada, up from 17 per cent a decade earlier. (As for portfolio investment, there has been little relative change in Europeans' holdings over the past decade.)

In sum, if one wanted to make an economistic, 'objective' case for the ongoing centrality of the North Atlantic Triangle to Canadian strategy, it would not be all that difficult. Nor would it have been difficult to do so even *prior* to the popping of the Asia-Pacific economic bubble.

What of the ethno-demographic content of *Innenpolitik*? The regionalist debate over contemporary Canadian grand strategy has occurred against the backdrop of a steady shrinkage in the proportion of Canada's population having European roots. Yet, while it may be that an increasingly multicultural and even 'post-modern' Canadian society looks less European with every passing year, it does not follow that Canadians whose ethnic origins are elsewhere than Europe are either indifferent or opposed to Canada's having—and defending—important transatlantic interests. Survey data reveal that Canadian public opinion remains solidly atlanticist and that only marginal differences exist in the support shown for atlanticism on the part of the country's 'Asian' or other non-European population (Buteux, Fortmann, and Martin, 1996: 159–60; Southam, 1998).

Moreover, and perhaps if history is any guide more importantly, one cannot and should not judge how a North American country will respond in its European policy simply on the basis of its ethnic mix. Thus, when Canada's postwar bout of Euro-fatigue first set in, during the 1960s, this country was much more European in ethnicity than it is today. Although it seems counter-intuitive, it might even be said that as Canadian society continues to take on more aspects of 'post-modernism' at the same time as the economy becomes more regionally integrated with the American one, we are witnessing a revival in significance of the North Atlantic area—and with it a renewal of interest in the Triangle metaphor, or at least its atlanticist dimension, for reasons that are not derived from economistic factors, but rather from the recent rise in importance of *Idealpolitik* in foreign and even defence policy.

CONCLUSION: THE NORTH ATLANTIC TRIANGLE IN 'POST-MODERN' GRAND STRATEGY

At this time, the NATO alliance is debating the future of its nuclear doctrine in an institutional context that seems to be moving more towards co-operative security pursuits. Some in Canada appear eager to force a revision in alliance thinking about the future of nuclear weapons. It is even possible that the Foreign Minister, Lloyd Axworthy, may see an opportunity for Canada to demonstrate leadership, perhaps in tandem with the new German government, on an issue (nuclear disarmament) that some liken to the successful campaign to ban anti-personnel landmines. Indeed, it may turn out that the 'Axworthy Doctrine' will constitute a fundamental revision of Canada's traditional approach of 'Pearsonian Internationalism' (Hampson and Oliver, 1998).

What is noteworthy at the moment is the degree to which Canada's defence commitments have become more focused on NATO, if only for the time being, and less on the United Nations or any of the myriad of regional security organizations. Whereas at the start of this decade most of Canada's military energies were being directed towards UN peacekeeping, today the country's peacekeeping effort is disproportionately concentrated on NATO. Some 85 per cent of all Canadian peacekeepers now serve in Bosnia, in an alliance-run mission (IFOR/SFOR) that has proceeded as smoothly as could have been imagined, especially when contrasted with the earlier involvement in Yugoslavia as part of UNPROFOR, to say nothing of Somalia.

It is too early to tell whether this reconcentration on NATO will persist; but if it does, it will be in no small measure as a result of a *rapprochement* with the ends and means of the alliance in an age increasingly characterized as being 'post-modern'. There seem to be three ways in which the concept of 'post-modernism' and grand strategy have become entangled with each other.

'Post-modernism' can be defined synonymously with a 'post-Westphalian' system of international relations, the latter meaning an order in which balance of power has become obsolete as a means of preserving peace within the group (as in, say, the Atlantic 'security community'). In this context, 'post-modern' really means post-balancing, and is applied to only a portion of the planet. Lands and peoples located outside the contemporary Western 'zone of peace' are relegated either to the modern or, worse, pre-modern zones, with all the sorrows and tribulations such situations connote (Cooper, 1996).

Post-modernism can furthermore conjure up leadership potential for countries that may not otherwise be militarily well endowed or 'powerful' in the conventional sense. In this sense post-modernism addresses the elevating effect of ideas and ideals as power assets (otherwise known as *Idealpolitik*)—what may be defined as 'soft power'. One of the most contentious debates in contemporary Canadian strategy revolves around the ability of Canada to rely on soft power—held to be the power to attract, not compel, others, and to do so through one's values and ability to communicate them—at the expense of investing in 'harder' assets, such as military forces or even economic assistance.

The Department of Foreign Affairs and International Trade seems convinced that Canada does possess and can employ soft power. This may well be the case. To the extent that this is so, it is worth stressing that Canada's power to attract inheres in its geopolitical setting as well as in the ideals it seeks to promulgate, and both are a function of atlanticism. The ideals that Canada promulgates derive pre-eminently from the North Atlantic Triangle, namely democratic governance, the rule of law, and respect for human rights. Insofar as contemporary Canadian peacebuilding efforts are concentrated on the promotion of those values, these signify in essence the *projection*—not the rejection—of the *Idealpolitik* embedded in atlanticism.

Post-modernism's impact on strategy can be traced to developments within Western societies, in particular to the rise of the 'politics of identity'. Just as NATO's evolution has made it a more congenial alliance for Canada, so has Canadian society's own evolution, paradoxically, made coalition-building a more important objective of Canadian defence policy. The thrust of the post-modern contention is that societies such as Canada, the United States, and parts of Western Europe are becoming characterized not only by the rise of identity politics, but also by a turning inward on the part of their publics, who are ever more attentive to their rights (and comforts) and less impressed by any obligations and responsibilities they might have.

Even if co-operative security is considered apart from post-modernism, there would still exist the shared aspiration—and it is a very important one—of reducing the burden that grand strategy imposes on domestic society. Barry Buzan and Gerald Segal have imaginatively likened foreign policy in Western post-modern societies to a beverage that is, strangely, much beloved by Americans: 'lite' beer. What the beverage and the policy have in common is that they are both insipid. On those rare occasions when something stronger is needed in the realm of strategy, post-modern states 'by their nature' will act only with others in coalitions of the willing. 'This means', argue Buzan and Segal, that 'military credibility requires standing coalitions. Thankfully, such a coalition, with standard operating procedures, already exists in the form of NATO. Because the United States, and to some extent even Britain, conducts exercises with other countries outside NATO . . . the NATO net is spread even wider' (Buzan and Segal, 1996: 8–9).

To sum up: post-Westphalianism, soft power, and the desire to minimize burdens, coupled with the zeal to preserve coalitions, all are pulling Canada back to its atlanticist centre of strategic gravity. As with the Bermuda Triangle of fable, the North Atlantic Triangle is proving to be an entity from which escape is not that easy. Canada is certainly not ending this century as a 'European' country. It remains, however, very much an atlanticist one.

REFERENCES

Bothwell, Robert, 1998. *The Big Chill: Canada and the Cold War.* Contemporary Affairs No. 1. Toronto: CIIA/Irwin.

Buteux, Paul, Michel Fortmann, and Pierre Martin. 1996. 'Canada and the Expansion of NATO: A Study in Élite Attitudes and Public Opinion', in David G. Haglund, ed., *Will NATO Go East? The Debate Over Enlarging the Atlantic Alliance.* Kingston: Queen's University Centre for International Relations, 147–79.

Buzan, Barry. 1991. *People, States and Fear: An Agenda for International Security Studies in the Post-Cold War Era,* 2nd edn. Boulder, Colo.: Lynne Rienner.

———— and Gerald Segal. 1996. 'The Rise of "Lite" Powers: A Strategy for the Postmodern States', *World Policy Journal* 13 (Fall): 1–10.

Christie, Keith H. 1995. 'The Four Amigos and Beyond: Towards the Free Trade Area of the Americas', *Policy Staff Paper* no. 95/10. Ottawa: DFAIT.

Coker, Christopher. 1988. 'The Pacific Century: Myth or Reality', *Washington Quarterly* 12 (Dec.): 5–16.

Cooper, Robert. 1996. *The Post-Modern State and the World Order.* London: Demos.

Copeland, Darryl. 1997. 'The Pacific Century: What's in it for Canada? (Part One)', *Behind the Headlines* 54 (Spring).

Daudelin, Jean, and Edgar Dosman. 1995. 'Introduction', in Daudelin and Dosman, eds, *Beyond Mexico: Changing Americas.* Ottawa: Carleton University Press/ Canadian Foundation for the Americas, 1–14.

Deudney, Daniel, and G. John Ikenberry. 1993/4. 'The Logic of the West', *World Policy Journal* 10 (Winter): 17–25.

DFAIT. 1995. *Canada in the World.* Ottawa.

————. 1997. Communications Strategies and Planning Division. 'Prime Minister Jean Chrétien in Washington, D.C., April 9, 1997', *The Week in Trade and Foreign Policy.* Ottawa, 7–13 Apr.

————. 1998. Communications Strategies and Planning Division. Sergio Marchi, Minister for International Trade, to the Canadian Council for the Americas, Toronto. *The Week in Trade and Foreign Policy.* Ottawa, 13–26 Apr.

Dobell, Peter C. 1972. *Canada's Search for New Roles: Foreign Policy in the Trudeau Era.* London: Oxford University Press/Royal Institute of International Affairs.

Gaddis, John Lewis. 1982. *Strategies of Containment: A Critical Appraisal of Postwar American National Security Policy.* Oxford: Oxford University Press.

Halstead, John G.H. 1993. 'Atlantic Community or Continental Drift?', *Journal of European Integration* 16 (Winter/Spring): 379–406.

Hampson, Fen Osler, and Dean F. Oliver. 1998. 'Pulpit Diplomacy: A Critical Assessment of the Axworthy Doctrine', *International Journal* 53 (Summer): 379–406.

Hettmann, Jens U. 1996. 'La politique extérieure canadienne vue de l'Europe: Fin de siècle pour les rapports canado-européens?' *Études internationales* 27 (June): 303–24.

Holmes, John W. 1992. 'Most Safely in the Middle', in J.L. Granatstein, ed., *Towards a New World: Readings in the History of Canadian Foreign Policy.* Toronto: Copp Clark Pitman, 90–105.

House of Commons. 1948. *Hansard.* 29 Apr.

Kennedy, Paul. 1991. 'Grand Strategy in War and Peace', in Kennedy, ed., *Grand Strategies in War and Peace*. New Haven: Yale University Press, 1–7.

Klepak, Harold P. 1996. '*Los Desconocidos se conocen*: Bridging the Knowledge Gap between Mexico and Canada', in Klepak, ed., *Natural Allies? Canadian and Mexican Perspectives on International Security*. Ottawa: Carleton University Press/Canadian Foundation for the Americas, 3–27.

Mackenzie, Hector. 1997. 'The Cold War and the Limits of "Internationalism" in Canada's Foreign Relations, 1945–1949', *YCISS Occasional Paper*, No. 47. Toronto: Centre for International and Security Studies, York University.

Morton, Desmond. 1992. *A Military History of Canada: From Champlain to the Gulf War*, 3rd edn. Toronto: McClelland & Stewart.

Nossal, Kim Richard. 1997. *The Politics of Canadian Foreign Policy*, 3rd edn. Scarborough, Ont.: Prentice-Hall Canada.

Roussel, Stéphane. 1998. 'Le 'moment kantien': La contribution canadienne à la création de la "communauté nord-atlantique" (1947–1949)', unpublished manuscript.

Ruggie, John Gerard. 1992. 'Multilateralism: The Anatomy of an Institution', *International Organization* 46 (Summer): 561–98.

Scott, F.R. 1932. 'The Permanent Bases of Canadian Foreign Policy', *Foreign Affairs* 10 (July): 617–31.

Senate. 1996. Standing Senate Committee on Foreign Affairs. *European Integration: The Implications for Canada*. Ottawa.

Southam. 1998. 'Moderate Support for a Defence Budget Increase amid Disagreement about How Unsafe to Feel', Southam News/Canadian National Committee of the IISS poll, May.

Weber, Steve. 1992. 'Shaping the Postwar Balance of Power: Multilateralism in NATO', *International Organization* 46 (Summer): 633–80.

10

The Global Issues Biz: What Gives?

DAVID M. MALONE

A little noticed by-product of Canada's 1994–5 Foreign Policy Review was the creation of a Global Issues Bureau in the Department of Foreign Affairs and International Trade (DFAIT), responsible for a variety of 'functional' (as opposed to geographic) issues. These included the environment, human rights, children's questions (e.g., child labour, children in war, sexual exploitation of children), gender issues, youth, humanitarian policy, conflict prevention and peacebuilding, terrorism, crime, and drugs (the so-called 'drugs and thugs' trio), health, population, migration and refugees, as well as circumpolar and Aboriginal issues. The unit was created, according to the government's foreign policy statement, *Canada in the World*, to bring greater 'coherence' to the government's capacity to address these interlinked and increasingly prominent issues (Canada, 1995: 50). The government's statement emphasized, in its introduction, the vast array of new security challenges, ranging from pandemics to global warming, requiring enhanced sensitivity to the risks as well as the opportunities presented by globalization. It also flagged the greater efforts needed to build lasting peace in countries emerging from (increasingly civil) war.

This new global issues prism through which a number of increasingly important issues would henceforth be dealt in DFAIT was the brainchild of Gordon Smith, previously Canada's Ambassador to the European Union, who returned to Ottawa as Deputy Minister of Foreign Affairs in mid-1994. On his return, he held several policy seminars with senior management, arguing that Canada's foreign policy should be constructed on three pillars: economic prosperity, global security, and action to counteract emerging threats to both. These internal debates took some account of the concurrent hearings conducted by a Special Joint Committee of Parliament Reviewing Canadian Foreign Policy, but the consensus that formed around Smith's schema was informed largely by the new government's strong emphasis on economic prosperity and employment through trade opportunities for Canadians and by an emerging nexus of 'non-traditional' security issues to which Smith, who previously had headed Canada's NATO mission, too, was particularly attuned. These he thought of and described as 'global issues'.[1]

Canada in the World responded to an encyclopedic parliamentary report that, not surprisingly given the Joint Committee's absence of operational responsibilities, failed to identify any particular priorities for Canadians among the myriad foreign policy issues it discussed. This foreign policy statement provided an opportunity to flesh out Smith's construct. One key challenge rapidly arose: whether and how to address international aid issues. Several DFAIT officials closely involved in the Foreign Policy Review favoured a separate statement on Canada's aid policy, as did some at the Canadian International Development Agency (CIDA). Others in both agencies viewed the government's international assistance program as an integral feature (if not merely a tool) of Canada's foreign policy and believed its guiding principles should emanate from the policy statement. André Ouellet, then Minister of Foreign Affairs, through and to whom CIDA reported, inclined to the latter view. Consequently, a chapter on international assistance was incorporated in *Canada in the World*. Ouellet also believed that DFAIT seriously undervalued the importance of Canadian culture as an international asset, and he directed that it be highlighted. This was done by equating Canadian culture with Canadian values in the third pillar, a somewhat lame effort further betrayed when DFAIT's funding for cultural programs was seriously slashed during subsequent rounds of Program Review cuts. Although departmental officials bravely stated that partnerships with the private sector would fund enhanced programs, this proved hard to square with the reality, in spite of sterling efforts by DFAIT's embattled cultural staff. Furthermore, the need to develop a third pillar centred on culture and values caused Gordon Smith's pillar on 'global issues' to disappear (although many of the global issues are value-based).

The Global Issues Bureau was the sole institutional initiative advanced by the statement. It came late in its concluding paragraphs, a bit of an orphan. Few commentators appeared to notice it. However, it mattered greatly to Smith.[2] He had noted the reorganization of a number of issues in the US State Department under an Under-Secretary of State for Global Issues, Tim Wirth (a former Senator from Colorado and State Department counsellor), earlier in 1994. The idea struck him as essentially sound, although his own design for DFAIT differed from the State Department scheme in a number of ways. One difference between the two was Canada's emphasis on international institutional reform while the US model highlighted the importance of science issues at the international level, something Canada, as a science and high-tech leader, should perhaps emulate. However, the US approach never really gelled at State. Smith appointed Marie Bernard-Meunier, one of DFAIT's strongest officers and recently chair of the United Nations Educational, Scientific, and Cultural Organization's (UNESCO's) council while Canadian Ambassador to that organization, as a new Assistant Deputy Minister for Global Issues and Cultural Affairs (an artificial pairing that did not long survive).[3] Smith wanted the new Global Issues Bureau to be more consultative (*vis-à-vis* Canadian civil society), more project-oriented, and less hierarchical than most DFAIT units. An additional rationale for a Global Issues unit in DFAIT was the difficulty the department had experienced in articulating a coherent and cohesive set of positions for the major United Nations conferences that marked the early 1990s: in Rio on environmental issues; in Cairo on population and development; in Vienna on human rights; in Beijing on women and development; and in Copenhagen on social development (a fuzzy issue, ill-defined even at the UN, which never really took off and yielded the weakest results of these large global jamborees).

Bernard-Meunier faced an uphill challenge: many of DFAIT's officers were uncomfortable with the apparently 'soft' mandate of the Global Issues Bureau, seen as touchy-feely in the interconnectedness of its issues. Few volunteered for service there, in spite of Bernard-Meunier's strong reputation. Undaunted, and with strong support from Smith and Lucie Edwards, the first Director-General for Global Issues (a very dynamic and effective former Ambassador in East Africa responsible for the UN Environment Program [UNEP] and a variety of countries including Rwanda and Somalia at the peak of their political convulsions), Bernard-Meunier set about hiring promising candidates wherever they could be found, resulting in Bureau composition atypical within a substantive DFAIT unit. It featured few foreign service officers (FSOs), but many talented 'non-rotational' (in terms of service abroad) individuals recruited from a variety of government departments, from non-govermental organizations (NGOs), and from academic backgrounds.

THE AXWORTHY ERA

The Bureau and its mandate received a huge boost with the appointment of Lloyd Axworthy as Minister of Foreign Affairs on 25 January 1996. Axworthy, Foreign Affairs critic of the Liberal Party when in opposition until 1993, and with a strong academic background and interest in international relations, hit the ground running with a personal agenda coinciding largely with the Global Issues Bureau's mandate.

Axworthy oriented much of DFAIT's attention to conflict prevention and peacebuilding, human rights and humanitarian issues, and key disarmament issues, including nuclear non-proliferation and the licit and illicit spread of small arms. He demonstrated very strong commitment, in his dealings with departmental officials, to gender equality and children's issues.[4] He did not seem much interested in bilateral relations as ends in themselves, but rather as conduits through which Canada's agenda could be advanced. He was consequently very open to multilateral diplomacy and to working through groups of like-minded countries and elements of civil society.[5] The triumph of this approach was signature in December 1997 by more than 100 governments of a multilateral treaty banning anti-personnel landmines, negotiated earlier that year beyond the confines of the UN, with strong support from a coalition of NGOs and other non-governmental actors. It was wholly unexpected only a year earlier in intergovernmental circles, given continuing inertia in several UN disarmament fora. The adoption of the statute of an International Criminal Court, much favoured by Canada, occurred in Rome in July 1998 after difficult negotiations chaired by DFAIT's legal adviser, Philippe Kirsch. The creation of such a court seemed highly unlikely only a few years earlier. Signal atrocities in the former Yugoslavia and genocide in Rwanda earlier in the decade combined with pressure from NGOs and other elements of civil society to create a groundswell of support for the court, catalysed within the negotiations by a like-minded group in which Canada played a key role.[6]

During a visit to Canada in the early spring of 1998 by Olara Otunnu, special representative of the UN Secretary-General for children and armed conflict, Axworthy committed Canada to play a prominent role internationally in tackling the problems of war-affected children. During the same visit, Minister of Defence Art Eggleton moved to codify the practice of not sending individuals under the age of 18 to combat. By late fall, the Department of National Defence was working on several key legislative amendments on the thornier issue of age and formal recruitment into the Canadian Armed Forces (relating also to military training for those under 18) to buttress Canada's role on the question internationally.

Axworthy and others referred often to the coalition of supporters for the landmine treaty, many of them from non-governmental worlds, as a manifestation of 'soft power'—the capacity of a good idea, if properly promoted, to force the hand of bureaucratic resistance in Canada and more widely. Kim Nossal, in an article unhelpfully titled 'Foreign Policy for Wimps', argued that this notion had little do to with power, but rather with 'persuasion or inducement' (Nossal, 1998a). In an uncharacteristically furious response, Axworthy underscored that he used the phrase 'soft power' in his speeches 'because it exemplifies the Canadian talent for drawing upon our skills in negotiating, building coalitions and presenting diplomatic initiatives; in other words, for influencing the behaviour of other nations not through military intimidation but through a variety of diplomatic and political tools' (Axworthy, 1998). Nossal later argued that Canada needed 'a full array of "power tools", including military forces that can be deployed in peacekeeping missions in Rwanda or Kosovo

[and] a well-maintained foreign service, to press Canadian interests abroad' (Nossal, 1998b). Ultimately, the exchange struck a number of observers as an unfortunate instance of two keen advocates of a leading Canadian role in international affairs talking past each other (Hampson and Oliver, 1998).

Both Axworthy's agenda and his preferred method of direct interaction with governments and non-governmental parties alike exploited the connections the Global Issues Bureau (soon renamed Global and Human Issues Bureau) had been set up to highlight and significantly strengthened the Bureau's hand within DFAIT. The Bureau, chronically underfunded since its launch in 1995, was at last adequately resourced in 1998 and enjoyed ever-stronger staffing under the tutelage of Ruth Archibald, Lucie Edward's accomplished successor, who had worked extensively on migration, population, and refugee questions as a director within the Bureau in its early years.

Those toiling on human security issues within DFAIT were acutely conscious that Canada's bid for a Security Council seat, 1999–2000, which was ultimately successful, would provide Canada with an opportunity to advance Axworthy's agenda in this key body.[7] Their hopes in this regard were qualified by the realization that the five permanent members of the Security Council largely ran this show and did not appear to favour an activist human security agenda. Thus, opportunities would have to be seized to register Canada's views and advance its positions, while taking advantage of the presidency of the Council that Canada would fill for a month each in 1999 and 2000 to draw attention to one or other of Canada's thematic (as opposed to crisis-related) priorities.

When appointed Foreign Minister, Axworthy was not given responsibility for Canada's International Assistance program. A full minister, Diane Marleau, was appointed with responsibility for CIDA. This generated some institutional friction between DFAIT and CIDA, with Axworthy pursuing a largely new agenda centred on human security, which DFAIT pressed on CIDA, while CIDA clung to the mandate set out for it in *Canada in the World* (and earlier) amidst severe budget cuts inhibiting its freedom of manoeuvre. Institutionally, much of the rivalry played out between DFAIT's Global Issues Bureau and CIDA's Policy and Multilateral branches, as documented by Cranford Pratt (1998). However, Axworthy and Marleau were able to agree on the launch, in 1996, of the innovative Peacebuilding

Initiative, under which $20 million of the International Assistance envelope would be devoted, over two years, to construction and promotion of the peace in developing countries (DFAIT, 1996). This was supplemented, within DFAIT, by a small ($1 million annually) but potent Peacebuilding Program, designed to invest in 'domestic capacity for peacebuilding' and in seed activities that did not fall within the parameters of Official Development Assistance (ODA) or the priorities of the $20 million Peacebuilding Fund (DFAIT, 1998a). By 1998, relations between DFAIT and CIDA were considerably more serene, thanks in large part to strenuous efforts to restore the peace by senior officials on both sides.

While DFAIT administers few programs relative to most federal departments, the Global Issues Bureau as of 1997 began overseeing a major portion of the Youth International Internship Program. Few would disagree with Disraeli's observation that 'the youth of a nation are the trustees of [its] posterity.' In today's economy, youth issues are quintessentially global, focusing on two broad areas of social policy development: preparation of youth for adulthood (e.g., education, employment, attachment to institutions) and measures to combat failures in these preparation efforts (e.g., Young Offenders Act, drug rehabilitation programs, re-entry to workforce). Ultimately, however, the youth issue of greatest concern to most Canadians is employment. Adaptability to technological and organizational change has been a key skills-set for young people. Increased concern over the transition between school and the workplace led to a proliferation of co-operative education programs in the 1980s and, in the case of Canada, the implementation of large, publicly funded internship programs in the 1990s. One of the unique elements of the Canadian Youth Employment Strategy (YES) was the inclusion of an international component to prepare a contingent of young Canadians to work in international organizations and in areas of growing Canadian exports.

Although the largest concentration of youth programming and policy development is in the Department of Human Resources Development Canada (HRDC), and HRDC retains the lead on youth issues in federal and international discussions, DFAIT came to administer over 1,100 of the total 3,700 youth internships abroad, for which the federal budgets in 1997–8 and 1998–9 provided $16.7 million, the belief being that such international employment would prepare promising university graduates for participation in today's increasingly global economy.

Preliminary audits suggest that 80 per cent of the interns have found permanent employment in the areas they targeted through their internships. This contribution to the future lives of young Canadians has been a tangible manifestation of DFAIT's growing ability to exploit the positive features of globalization and represents a singularly exciting component of the work within the Global and Human Issues Bureau.

SOME KEY ISSUES

The Global and Human Issues Bureau's policy files themselves were diverse, and the linkages between them were sometimes more apparent than real. Eventually they congealed into clusters, with synergies developing (or not) in fairly haphazard fashion. The scope of this chapter does not permit a detailed discussion of them all, but several salient ones are highlighted below. The largest, most complex, and most economically significant issue addressed by the Bureau has been the environment.

A host of environmental issues competed for attention but the most demanding was climate change. Following the adoption of the UN Framework Convention on Climate Change in the run-up to the 1992 Rio Earth Summit, lethargy set in among many of its signatories with respect to follow-up. The anti-climax following the end of a very intense negotiating process was accompanied, in Canada, by relentless budget cuts, affecting the federal Environment Department very seriously and ensuring that the federal 'Green Plan' set in place to implement commitments at Rio was renewed in 1997 at only 66 per cent of previous levels, with no funding provided for continuation of its activities at the international level overseen by DFAIT. The government, within which a strong environmental lobby had always existed, had necessarily focused on deficit reduction since 1993, and seemed to be taken off guard in the lead-up to the Kyoto negotiations on greenhouse gas emissions of December 1997. Industrialized countries committed to an overall target of 5.2 per cent below 1990 levels by the years 2008 to 2012, with the EU target set at 8 per cent, the US at 7 per cent, and Russia agreeing to stabilize emissions by then. Canada negotiated hard at Kyoto and emerged with a reduction target of 6 per cent (the same as that of Japan). The developing countries refused to commit themselves to reductions, arguing for economic assistance and preferential transfer of technology from the industrialized countries in exchange for such commitments. Means of bringing these countries to reduce greenhouse gases were a major agenda item for the Buenos Aires November 1998 resumption of talks among states party to the Climate Change Convention.

Against 'business as usual' projections for 2010, Canada's target represented a 21 per cent lowering of greenhouse gas emissions. Intensive consultations among Ottawa, the provinces and territories, business, labour, and NGOs preceded and followed Kyoto. With the nation's and government's focus remaining locked on employment figures, these consultations were difficult. While the federal ministers for the environment and for natural resources took the lead domestically, DFAIT negotiators played key roles at and following Kyoto. Because of the urgency of international action at a time when the effects of global warming were coming to be more widely recognized (including by China, afflicted by devastating floods throughout the summer of 1998) and because of the economic stakes at play, particularly those affecting Canada's competitive position *vis-à-vis* key trading partners, notably the United States, climate change was the single hottest issue for the Global and Human Issues Bureau. Paul Heinbecker, Assistant Deputy Minister for Global and Security Policy and Canada's chief negotiator at Kyoto, supervised Canada's response in this issue-area.[8]

Forests, freshwater resources (i.e., mainly fish), oceans (1998 was the International Year of the Oceans), and persistent organic pollutants (POPs), all involving detailed consultations and some negotiation with major partners and multilaterally, also vied for DFAIT attention and resources. As always, Canada played a significant role in developing the international institutional framework to address these and other challenges, strongly supporting the new Intergovernmental Forum on Forests. Indeed, international institutional reform and construction were a leitmotif in this work. This included support for the new executive director of UNEP, Klaus Töpfer, who was tackling funding problems (with which Canada had not been able to help much during the years of Program Review, having halved the size of its contribution to this UN agency); support for UNEP's poorly functioning governance system, which had preoccupied Töpfer's predecessor, Elizabeth Dowdeswell of Canada; and the need for greater coherence within the UN system on environmental issues.

Related closely to the condition of the global commons have been issues of population, migration, and refugees. For example, were it not for the devastating deforestation and consequent soil erosion that have marked Haiti's economic development since the mid-nineteenth century, there is little doubt that it could feed much of its current population of approximately 7 million. However, given the poor returns from the subsistence agriculture and barren mountainsides that now characterize much of the country, it is not surprising that waves of refugees from Haiti have become a destabilizing factor throughout the Caribbean in this century. Thus, environmental, population, and migration challenges are very real. In 1997, Canada's acceptance rate of refugee applicants remained high, at 40 per cent, prompting complaints from the United States and some other countries that Canada has a defective screening system. The Global and Human Issues Bureau, which leaves refugee determination policy to Citizenship and Immigration Canada (CIC), nevertheless addressed energetically the international assistance and protection provided to refugees and other displaced persons abroad. In partnership with the United Nations High Commission for Refugees (UNHCR) and other donors, it focused particularly on prevention of mass population flows driven by war, oppression, and human rights abuses. In a year when UNHCR was beset by accusations of mismanagement, the Bureau continued to focus on support for the UN Secretary-General's efforts to achieve better management system-wide for emergency humanitarian assistance, most recently through the creation of the Office for the Co-ordination of Humanitarian Affairs (OCHA) and the appointment of a promising undersecretary-general, Sergio Vieira de Mello, to lead it.[9] Of particular concern in DFAIT, as in CIDA, was the issue of protection of humanitarian workers and means to ensure greater respect for international humanitarian law. Between 1 January 1992 and 31 August 1998, for instance, 153 UN international and local staff members lost their lives—35 engaged in humanitarian operations. Numerous NGO staff engaged in humanitarian relief activities, including Red Cross personnel, also lost their lives during this period.

The Bureau also focused on how reintegration of those returning to their homes can best be accomplished, often in the face of heavy odds, as in Bosnia. At a time when many countries have been declining to support UNHCR on international protection principles, Canada lobbied hard to stem this tide. Of even greater importance to Canada as a whole, the Citizenship and Immigration Minister, Lucienne Robillard, undertook national consultations with a view to enacting new immigration legislation as a result of an advisory report received on 6 January 1998. For DFAIT, this review provided an opportunity to flag several of its own concerns, one of which was the rigidity of current legislation militating against access to Canada for all individuals with criminal records. Although the government will wish to continue screening out those with terrorist ambitions, it is obvious that circumstances have changed for a number of individuals, such as Nelson Mandela (who visited Canada in September 1998 on his last state visit before retirement). In brief, DFAIT worked to ensure that any new Immigration Act retained some degree of flexibility (with appropriate safeguards) to allow for foreign policy imperatives.

Another question enjoying a high public profile and generating occasional controversy was human rights. DFAIT had come a long way since the early 1980s, when a single officer at headquarters attempted to inject human rights considerations into Canada's foreign policy while underpinning Canadian participation in a broad range of UN activities and fora. By 1998, the Human Rights, Humanitarian Affairs, and International Women's Equality Division featured officers responsible not just for UN activities but also for Canada's bilateral relations. In 1996 and 1997, Canada launched in-depth dialogues with China, Cuba, and Indonesia on human rights questions, covering a broad range of subheadings such as freedom of expression, the rights of children, and impunity. The dialogue with China, in particular, seemed promising, with relaxed, open, and substantive exchanges during July and October sessions between officials in Ottawa and Beijing. This positive atmosphere and seriousness of intent were also on display during the March 1998 Plurilateral Symposium hosted by Canada and China in Vancouver, which was attended not only by several national human rights institutions but also by a number of Asia-Pacific governments, including Thailand, Philippines, Indonesia, Malaysia, and Mongolia. Chinese interlocutors, several of them scholars more than officials, increasingly appeared to recognize that China's economic expansion can only proceed in tandem with greater respect for the rule of law and international regulatory frameworks, a realization perhaps yielding new interest in the expertise of other countries in these fields.

The appointment by the new UN Secretary-General, Kofi Annan, of Mary Robinson, then president of Eire, as High Commissioner for Human Rights gave new impetus to the UN's role as protector and promoter of human rights globally.[10] Robinson's predecessor, José Ayala Lasso, a thoughtful Ecuadorian diplomat and foreign minister of the old Latin American tradition, had failed to enliven this new position while enduring rivalries from elsewhere within the UN system, including the Centre for Human Rights. Axworthy rapidly established a strong connection with Robinson, undertaking to support her efforts at reshaping the dedicated but sluggish UN human rights machinery. Her visit to Canada in November 1998 represented a highlight of the celebrations surrounding the fiftieth anniversary of the Universal Declaration on Human Rights, in the drafting of which John Humphrey, a Canadian, had played a key role.

Axworthy and his Secretary of State for Latin America and Africa, David Kilgour, attached real importance to dialogue with NGOs and the public on human rights issues, with both reaching out at the mushrooming annual NGO consultations on human rights in Ottawa in February 1998. Axworthy launched a review of Canada's international human rights policy in consultation with key NGO and civil society leaders in the summer of 1998, focusing on strategies for further engaging Canadians in shaping objectives to advance human rights. Although the seriousness of this dialogue was appreciated, it was clear that a number of human rights activists remained perturbed over the perception that Canadian foreign policy was driven largely by trading concerns, with Burma and Nigeria the focus of considerable Canadian attention and with criticism of Chinese practices more muted. To this Axworthy responded that Burma and Nigeria refused all dialogue, while serious talks and some progress were occurring with China. The release to Canada of a number of Cuban dissidents and their families following visits to Havana by Pope John Paul II and Prime Minister Jean Chrétien in early 1998 was seen by many as a response, although still an insufficient one, to extensive Canadian lobbying on human rights issues *vis-à-vis* an often indifferent and defensive Cuban *apparat*. The fairly radical transition in Nigeria in mid-1998 from the thuggish practices of the Abacha regime to the more conciliatory interim rule of General Abubakr also seemed in part to reward the stern approach, in keeping with the Harare principles, that Canada had adopted within the Commonwealth Ministerial Action Group (CMAG) against any compromise on democratization and human rights issues.

In February 1998, an Aboriginal and Circumpolar Affairs Division of DFAIT was created, under Wayne Lord, a Métis foreign service officer, in part because these issues were gaining an increasing profile within Canadian foreign policy overall and in part because

Canada's Ambassador for Circumpolar Affairs, the widely respected Mary Simon, and its newly appointed Counsellor for International Indigenous Affairs, Blaine Favel (an energetic and committed young former Chief of the Federation of Saskatchewan Indian Nations), needed more substantive support as the importance of their files grew.[11] Favel focused on the benefits to be derived by Aboriginal communities from enhanced international economic ties among them, in effect creating wealth in indigenous communities through international trade opportunities. He offered DFAIT a great deal in terms of his access to Aboriginal networks on governance, human rights, and self-determination issues. Simon had her hands full with preparations for a ministerial meeting of the Arctic Council in Iqaluit, 17–18 September. She had chaired the Council during its first two years of existence and worked hard to develop a substantive agenda for its future work in the face of considerable reluctance, *inter alia*, on the part of the US to commit to significant spending in these areas.

The Arctic Council meeting launched plans for an Arctic university, marked distinct progress on sustainable development and environmental protection issues, and consolidated the institutional structures that participating governments and permanent participants had developed since 1996.[12] On 17 September, Axworthy released a framework consultation document on a Northern Foreign Policy, laying out elements for debate in the North (and elsewhere), having the previous day issued the report on the 1998 National Forum on Circumpolar Relations (DFAIT, 1998b, 1998c). Both documents make clear how much sensitivity remains in the North on policy suggested or imposed from the South, and the extent to which the consensus-based policy development processes favoured by Simon and others in the circumpolar world will continue to dominate Arctic negotiations.

The crime, drugs, and terrorism cluster of issues attracted growing attention throughout 1998, spurred by Birmingham G–8 summit discussion of international organized crime, the UN General Assembly Special Session on the World Drug Problem (UNGASS), and the Summit of the Americas, which focused extensively on the narcotics trade and an assortment of terrorist outrages, not least the August bombings of US embassies in Nairobi and Dar es Salaam.

An activist posture by Canada on narcotics issues in the Western hemisphere was signalled by Deputy Solicitor-General Jean Fournier's election to chair a key working group of the Inter-American Drug Abuse Control Commission (CICAD). The Prime Minister, at the

Santiago Summit of the Americas in April 1998, announced the creation of a ministerial dialogue group to grapple with the significant collateral impact of the drug problem. More broadly, the government addressed the growing gap between its international obligations in the drug field (e.g., on precursor chemicals[13]) and its ability to regulate movement of key substances through an emergency allocation of funds authorized by the Prime Minister. At UNGASS, Canada hosted the international youth conference, Youth Vision Jeunesse, which will lead to a worldwide network on best practices for youth drug abuse prevention and also was instrumental in launching (and funding) the first expert group meeting on the declaration on the guiding principles of drug demand reduction, which was adopted by the conference, the first instance of international consensus on drug demand reduction. Canada and other countries detected some welcome movement of the US away from a monolithic focus on supply reduction internationally to the more sophisticated integrated approach represented by so-called alternative development, in which crop substitution and supply reduction play only a small part relative to the more fundamental retooling of societies and economies at large (in which demand reduction is also understood to play a major part). This came to light in discussions between the new Colombian President and US officials in Washington in mid-1998.

On 12 January 1998, Canada signed the Convention on the Suppression of Terrorist Bombings, negotiation of which had also been chaired by Philippe Kirsch (fast becoming the chair of choice for key UN-related multilateral negotiations). Canada participated actively in work on a new convention for the suppression of nuclear terrorism (a Russian initiative) and co-operated with France in considering the elaboration of a new convention against fund-raising for terrorism. It also worked closely on the elimination of terrorism not only with the US but also with Mexico and others in the Western hemisphere. The Organization of American States (OAS) is quite active in this sphere, having organized a regional meeting on terrorism in Lima, Peru, in April 1996. Argentina hosted a second OAS conference on terrorism in Buenos Aires in November 1998.

International organized crime attracted public and media attention, as Russia's economy was increasingly understood to be seriously penetrated, and in some sectors dominated, by criminal elements and as organized crime syndicates seeped from and through Eastern

Europe into other parts of the world. Not the least of the phenomena newly prominent was trafficking in people. Canadian efforts, in part through the G–8 Lyon Group, focused on improving mutual legal assistance and extradition, promoting co-operation among enforcement agencies, improving tools to fight money-laundering, including asset confiscation, and developing a plan of action on high-tech crime. Multilaterally, Canada worked to advance a UN convention against transnational crime and spearheaded efforts to focus the convention on specific tools and protocols, helping to develop protocols on trafficking in women and children for purposes of sexual exploitation, trafficking in migrants, and trafficking in illegal firearms. A dynamic new head of UN operations at the Vienna headquarters, Pino Arlacchi of Italy, provided considerable support for such international efforts, although Canada and some other countries also pressed for additional focus on crime prevention, criminal justice, and prison conditions.

CONCLUSIONS

To my regret, I spent only eight months as Director-General of the Global and Human Issues Bureau. During this period, my predecessor, Ruth Archibald, while preparing for a foreign assignment, agreed to continue her leadership of international crime issues while I combined the rest of the global and human issues portfolio with co-ordination of efforts to secure a UN Security Council seat for Canada in 1999–2000. Never, in a 23-year career in DFAIT, had I grappled with so diverse a range of interlinked policy issues, nor had I experienced as much pressure (and support) from a minister's office and senior management to achieve tangible results on so many policy fronts. At times, Canada got somewhat ahead of itself, as when it proposed only days before a conference on small arms in Oslo that participating countries focus on a convention on the licit trade of such weapons, taking the Norwegian hosts (who reacted graciously) and others very much by surprise. On the whole, however, the drive and advocacy from the top, the very high quality of our staff, and the support of colleagues throughout the department and at our diplomatic missions abroad allowed us to launch a number of major new departures in foreign policy that should remain with Canada for some years to come. The Global and Human Issues Bureau has taken root firmly within DFAIT, nurturing new issues as they arise and spinning off others as they mature. It has been a successful experiment and one attracting considerable attention abroad. As I depart Ottawa for the International Peace Academy in New York, it is good to see the global issues biz booming at DFAIT.

NOTES

1. Smith had been approached about the deputy minister slot in May 1994 and had a couple of months to read and to reflect on where he wanted to take the DFAIT machine. 'Foreign Ministers traditionally dealt mainly with political and security issues, while governments as a whole were increasingly interested in economic ones. Neither were prepared for the third, emerging, wave of challenges. Once I became G–7 Sherpa [for Prime Minister Chrétien], I was reinforced in this view: leaders spent more time struggling with these emerging issues than with classic economic or political ones. They spent more time on issues such as the environment and nuclear safety than observers realized. At Denver [in 1997] they decided that they wanted to concentrate on organized crime at Birmingham [in 1998], with one leader commenting that crime was organizing faster than our countries could fight it. They were particularly concerned over the technology angle, what role it was playing in the growth of organized crime and how it could help us. The lengthy discussion at Denver on infectious diseases was driven by questions they had over how these could be combated at the global level.' (Smith interview, 10 Sept. 1998.)

2. Ouellet was not hard to convince on this score, and the idea was actively supported by his influential policy adviser, Michael Pearson. The economic and trade policy branch of DFAIT was loath to lose the environment file, but Smith overrode strong objections from this source.

3. DFAIT's International Cultural Relations Bureau in mid-1998 reported through the Assistant Deputy Minister for Communications and Policy Planning.

4. Axworthy instituted a system of briefings through which he met regularly with small groups of DFAIT officials at all levels, always including the deputy minister, on any issues of current concern. These sessions left officials with little doubt as to where the minister wished to drive Canadian policy, but also provided officials with an opportunity to help shape his views and created much greater transparency and responsiveness in both directions than had been the norm in DFAIT in relations between the minister and officials under most previous regimes.

5. This led, notably, to the adoption of the so-called Lysoen Declaration on 11 May 1998, an agreement between Canada and Norway to work together with other like-minded countries on a 'partnership for action' on such issues as human rights, humanitarian law, the prevention of conflict, and the promotion of democracy and good governance. On the margins of the UN General Assembly, in September 1998, the foreign ministers of Thailand, Slovenia, Chile, Austria, Ireland, Switzerland, and South Africa met with their Norwegian and

Canadian counterparts to explore what joint action could be undertaken to give effect to the Lysoen Declaration.

6. The Global Issues Bureau played an important role at the outset in DFAIT's work on landmines and on international criminal justice, but increasingly these very demanding files were managed by the International Security Bureau and the Legal Branch, respectively.

7. The election, in which Greece, the Netherlands, and Canada vied for two Western non-permanent seats, took place on 8 October 1998, with successful results for Canada and the Netherlands.

8. So important were environmental questions within DFAIT and so considerable the resources devoted to them that, in the fall of 1998, a separate bureau was created to address them alongside the Global and Human Issues Bureau. Within it, a full division was established to deal with climate change.

9. Efforts to institute genuine, effective humanitarian co-ordination within the UN have a long history. In 1991, the General Assembly returned to the charge, creating a Department of Humanitarian Affairs of which Jan Eliasson (Sweden) was the first leader, in 1992. For a variety of reasons, many relating to bureaucratic trench warfare, neither he nor his successors, Peter Hansen and Yasushi Akashi, were successful. OCHA's prospects looked highly uncertain as of late 1998. The attacks on UNHCR management, spearheaded by an uncharacteristically hyper-ventilating (London) *Financial Times*, drew on a leaked audit report alleging considerable waste and some fraud. More systemic criticism of UNHCR, articulated by several governments, related to its reluctance to downsize at a time when donor funding for its activities was in sharp decline. However, the much-admired High Commissioner for Refugees, Sadako Ogata, was re-elected for a two-year term by the General Assembly late in the year. In October, UNHCR had announced staff reductions of approximately 1,000.

10. Robinson's appointment was followed in early 1998 by that of Louise Fréchette, a former Canadian Permanent Representative to the UN and Deputy Minister of Defence, as Deputy Secretary-General of the UN. With the election of Gro Harlem Brundtland as Director-General of the World Health Organization, the UN was finally leading by example on gender equality with these strong, competent, widely admired women in the vanguard of Annan's team.

11. Minister Axworthy's external Advisory Board (chaired by Professor Janice Stein) in early 1998 played a valuable role in signalling to DFAIT that it was not sufficiently ventilating Arctic foreign policy debates through northern communities, with which one of the Board's members, Christine Lee, executive director of the Walter and Duncan Gordon Foundation, had significant experience. The existence of this Board since 1995, and the extensive use that Lloyd Axworthy makes of it and other, more informal, networks of advisers, underscores the degree to which academic, NGO, and civil society voices are now heard (and acted on) in high places within DFAIT.

12. The permanent participants in the Arctic Council are several organizations representing indigenous peoples of the region.

13. These chemicals are used in the manufacture of drugs (e.g., opium and heroin) from plant-based sources or in the manufacture of synthetic drugs (e.g., ecstasy, LSD).

REFERENCES

Axworthy, Lloyd. 1998. 'Why "Soft Power" is the right policy for Canada', *Ottawa Citizen*, 25 Apr., B6.

Canada. 1995. *Canada in the World*. Ottawa: Government of Canada.

Canadian Centre for Foreign Policy Development. 1998. *Circumpolar Relations*. 1998 National Forum on Canada's International Relations. Ottawa: Canadian Centre for Foreign Policy Development.

Department of Foreign Affairs and International Trade (DFAIT). 1996. 'Canada to Establish a New Peacebuilding Fund', Press Release No. 201, 30 Oct.

———. 1998a. *Canadian Peacebuilding Initiative, 1997–98*. Ottawa: DFAIT and CIDA. Available at: <www.dfait-maeci.gc.ca/peacebuilding/> <www.acdi-cida.gc.ca>.

———. 1998b. *Toward a Northern Foreign Policy*. Ottawa, 17 Sept.

Hampson, Fen Osler, and Dean F. Oliver. 1998. 'Pulpit Diplomacy: A Critical Assessment of the Axworthy Doctrine', *International Journal* 53, 3 (Summer): 379–406.

Nossal, Kim Richard. 1998a. 'Foreign Policy for Wimps', *Ottawa Citizen*, 23 Apr., A19.

———. 1998b. 'Our Insecure Foreign Policy', *Ottawa Citizen*, 14 Oct.

Pratt, Cranford. 1998. 'DFAIT's take-over bid of CIDA', *Canadian Foreign Policy* 5, 2 (Winter): 1–14.

11

Present at the Creation? Human Security and Canadian Foreign Policy in the Twenty-first Century

ROBIN JEFFREY HAY

The concept of human security has come of age. Many have con-cluded that the causes and nature of armed conflict are changing, requiring a new set of responses. As Foreign Minister Lloyd Axworthy, the leading Canadian proponent of the human security doctrine, explains:

> The face of war has been transformed. The majority of conflicts occur inside states rather than between them. Regardless of where these conflicts hap-pen, civilians are now increasingly the main victims and targets—especially the most vulnerable. As a result, the world has witnessed human tragedies of devastating proportions—massive refugee flows and the grossest viola-tions of humanitarian law, including genocide.

This 'new reality', Axworthy concludes, puts the security of the indi-vidual at the front and centre of world affairs:

> Our basic unit of analysis in security matters has shrunk from the state to the individual. This human security lens produces new priorities—everything from countering terrorist bombs to child labour and climate change. These issues have now become the daily concern of foreign ministers and governments. They are the human security agenda. (Axworthy, 1998c)

Without completely dispensing with traditional security concerns, the Minister of Foreign Affairs has noted that human security is rapidly becoming the main issue in global affairs. And in Canadian foreign affairs, too, he might have added. In the few short years since Lloyd Axworthy replaced André Ouellet as Foreign Minister, the Chrétien government appears to have shifted the focus of Canada's foreign policy from trade to human security.

As a result of this shift, Canada has been reshaping and refocusing its foreign policy priorities to deal with the concerns of the individual. The highest-profile elements of this shift include a reliance on soft power, which Axworthy has called the art of persuasion rather than coercion; an emphasis on peacebuilding—a package of initiatives delivered at the appropriate moment after the fighting has stopped that can develop the social infrastructure of war-torn societies and break the cycle of violence; and a number of specific initiatives in discrete but related areas: the anti-personnel landmines campaign and treaty, efforts to control the proliferation of military small arms and light weapons, the creation of an International Criminal Court, and efforts to address the plight of war-affected children.

Human security provides the framework for these high-profile initiatives and the rationale for a reliance on soft power and the emphasis placed on peacebuilding. It has also provided a target for Axworthy's critics, who have accused the minister of engaging in everything from 'pulpit diplomacy' to a 'foreign policy for wimps'.

In this chapter I, too, will take a critical look at the concept of human security, reviewing both its general origins in development thinking (and in security thinking) and its specific evolution in relation to Canadian foreign policy. Then I will examine how human security fits with the changing dynamics of the international system in the post-Cold War. Next, I will consider some of the measures that Canada has undertaken to promote its agenda and assess whether or not they can fulfil the requirements of human security. Finally, I will outline what it will take for Canada truly to advance a human security agenda as we head into the twenty-first century.

ORIGIN OF THE SPECIES

The Development Roots

Ironically—though not unexpectedly—the concept of human security has its primary origins not in thinking about security but in thinking about development. It originated and was first elaborated in the 1994 version of the United Nation's Development Program's annual *Human Development Report*. The report cited Albert Einstein, who, 50 years earlier in response to the dawn of the nuclear age, called for a substantially new manner of thinking for mankind to survive. Five decades later, the *Report* noted, 'we need another profound transition in thinking—from nuclear security to human security.' The report complained that for too long the focus on security has been on nation-states and territory rather than on people who seek security in their daily lives. Human security is not concerned with weapons, then, but with human life and dignity: 'a child who did not die, a disease that did not spread, a job that was not cut, an ethnic tension that did not explode in violence, a dissident who was not silenced' (UNDP, 1994: 22). The report was careful to note that human security should not be equated with human development. The latter involves widening the range of people's choices, while the former means they can exercise those choices safely and freely, confident that the opportunities they have today will not disappear tomorrow.

The human security concept was a natural outgrowth of the shift in development thinking that began in the 1970s, marking a movement away from an exclusive focus on economic growth to a broader understanding of development. That broader understanding included such components as social justice, political development, gender equity, and, most importantly, the environment. The shift reached its apex with the publication in 1987 of *Our Common Future*, the report of the World Commission on Environment and Development, popularly known as the Brundtland Report.

The Brundtland Report introduced into common parlance the notion of sustainable development, noting that development can only be sustained if it fulfils today's needs without compromising the capacity of future generations to fulfil their own needs. As the head of the commission whose report bears her name has noted, the most important contribution of the report was to shift development away from compartmentalized thinking by defining sustainable development as a process of change where social, economic, political, and environmental concerns had to be harmonized (Brundtland, 1996: 174).

The Brundtland Report not only broadened the concept of development, it provided a link between sustainable development and peace and security, arguing that environmental stress is both a cause and an effect of political tensions and armed conflict.

The Security Roots

The Brundtland Report began an evolution in development thinking that progressed from sustainable development to sustainable human development—placing people and their needs squarely at the centre of the development process. This process branched off to include sustainable human security, which also places people squarely at the centre of its concerns. In security studies a similar evolution has been taking place, though for many analysts the debate remains open.

A critical document in this process was another commission report named after a world leader. As one analyst has noted, the Brandt Commission Report of 1983 marked a horizontal expansion of the scope of security by including economic security as a necessary condition for the maintenance of political security (Prins, 1998: 788; see also Ullman, 1983).

Soon, other academics began to call for a broadened concept of security beyond the purely military. Barry Buzan, for instance, suggested that security should be thought of, generally, as the pursuit of freedom from threat—threats that emanate as much from the political, economic, and social spheres as from the military. Military security, according to Buzan, must be seen as part of a larger picture (Buzan, 1983). Similarly, Ken Booth argued that true international security entails that humankind must not only be emancipated from war or the threat of war, but also from poverty, poor education, political oppression, scarcity, overpopulation, ethnic rivalry, environmental destruction, and disease (Booth, 1991). More recently, Thomas Homer-Dixon's controversial work on environmental scarcity and violent conflict, popularized by Robert Kaplan in his 1994 *Atlantic Monthly* article, 'The Coming Anarchy', brought the debate full circle, ending up, from a security standpoint, where the Brundtland Report began.

POLICY CONVERGENCE

What was mostly an academic debate over security and its links with development began to seep into policy circles with the end of the Cold War and the rise of intrastate conflict. A seminal document in this regard was the publication of *An Agenda for Peace*, by UN Secretary-General Boutros Boutros-Ghali, in which he redefined threats to global security:

> A porous ozone shield could pose a greater threat to an exposed population than a hostile army. Drought and disease can decimate no less mercilessly than the weapons of war. . . . the efforts of the Organization to build peace, stability and security must encompass matters beyond military threats in order to break the fetters of strife and warfare that have characterized the past. (Boutros-Ghali, 1992: 7)

This type of thinking was reflected in Canadian policy circles as well. In late 1994 and early 1995 the Chrétien government issued successive White Papers on defence and foreign policy. Both documents made reference to non-traditional threats to security. In its statement on foreign policy the government used language reminiscent of that used by the UN Secretary-General, noting that the international context had changed, bringing with it threats to security that transcended borders and affected whole regions or even the globe. Crime, disease, mass involuntary migration, social inequity, environmental degradation, overpopulation, and lack of economic opportunity— these were among the new threats the government began to contemplate. Thus, security needs were changing, moving away from concerns about the security of the state and focusing on the economic, social, and political needs of the individual.

The foreign policy White Paper called for a response to security issues beyond those of a strictly military nature. The promotion of democracy and good governance, of human rights and the rule of law, and of prosperity through sustainable development were seen as the appropriate kinds of responses to new international threats. Significantly, the paper highlighted the fact that sustainable development is a precondition for human security: 'Problems such as environmental degradation and growing disparities between rich and poor affect human security around the world and are areas where Canada can make an effective contribution by promoting sustainable development through its program of development cooperation' (DFAIT, 1995).

This foreign policy statement, *Canada in the World*, provided the navigational guideposts for a new bearing in Canadian foreign and security policy that began to take shape, we should remember, under André Ouellet, though it is most closely associated with Foreign Minister Axworthy. More significantly, as David Malone describes in Chapter 10, the government statement also provided an institutional framework for human security by calling for the establishment of a Global Issues Bureau within the department to deal with new, non-traditional threats to security.

What is noteworthy about the creation of the Global Issues Bureau, according to Malone, is that, like the foreign policy White Paper, it was the brainchild of a senior Foreign Affairs bureaucrat—Gordon Smith—not a politician, and its establishment preceded Axworthy's term as Foreign Minister. This is noteworthy because the human security agenda is often portrayed as a personal crusade of Axworthy's that may very well disappear when he leaves the department (Green, 1999; Knox and Sallot, 1999). While Axworthy has been a forceful proponent of human security, the genesis of the Global Issues Bureau and the commitments in the White Paper would seem to indicate that the concept will almost certainly survive his departure, though its profile might be lowered.

THE HUMAN SECURITY AGENDA

It *is* fair to say that with the appointment in 1996 of Lloyd Axworthy as Minister for Foreign Affairs, the human security agenda took off. Taking the government statement on foreign policy as his point of departure, Axworthy began to shape, articulate, and advance the idea of human security like no one else in or out of government. In an article in *International Journal*, published in 1997, the Foreign Minister provided the rationale and outline for what is often described as his personal agenda. He noted that the Cold War approach to security was inadequate. Human security was much more than the absence of military threat:

It includes security against economic privation, an acceptable quality of life, and a guarantee of fundamental human rights. This concept of human security recognizes the complexity of the human environment and accepts that the forces influencing human security are interrelated and mutually reinforcing. At a minimum, human security requires that basic needs are met, but it also acknowledges that sustained economic development, human rights and fundamental freedoms, the rule of law, good governance, sustainable development, and social equity are as important to global peace as arms control and disarmament. (Axworthy, 1997: 184)

Axworthy was careful to link the human security agenda to Canadian foreign policy traditions such as peacekeeping and development assistance. He also drew direct links between peacekeeping and peacebuilding, noting that the concept of the former was evolving to incorporate aspects of the latter in an effort to provide longer-term solutions to conflict. The landmines campaign, too, could be viewed as an outgrowth of Canada's long tradition to promote arms control and disarmament. Canadian aid policy was also being harnessed in an effort to promote human security in the developing world through programs as diverse as food security, income generation, judicial training, and support for health care. Axworthy described a new integrated approach linking foreign policy to assistance priorities, an approach that he said was manifest in the involvement of the Canadian International Development Agency (CIDA) in the Canadian Peacebuilding Initiative. Even the emphasis on soft power was linked to Canada's middle-power diplomatic tradition, which, as he wrote, always stressed the importance of coalition-building and fostering consensus.

Since 1997, Axworthy has elaborated several times on what the human security approach to international relations means for Canadian foreign policy. It entails engagement in the world, not isolationism; it relies on new innovative partnerships with civil society organizations, not just nation-states and diplomats; it calls for new tools and instruments and the revitalization of old ones; and, as the minister continued to emphasize at every opportunity, 'the use of soft power—negotiation rather than coercion, powerful ideas rather than powerful weapons, public diplomacy rather than backroom bargaining—is an effective means to pursue the human security agenda' (Axworthy, 1998c).

The minister has also proudly pointed to a number of initiatives that Canada has taken to promote the human security agenda: the landmines campaign that resulted in December 1997 in the Ottawa Convention to ban anti-personnel mines; support for the establishment of an International Criminal Court; efforts to prevent the proliferation of small arms and light weapons; and activism in the area of child soldiers and war-affected children.

Other chapters in this volume are devoted to discussing some of these specific initiatives in detail, while others were addressed in last year's edition (see Lawson, 1998), so it would be redundant to take them up in any detail here. In the concluding section they will be addressed broadly in an assessment of the government's efforts to fulfil the human security agenda. But before turning to an examination of the human security concept and its relationship to international circumstances today, it is worth noting that the idea, which was formulated almost exclusively to deal with the situation in developing countries, has been expanded to include North America.

At a meeting before the Mid-America Committee in Chicago in September 1998, the minister referred to the familiar initiatives cited above before turning to human security in the North American context. In his speech Axworthy encouraged the development of a common North American response to human security issues such as crime, terrorism, drugs, and the environment. He called for a closer look at border operations, trade and transportation corridors, and labour mobility. We need to update our instruments, he said, to deal with everything from a shared environment to the movement of goods and people, to education and human resources.

These sentiments were echoed the following month when, at a CIIA conference, Axworthy again addressed North American human security. Once more he called for co-ordination and co-operation in a number of areas, including: education, research and culture, the sound management of environmental and natural resources, integrated management of shared watersheds, climate change, and border management in a way that lets in people and goods and keeps out crime and drugs. He has called for no less than a North American community comparable to the European Union model.

HUMAN SECURITY AND ITS CRITICS

While Axworthy has developed a large following and support in the non-governmental community, his elaboration of human security, or certain aspects thereof, was assailed by a number of academics and

Canadian foreign policy experts. Kim Nossal derided the notion of soft power, or at least that it could be applied in the Canadian context, arguing that soft power is not power at all, especially not without hard-power assets such as military forces to back it up. He accused Axworthy of conducting foreign policy on the cheap and misleading Canadians to believe that all this country needs in world politics is a few good ideas that will get others to want what we want (Nossal, 1998: A19).

The notion of soft power came under similar attack in an article by Fen Hampson and Dean Oliver in the same journal where Mr Axworthy first articulated the human security concept in 1997 (Hampson and Oliver, 1998). Like Nossal, Hampson and Oliver criticized the Foreign Minister for inappropriately borrowing the notion of soft power from the American context, where it was more applicable. They also agreed with Nossal that soft power needs hard power to back it up if it is to succeed, and cited Axworthy's apparent reluctance to support Canadian involvement in such organizations as the North Atlantic Treaty Organization (NATO) and the North American Air Defence Command (NORAD).

Hampson and Oliver were also critical of the fact that DFAIT's human security approach in international affairs is predicated on the idea that intrastate conflict, fuelled by non-traditional threats to security, is on the rise while interstate conflict is on the wane. This is hardly the case, they argue, and cite potential or recent interstate troubles between Indian and Pakistan over Kashmir, between Peru and Ecuador, in the Middle East, and between China and many of its Asia-Pacific neighbours over the Spratly Islands, to name a few. Mr Axworthy is criticized, then, for developing a foreign policy based on the assumption that such interstate conflicts will not occur.

A former DFAIT diplomat, Graham N. Green, also poured cold water on the notion that Canada could advance the human security agenda at the UN during its two-year membership on the Security Council beginning in January 1999. Green bluntly warned that any attempts to champion non-traditional issues will almost certainly end in failure and, worse, would weaken Canada's international credibility and influence. He advised Canada to pursue the achievable at the expense of the desirable (Green, 1999: 137).

Mr Axworthy's response to this criticism, at least in the case of his response in the *Ottawa Citizen* to Nossal's article, was decidedly churlish, betraying perhaps his insecurity about human security and

revealing to his critics the depth of his personal (political?) investment in the notion. He needn't have been either insecure or churlish. In fact, he would have been wise to embrace the criticism, since
a careful reading of these articles reveals that they are not disparag-
ing of the notion of human security in principle, but simply calling
for a more analytical and balanced approach to adopting it as a major
plank of Canadian foreign and security policy.

In fact, there is plenty of reason to believe that a balanced human
security agenda, including a proportionate emphasis on both hard
and soft power, is a defensible, even realistic, approach to international relations today. Nor should we automatically conclude that
such a formulation of human security will fall on deaf ears among
Canada's principal allies.

HUMAN SECURITY IN TODAY'S CONTEXT

Viewed more closely, the human security concept is a rational
response to international developments as we enter the twenty-first
century. At its root, human security springs from the notion that
spreading democracy is the surest way to peace, an idea as old as
Immanuel Kant and as modern as the writings of R.J. Rummel,
Michael Doyle, and Bruce Russet attest. The basic argument is that
democracies don't fight each other (Kant called it a liberal peace).
Nor do its citizens resort to violence within the state. Generally, it is
argued, democratic government provides opposition groups with the
freedom to express their dissenting opinions and the people with the
mechanisms and the opportunity to change their government peace-
ably should its policies and programs not meet their needs. Thus, in
a functioning democracy, there is less need, motivation, or room for
citizens to resort to political violence. Human security, as explained
by Axworthy, is essentially about the spread of democratic values:
human rights and fundamental freedoms, the rule of law, good governance, sustainable development, and social equity.

It is an argument that was taken to heart in the early days of the
Clinton government in the United States, especially by Anthony Lake,
the President's first national security adviser. Lake proposed that the
United States should pursue a strategy of *enlargement* (of the world's
market democracies) to replace the now outmoded Cold War doctrine of *containment* (of the Soviet Union). He predicated this strategy on US security, noting that to the extent democracy and market

economics hold sway in other nations the United States will be more secure, prosperous, and influential, while the broader world will be more humane and peaceful (Lake, 1993: 4).

And like Axworthy, the Clinton administration was criticized for this approach to foreign policy, especially as it manifested itself in US intervention in Bosnia, Somalia, and Haiti. Michael Mandelbaum called those efforts a misguided attempt to help the helpless. Applying the standards of Mother Theresa to foreign policy, he concluded, is an expensive proposition. And like Green on Axworthy, Mandelbaum argued that such an approach to foreign policy only alienated vital allies (Mandelbaum, 1998).

While the US seems to have backed off, at least explicitly, from the strategy that led it into Bosnia, Somalia, and Haiti, Britain under the Labour government of Tony Blair is formulating an approach to foreign policy remarkably similar to the Axworthy doctrine. Like Axworthy, Britain's Foreign Secretary, Robin Cook, is putting human rights at the centre of a foreign policy that has been dubbed the 'third way'. It is an approach that finds its precursor in the 'good international citizenship' of Gareth Evans, Australia's Foreign Minister from 1988 to 1996.

The Cook doctrine is, as one commentator remarked, wholly unrecognizable when looked at through the traditional realist-cum-pragmatist lens.

> There is no talk of sovereignty, of which we heard so much from the previous administration, no mention of 'threats' to national security, no elevation of the principle of non-intervention in Britain's domestic affairs; in their place, one finds 'internationalism', 'promoting democracy', 'promotion of our values and confidence in our identity', 'a people's diplomacy' and so on. (Frost, 1998)

He might almost have been talking about Axworthy's human security agenda. Indeed, Robin Cook appears to have taken a page from Axworthy's book, calling for an ethical dimension in foreign policy, putting human rights at the centre, focusing on such issues as child labour and sex tourism, and advocating openness in foreign policy-making that includes NGOs in its implementation and formulation.

In short, given the US and British experience it would be wrong to conclude that Axworthy's human security agenda is a solitary candle blowing in the realist wind. Indeed, a more carefully contrived and balanced approach to human security may find a welcome reception among at least two permanent members of the United Nations Security Council.

And with good reason. The human security agenda responds to a number of developments in the post-Cold War environment that makes it a tempting and even logical strategy for Canada—a middle power with a traditional preference for multilateral action—to pursue. First, as has often been noted, intrastate conflicts in the developing world are a remarkably prominent feature of the international landscape in the 1990s. While the potential for interstate conflict remains and should not be ignored, peace support operations since 1990 have responded more often to conflicts within states than to wars between them. Canada has long been a leading proponent and participant in UN peacekeeping, and cannot afford to discount this trend or the emphasis given to peacebuilding in those operations.

Second, while Graham Green's critique about the pursuit of human security issues during Canada's tenure on the Security Council is well taken, we cannot ignore the fact that the United Nations, at least since the 1989 peacekeeping operation in Namibia, has taken on the promotion of democratization as one of its core missions. Today, UN peace support operations, mandated by the Security Council, are dominated by civilians performing a host of human security tasks, such as training police in democratic methods, creating and supporting effective judiciaries, civil services, and human rights bodies, and reintegrating combatants into civilian life. It would also be a mistake to assume that non-traditional subjects such as crime, terrorism, and drugs are not an appropriate subject for either the Security Council or the General Assembly (Ruggie, 1998). While Mr Axworthy may have to approach these issues pragmatically, it would be wrong to conclude that they should be dropped entirely during Canada's tenure on the Security Council. Rather, as Green suggests, human security issues need to be pursued in terms of what is realistically achievable. A healthy dose of realism is what the Axworthy doctrine is missing and ignores at its own peril.

Third, globalization is a pervasive trend that enriches some people while marginalizing most others. It is the negative effects of globalization that the human security approach purports to respond to. As Gwyn Prins has argued, these negative effects can be seen in conflicts in Europe, Asia, and Africa, where globalization has fostered alienation and isolation rather than unification and empowerment

(Prins, 1998: 797). Human security is formulated in part as an appropriate response to what Axworthy has called the dark side of globalization: transnational crime, terrorism, the drug trade, transboundary environmental pollutants, and economic inequities.

Fourth, while many analysts have concluded that democracies rarely go to war against each other, these days they also seem loath to send troops abroad for almost any reason. Edward Luttwak has called this the age of post-heroic warfare, in which, for demographic reasons (low birth rates), casualties will not be tolerated. Michael Mandelbaum, too, has concluded that war for the major powers is fast becoming obsolete:

> At the end of the nineteenth century, war was a normal activity of sovereign states. Military conscription was a standard practice and military service a normal obligation of citizenship. By the end of the twentieth century, serving in the armed forces was no longer seen as an important civic duty and conscription had been abolished in many places. And while 100 years ago acts of war were considered legitimate, necessary, even heroic, war has now come to be widely regarded as something approaching a criminal enterprise. (Mandelbaum, 1998)

Given these arguments, one wonders if human security is not a prudent and realistic approach to international relations, especially for a middle power such as Canada. Although the United States can afford to develop high-technology weapons that enable it to wage war from afar without risking casualties—for instance, using cruise missiles against Iraq—Canada and many other nations cannot afford such 'luxuries'. Canada could and should do more to develop its hard-power assets. But the reality is that there are real limits to what we can do in this regard. Human security has to be developed as a necessary complement to our hard-power obligations and as a realistic response to a world in which Western societies are reluctant to commit their sons and daughters to military adventures abroad.

Fifth, the world, and the way we think about it, has changed. Non-traditional threats to security are being discussed in the halls of power and in mainstream foreign policy and security journals (Garrett, 1996). The ascendance to power on the international scene of actors or agents other than the state, including civil society actors, is garnering increasing attention (Matthews, 1997; Zakaria, 1999). The tendency for Axworthy to confront these threats and embrace many of those actors to advance human security would appear to be nothing less than an appropriate reflection of this new reality.

THE AXWORTHY INTERPRETATION:
DOES THE EMPEROR HAVE CLOTHES?

Human security is a valid concept and may even be a necessary, if not sufficient, contribution to international affairs. But the question is, does Axworthy's application of the doctrine match its formulation? Here, it is hard not to be sympathetic to his critics.

The human security agenda is arguably the most ambitious agenda of any Foreign Minister in history. By conceiving security in both horizontal and vertical terms it could, in the extreme, commit Canada to the micromanagement of human affairs across the globe, in both developing and developed countries. Consider for a moment what is on the human security agenda as described in the UN's *Human Development Report*: jobs, unemployment, death by industrial and traffic accidents, diseases of the circulatory system, health insurance, violent crime, violence in the home, a stable family life, community security, and so on. Consider, too, the *Report*'s argument that a threat to one element of human security is likely to travel like an angry typhoon to all forms of human security. If Axworthy's human security agenda is not defined within explicit parameters, Canada may find itself cast as a Boy Scout imperialist, the busybody of international politics with a right to butt into everyone's business.

Clearly, the Foreign Minister has no intention of going this far. But even the issues he champions explicitly—crime, drugs, human rights, poverty reduction, child labour, environmental degradation, and so forth—will demand an enormous increase in financial resources if they are to be addressed substantively. And this is a time when the budgets for foreign affairs, defence, and development have been shrinking annually at an alarming rate. Also, given Finance Minister Paul Martin's tendency to husband the government's resources, even in an era of zero budget deficits, meaningful increases in funding for human security are unlikely to be forthcoming anytime soon.

The problem with human security is not with the validity of the concept but with the size of the ambition. To be fair, the minister has no intention of tackling this agenda alone but has proposed to move in co-operation with other like-minded countries. In May 1998 he took the first step, signing an agreement with Norway—the Lysoen

Declaration—pledging co-operation on a host of the minister's favourite issues: landmines, the International Criminal Court, human rights, women and children in conflict, small arms, and child soldiers.

To his credit, the minister has been pursuing these issues with zeal. The Ottawa Process, as it was called, culminated in the signing of the Anti-Personnel Mines Convention in December 1997. In the summer of 1998, with active Canadian support, a framework establishing an International Criminal Court was agreed upon in Rome. An Optional Protocol to the Convention on the Rights of the Child that would ban the recruitment of child soldiers under the age of 18 is being eagerly, if so far unsuccessfully, pursued with Canadian government support. Canada has made the proliferation of small arms and light weapons a high priority among human security issues.

These are all noble and worthwhile pursuits that draw attention to the human security dilemma experienced by people in many parts of the world. Axworthy's relentless beating of the drum on behalf of these and other human security 'causes' has done much to rehabilitate the image of the department in Canada and abroad, providing a healthy corrective to the widely held perception that DFAIT, under Ouellet, was only interested in international affairs insofar as they had commercial benefits for Canada.

But these causes are only the symptoms or manifestations of human insecurity. They are low-risk, low-cost pursuits that easily lend themselves to rhetorical flourish and leave the rhetorician vulnerable to charges of pulpit diplomacy. Save for the International Criminal Court, one would be hard-pressed to point to any one of these issues that addresses the root causes of human insecurity.

Having committed itself to such an ambitious agenda, Canada now has to demonstrate its seriousness. Championing good causes is fine, for a while. But without a grand strategy that establishes the extent and limits of our commitments, describes how we are going to meet them, and provides the necessary resources to do so, Canada will soon begin to resemble a dilettante, frittering away at the fringes while others do the dirty work.

Canada can and should take a number of meaningful initiatives. First, it needs to get beyond symptomatic issues and address the root causes of conflict. This means increasing the budget for development and for peacebuilding. At the very least, Canada should increase the aid budget to the OECD prescribed 0.7 per cent of GNP. Here Axworthy is going to have to convince Paul Martin to loosen the purse-strings.

Second, Canada needs to develop a framework for human security that specifies our commitments and obligations. This would put meat on the bones of what is now an open-ended conglomeration of analyses, ideas, and prognostications. That framework should also reconcile our human security obligations with our obligations to more traditional security concerns. Neither can be ignored in a world in transition, and each complements the achievement of the other.

Third, and related to the last point, Canada should increase the resources it devotes to Foreign Affairs and Defence. Hard-power assets are still the currency in many parts of the world and among most of Canada's allies. We need to be able to contribute a respectable amount of those assets not only to retain the respect of our allies, whose support we will need in the human security sphere, but to lend our soft-power undertakings the requisite muscle.

Finally, Canada should include Britain among the like-minded nations it wants to co-operate with in pursuit of human security. As a nuclear power, a permanent member of the Security Council, a country committed to many of the same issues that Axworthy champions, and the leader of the Commonwealth, Britain could be a valuable ally in Canada's pursuit of a human security agenda.

In a speech to the National Forum in Montreal in January 1999, Axworthy belatedly and somewhat reluctantly acknowledged the need for hard-power assets and robust actions, when necessary, to promote human security. He argued that Canada's focus on human security should not be mistaken for softness. Yet, in the federal budget released less than a month later, there was precious little spending on defence, save for an additional $175 million a year over three years to be devoted to much-needed pay raises and benefits for soldiers. Most defence analysts agree that this falls short of what the Defence Department needs to maintain even our present, inadequate level of defence forces (Sallot, 1999).

The fact is that Paul Martin continually fails to put the government's money where Lloyd Axworthy's mouth is on human security. Aid spending, too, fell far short of this year's budget, adding only $237 million to a $2.5 billion budget and bringing the development envelope to a paltry 0.29 per cent of gross domestic product, less than half the OECD-mandated level. Like defence analysts, aid specialists were disappointed (Gee, 1999).

If something is not done to correct this situation in the year 2000 budget, Canada can expect to be laughed out of the room when it lends its voice to any serious discussion of security, human or military, soft or hard.

REFERENCES

Axworthy, Lloyd. 1997. 'Canada and human security: the need for leadership', *International Journal* 52, 2: 183–96.

———. 1998a. 'Canadian Foreign Policy and Human Rights', *Human Rights Research and Education Bulletin* (Ottawa) 35: 1–6.

———. 1998b. 'Global Action, Continental Community: Human Security in Canadian Foreign Policy'. Notes for an address by the Minister of Foreign Affairs to a Meeting of the Mid-America Committee.

———. 1998c. Notes for an address by the Minister of Foreign Affairs to the Canadian Institute of International Affairs Foreign Policy Conference, Ottawa, 16 Oct.

Booth, Ken. 1991. 'Security and Emancipation', *Review of International Studies* 17, 4 (Oct.).

Boutros-Ghali, Boutros. 1992. *An Agenda for Peace*. New York: United Nations Department of Public Information.

Brundtland, Gro Harlem. 1996. 'Our Common Future Revisited', *The Brown Journal of World Affairs* 3, 2 (Summer/Fall): 174.

Buzan, Barry. 1983. *People, States and Fear*. Brighton, Sussex: Wheatsheaf.

Department of Foreign Affairs and International Trade. 1995. *Canada in the World*. Ottawa: Department of Supply and Services.

Garrett, Laurie. 1996. 'The Return of Infectious Disease', *Foreign Affairs* 75, 1: 66–79.

Gee, Marcus. 1999. 'World's poor overlooked as foreign aid stays low', *Globe and Mail*, 18 Feb., A14.

Green, Graham N. 1999. 'Canada's formula for failure', *Ottawa Citizen*, 2 Jan., B7.

Hampson, Fen Osler, and Dean F. Oliver. 1998. 'Pulpit Diplomacy: A Critical Assessment of the Axworthy Doctrine', *International Journal* 53, 3 (Summer), 379–406.

Kaplan, Robert D. 1994. 'The Coming Anarchy', *Atlantic Monthly* 273, 2: 44–76.

Knox, Paul, and Jeff Sallot. 1999. 'Axworthy's maxim: All politics are local', *Globe and Mail*, 1 Jan., A1, A9.

Lake, Anthony. 1993. 'Address at Johns Hopkins School of Advanced International Studies (21 September)'. Ottawa: United States Embassy. Text (24 Sept.).

Lawson, Robert. 1998. 'The Ottawa Process: Fast-Track Diplomacy and the International Movement to Ban Anti-Personnel Mines', in Fen Osler Hampson and Maureen Appel Molot, eds, *Canada Among Nations 1998: Leadership and Dialogue*. Toronto: Oxford University Press.

Luttwak, Edward. 1995. 'Toward Post-Heroic Warfare', *Foreign Affairs* 74, 3: 109–22.

Mandelbaum, Michael. 1996. 'Foreign Policy as Social Work', *Foreign Affairs* 75, 1 (Jan./Feb.): 16–32.

———. 1998. 'Is Major War Obsolete', *Survival* 40, 4: 20–38.

Matthews, Jessica T. 1997. 'Power Shift', *Foreign Affairs* 76, 1: 50–66.

Nossal, Kim Richard. 1998. 'Foreign Policy for Wimps', *Ottawa Citizen,* 23 Apr., A19.

Prins, Gwyn. 1998. 'The four-stroke cycle in security studies', *International Affairs* 74, 4: 781–808.

Ruggie, John Gerrard. 1998. 'The New United Nations: Continuous Change and Reform', *Behind the Headlines* 56, 1: 16–19.

Rummel, Reinhart J. 1995. 'Democracies Are Less Warlike Than Other Regimes', *Journal of International Relations* 1, 4: 457–79.

Russett, Bruce. 1993. *Grasping the Democratic Peace: Principles for a Post Cold War World*. Princeton, NJ: Princeton University Press.

Sallot, Jeff. 1999. 'Gag order silenced military critics', *Globe and Mail*, 18 Feb., A4.

Ullman, Richard. 1983. 'Redefining security', *International Security* 8, 1: 129–53.

United Nations Development Program. 1994. *Human Development Report*. New York and Oxford: Oxford University Press.

Wheeler, Nicholas J., and Tim Dunne. 1998. 'Good international citizenship: a third way for British foreign policy', *International Affairs* 74, 4: 847–70.

Zakaria, Fareed. 1999. 'Back to the Future: The coming year will show the waning power of the state', *Report on Business Magazine* 15, 7: 34–5.

12

Taming the South Asian Nuclear Tiger: Causes, Consequences, and Canadian Responses

LOUIS A. DELVOIE

Nuclear weapons tests conducted by India and Pakistan in May 1998 sent shock waves around the world. They instantly evoked ringing condemnations, political grandstanding, and gloomy editorials, to say nothing of outbursts of popular enthusiasm in the subcontinent itself. In terms of public and media attention outside of South Asia, however, the figurative shock waves were almost as brief in their impact as the physical ones. They receded into the background as pride of place was once again accorded to the boudoir scandals in Washington and to the political-economic woes of Russia and East Asia.

While it did last, the attention paid to the tests in most Western countries focused on them as discrete phenomena linked only to the current state of the hostile relationship between India and Pakistan. The policy responses adopted by many Western countries, including Canada, reflected this focus. And yet the decisions of the Indian and

Pakistani governments to conduct these tests, and their positions on the question of nuclear proliferation, are deeply rooted in the ideology, politics, and security concerns of both countries, as well as in their relations with China. While it may prove easier to ignore these complexities of the situation in formulating policy responses, doing so only ensures that those policy responses are inadequate and ineffective. So, too, is any approach that minimizes the consequences, real and potential, of the tests in terms of the seriousness of purpose with which they should be addressed.

This chapter examines some of the factors that led India and Pakistan to conduct these tests and will assess some of their implications. It will also assess the Canadian government's response to the tests and propose a more promising alternative in light of Canada's security interests and objectives. Finally, it will suggest that the Canadian government should re-examine the relative priority of the concepts of 'soft power' and 'human security' in its declaratory foreign policy if it is effectively to address security issues such as the proliferation of weapons of mass destruction.

CAUSAL FACTORS: INDIA

Through its formative years as an independent state, India's foreign policy was dominated by the ideology and thinking of its first Prime Minister, Jawaharlal Nehru. Much of that thinking emanated from Nehru's exposure to and espousal of the tenets of Fabian socialism. In foreign policy that meant, among other things, a constant and repeated insistence on the sovereign equality of all independent nations and a rejection of the notion that any nation should enjoy a distinct or privileged position in the international system by virtue of its wealth or power.[1] Adherence to this precept led India and Nehru to contest the leadership roles exercised by the two superpowers, to refuse to adhere to the blocs they dominated, and to opt instead for a policy of non-alignment in international affairs, which became the hallmark of India's foreign policy (Nehru, 1961: 24–85).[2]

This basic ideological orientation in India's foreign policy not unexpectedly found expression in India's approach to nuclear relations with other countries. Already in 1954, Nehru had condemned the principle of international control and inspection of nuclear facilities as yet another attempt by big powers to dominate the world by curtailing the legitimate aspirations of economically and technically underdeveloped nations (Morrison and Page, 1974: 25). When what India saw as discrimination in practice came to be enshrined in law in the form of the nuclear Non-Proliferation Treaty (NPT) of 1970, its reaction was eminently predictable. India rejected the notion that the world should be divided by treaty into two classes of countries, those who had nuclear weapons and could retain them against vague promises of pursuing disarmament, and those who did not have them and were forbidden to acquire them. India simply 'refused to obey the rules of what it regards as a club organized by the "haves" which is trying to impose [its] rules on the "have nots"' (Bradnock, 1990: 89).

If the idea of 'international egalitarianism' goes a long way towards explaining India's stand on nuclear proliferation, it can also be explained in terms of another equally important, albeit somewhat contradictory, trend in Indian foreign policy thinking. Put succinctly, this involves the search for recognition and status as an important country in the international community, which is not a new or recent phenomenon. Shortly after independence, Nehru declared that 'India is a great country, great in her resources, great in manpower, great in her potential, in every way. I have little doubt that a free India will play a very big part on the world stage' (Ghoshal, 1996: 33). Given these sentiments, it is perhaps no coincidence that one of the very first works on foreign policy published in India after independence is entitled *India as a World Power* (Ghopal, 1948).

India's ambition to be viewed as a major power was, however, largely frustrated for several decades. Throughout the years of the Cold War, the superpowers treated India as a leading regional or sub-regional actor, but paid it scant attention in matters of global importance (Bajpai and Cohen, 1993: 109–10). For its part, India considered that it deserved an international status equivalent to that of China. Indian leaders were particularly sensitive to the fact that, despite its weak economic base, China's status had been greatly enhanced when it first exercised its nuclear option in 1964 (Bradnock, 1990: 7–8; Ghoshal, 1996: 39). In the words of one scholar, India became progressively convinced that it 'must become a nuclear power in order to attain the much desired status of more than a regional power' (Pervaiz Cheema quoted in Ghoshal, 1996: 113).

If China figured prominently in India's foreign policy ambitions, it certainly figured no less prominently in India's security concerns and calculations. In seeking to explain the nuclear tests conducted by India in May 1998, media and academic commentators placed great emphasis on the hostile relationship between India and Pakistan and on the fact that the two countries had fought three wars against each other. What they usually failed to mention was that India had won all three of those wars with relatively little difficulty, that India had derived considerable political benefits from those wars, and that, in any event, India's conventional military capabilities were vastly superior to those of Pakistan. On the other hand, India's situation *vis-à-vis* China is remarkably different. In the only war it fought against China (1962), it suffered a humiliating defeat. China not only has a much larger conventional army than India but also has a fully deployed nuclear arsenal.

The security imperative that has shaped India's nuclear weapons policy since the 1960s is the existence of China's nuclear weapons capability and the uncertainty surrounding Indo-Chinese relations. This is not just a historical phenomenon; it is also a contemporary reality. As the head of India's leading strategic studies centre put it recently:

> While China-India relations have been improving in recent years, there are major uncertainties about the future strategic scenario. China is deeply engaged in a qualitative and quantitative buildup of its nuclear arsenal. This modernization is likely to increase in future. (Jasjit Singh, 1996: 344–5)

But it is not merely the existence of China's nuclear arsenal that pre-occupies India, it is also the nature of that arsenal. 'China's nuclear arsenal is basically one of regional effectiveness and therefore figures primarily in the threat perceptions of its immediate neighbours' (Bajpai and Cohen, 1993: 178). India's genuine security concerns *vis-à-vis* China are, of course, only compounded by the fact that China has been a significant supplier of nuclear and missile technology to Pakistan (Jasjit Singh, 1996: 845; Tucker, 1998: 247).

Finally, it must be recognized that the Indian political scene has undergone a fundamental change in the 1990s. During the first 40 years of India's existence as an independent state there existed a broad consensus among the national political parties that India should adhere to the ideology of its founders and remain a secular democratic state, but the 1990s have seen that consensus challenged by the meteoric rise of the Bharatiya Janata Party (BJP), the political expression of Hindu nationalism. While the factors accounting for the upsurge in Hindu nationalism and for the success of the BJP are numerous and varied, two of them are directly relevant to the present discussion. The BJP has played heavily on India's historical experience of Muslim rule under the Mughals and on the injustices and humiliations suffered by Indians in bygone centuries. It has also reactivated and exploited the perception of a Hindu India surrounded on all sides by hostile Muslim nations, a task made that much easier by the resurgence of political Islam in the Middle East and Southwest Asia (Sarhadi, 1979: 160–84). The apparent success of this appeal to Indian fears and insecurities, combined with some of the more assertive aspects of Hindu nationalist ideology, also led the BJP to become, among all Indian political parties, the most enthusiastic advocate of India becoming a full-blown nuclear weapons state. In the defence of a Hindu India, the BJP made clear its 'resolve to give nuclear teeth to the Indian armed forces' (Ghoshal, 1996: 112).

Although this ideological element was clearly present in the decision of India's BJP-led government to conduct nuclear weapons tests in 1998, the decision was largely justified on the grounds that it was dictated by India's security situation and its basic security interests. BJP spokesmen put forward a series of interconnected arguments that can be summarized as follows: (a) in the post-Cold War era nuclear weapons continue to remain a key indicator of state power and are the currency of power relationships in vast areas of the world; (b) the existing nuclear weapons states refuse to abandon their nuclear weapons on the grounds that they need them for their deterrent value; (c) India is unique in being 'sandwiched' between two states, China and Pakistan, with well-known nuclear weapons capabilities; (d) new evidence of Sino-Pakistani nuclear weapons collaboration proved beyond any doubt that the non-proliferation regime had collapsed in India's neighbourhood; (e) under these circumstances, India had not only the right but the duty to become a nuclear weapons state in order to deter a possible nuclear threat to it by its neighbours; (f) in so doing, India had violated no treaties, since it was party to neither the NPT nor the Comprehensive Test Ban Treaty (CTBT), and remained committed to nuclear disarmament on a universal and non-discriminatory basis (Jaswant Singh, 1998: 41–52).

Although vigorously denied by the BJP, it is difficult for an outside observer to escape the conclusion that the Indian tests and their timing were dictated not only by ideological and security considerations, but also by domestic politics. The BJP-led government was a coalition of 12 different parties and by the spring of 1998 disputes among the member parties threatened its survival. Speculation was rife in India and abroad as to how long it could last and whether the BJP could retain its dominant position in a new government emanating from fresh elections. The outburst of Indian popular enthusiasm that greeted news of the nuclear tests certainly served to strengthen the hand of the BJP within the government and to prolong the life of the government. Whether intended or not, the tests were a short-term political godsend to the BJP (Mehta, 1998: 403–4).

CAUSAL FACTORS: PAKISTAN

The factors that led Pakistan to conduct nuclear tests in 1998 are in many ways different from those that motivated India. Pakistan has never aspired to world power status and has not, as a matter of principle, rejected the leadership role played in international affairs by the major powers; quite the contrary, Pakistan aligned itself solidly with the United States and the West throughout most of the Cold War period. Nor does Pakistan reject the NPT on principle as an inherently discriminatory treaty. Rather, it proclaims its willingness to adhere to the NPT if and when India does so, i.e., its position is eminently pragmatic and relates to what it sees as a specific security threat. Finally, Pakistan sees no threat to its security emanating from China, with which it has traditionally maintained close and friendly relations. These important differences do not, however, mean that Pakistan's position on nuclear weapons is not also the product of a fairly complex combination of ideological, political, and security factors.

The partition of the subcontinent in 1947 was a traumatic experience for both Pakistan and India. The results of partition, however, appeared far more threatening to Pakistan than they did to India. Pakistan, as the smaller and less populated country, was destined to live in a state of ongoing inferiority side by side with a much larger, more powerful, and hostile neighbour. More important was the conviction held by many Pakistanis that Hindu India had never voluntarily accepted the partition scheme devised and imposed by the British; sooner or later India would act to reverse the effects of partition and to reincorporate the territory of Pakistan into India, and it would do so by military force if necessary (Sarhadi, 1979: 86; Sherwani, 1964: 33–41). Thus Pakistan saw in its hostile relations with India not merely a threat to its interests, but a threat to its very existence as a nation.

The first Indo-Pakistani war of 1947–9 only served to enhance Pakistani fears. Not only did it result in a political and military defeat for Pakistan, it created in relation to Kashmir a situation that tended to undermine the ideological foundations of Pakistan as a separate and sovereign state. Pakistan had been created to provide a home-land for the Muslims of South Asia, a homeland in which Muslims could develop their separate cultural ethos free of Hindu domination. To fulfil that geopolitical vocation, Pakistan needed to absorb all Muslim majority regions in the subcontinent, including Kashmir. India's occupation and eventual annexation of Kashmir thwarted that purpose and left Pakistanis with the sentiment that their nation was somehow incomplete (Ganguly, 1994: 10–11, 37–40). This factor, more so than any territorial or strategic imperatives, explains the cen-trality of the Kashmir question in Pakistani foreign policy and Pakistan's enduring hostility towards India and India's position on Kashmir.[3] Two more Indo-Pakistani wars, and India's role in the dis-memberment of Pakistan in 1971, only served to solidify Pakistan's fears and hostility.

These Pakistani concerns accounted in large measure for Pakistan's early alignment with the United States as a source of political and military support. Of even greater importance in the context of the nuclear weapons question, they also gave rise to Pakistan's ever closer relations with China. At first sight the two countries appeared to be somewhat unusual bedfellows. There were, after all, few ide-ological affinities between an Islamic republic and a Communist state that was officially atheistic. But any difficulties these differences might pose were easily overcome in the mutual pursuit of national interest and in deference to the old but tried proposition that 'the enemy of my enemy is my friend'. The Sino-Pakistani relationship solidified and flourished in response to a series of interconnected geopolitical phenomena of the Cold War era: (a) the estrangement of China from the Soviet Union; (b) the outbreak of war and hostile relations between China and India; (c) the *rapprochement* between India and the Soviet Union; and (d) the *rapprochement* between the United States and China. And despite all of the realignments that have occurred in and around South Asia in the post-Cold War period, the Pakistan-China relationship remains solid; in fact, China has proved to be both Pakistan's most reliable ally and its principal for-eign source of nuclear and missile technology (Munro, 1993: 80–4; Tucker, 1998: 247). Pakistan is most unlikely to turn its back on this relationship, for it now represents its only counterweight to the pre-ponderant position of India in the subcontinent.

If Pakistan's nuclear weapons program was initially grounded in the country's security concerns and in what it saw as the need to equip itself with a deterrent against India's vast superiority in con-ventional forces,[4] the program also assumed an important ideologi-cal dimension in Pakistan's domestic politics. When Prime Minister Zulfikar Ali Bhutto launched the program in earnest in the aftermath of the Indo-Pakistani war of 1971, he chose to give it an 'Islamic' character by pointing out that among the world's major civilizational groups, only the Islamic world did not have a nuclear weapons capa-bility. While Bhutto's characterization of what came to be known in media parlance as the 'Islamic bomb' was largely prompted by an interest in securing support from the Muslim countries of the Middle East and North Africa (Wolpert, 1993: 207–25), the idea was seized upon by Pakistan's Islamist political parties. Like their Hindu nation-alist counterparts in India, these parties became the most ardent and outspoken advocates of Pakistan's nuclear weapons program (Delvoie, 1996: 133–4). Their advocacy, combined with the Pakistani population's broadly based fear of India, contributed to creating a near consensus among Pakistanis in favour of the nuclear program. The Islamists also portrayed support for the program as the litmus test of loyalty and patriotism on the part of political leaders, and warned of 'dire consequences' for any leader who did not whole-heartedly endorse it, which only reinforced the political and military pressures to which Pakistani governments were constantly subject (Thomas, 1993: 71–2; Ispahani, 1990: 36–7). Given these realities, it was eminently predictable that the sitting Pakistani government, already confronted by staggering domestic challenges, would respond in kind to the Indian nuclear tests of May 1998.

CONSEQUENCES AND IMPLICATIONS

If the factors that gave rise to the Indian and Pakistani tests are var-ied and multifaceted, so, too, are the consequences and implica-tions of the tests. While much of the public commentary following the tests focused on the threat they posed to regional peace and secu-rity in South Asia, the foreign ministers of the G–8 countries quite correctly also labelled them a 'global challenge' (G–8 Foreign Ministers, 1998: 1).

In an article published in 1996, *The Economist* stated rather starkly that 'Bad blood between India and Pakistan makes South Asia the likeliest place for a [nuclear] bomb to be detonated in anger—especially as the two are on the verge of a missile race that would bring a new hair-trigger instability to a future crisis.' While this statement seemed somewhat overly dramatic when it appeared, the apprehension it conveyed has become more solidly founded as a result of the tests. In abandoning all pretence that they do not possess nuclear weapons and in taking a decisive step in moving from a 'non-weaponized' capability in the direction of a 'weaponized' capability, both India and Pakistan have greatly enhanced the risks that nuclear weapons could be used in South Asia, whether deliberately or accidentally. At least two strategic options have become that much more real as a result of the tests and of the missile development programs being pursued by both countries. On the one hand, the temptation exists to resort to a pre-emptive first strike in the hope of totally incapacitating the other side's nuclear weapons systems at the outset of a conflict. On the other hand, the resort to nuclear weapons in the face of imminent defeat in a conventional war is a real possibility. The first would be an option for either India or Pakistan in a war between the two; the second would be primarily an option for Pakistan in a war with India or for India in a war with China. As a result, any future armed conflicts involving these three countries would be inherently far more dangerous to regional and international peace and security than they have been historically.

It has been suggested by some observers that these concerns are misplaced. They argue that what may result is a situation of stable nuclear deterrence between India and Pakistan, comparable to that which existed between East and West during the Cold War (e.g., Kapur, 1995: 5–22; Jaswant Singh, 1998: 43). This view relies heavily on a rather theoretical strategic logic, at the expense of a close examination of military, technological, and political realities. Stable nuclear deterrence relies in part on an assured second-strike capability, which neither India nor Pakistan now possesses or is likely to acquire in the foreseeable future. It also relies on a mix of highly sophisticated systems for the secure storage, deployment, and command and control of nuclear weapons and their delivery systems to avoid their accidental or unintended use; it is by no means clear that India and Pakistan have all the requisite systems. Finally, stable nuclear deterrence requires well-established political institutions that can provide

a series of checks and balances against arbitrary or overly hasty decision-making,[5] as well as a reasonably well-developed tradition of
civilian control over the military. While India may have most of these
political attributes, Pakistan certainly does not. Pakistan has weak
institutions, has spent nearly half of its existence as a nation under
military rule, and even during the past decade (1988–98) of civilian
government the army has been actively involved in the removal from
office of two presidents and at least one prime minister. Given all of
these factors, the prospect of the instauration of a stable nuclear
deterrence regime in South Asia must remain little more than a hope
(see *The Economist*, 1998: 45). Unfortunately, the field of international relations is strewn with the debris of dashed hopes.[6]

Thus, the concerns expressed about the implications of the tests
for regional security in South Asia would seem well founded, but
they are essentially related to longer-term perspectives, given the current state of relations between India and Pakistan and between India
and China; there is no evidence to suggest that any of these countries are about to engage in military hostilities in the near future. In
contrast, the impact of the tests on the global non-proliferation
regime was far more immediate, in that they served to undermine
the basic assumptions on which the nuclear NPT rests.

When initially negotiated, the NPT was founded on the assumption that the nations of the world and adherents to the treaty could
be divided into two separate categories: five nuclear weapons states,
and all the rest that were deemed non-nuclear weapons states. While
reasonable at the time, that assumption became increasingly a fiction
in the ensuing decades as it became evident that Israel, India, and
eventually Pakistan had developed nuclear weapons capabilities. The
fiction could, however, be sustained as a basis for policy by adherents and supporters of the treaty so long as those three countries
either denied or refused to admit that they had nuclear weapons.[7]
The fiction was, however, blown to smithereens by the tests conducted in Pokharan and Baluchistan and by the accompanying statements issues by the Indian and Pakistani governments (IDSA, 1998:
1091–6).

Although the UN Security Council was no doubt legally correct in
asserting that these developments did not confer on India and
Pakistan the status of nuclear weapons states in accordance with the
NPT (UNSC Resolution 1172 of 6 June 1998), the Council not unexpectedly avoided addressing the concomitant reality, which is that by

any empirical standard, India and Pakistan can no longer be deemed to be non-nuclear weapons states. This would seem to constitute a dilemma that can be dealt with in one of only two ways. On the one hand, a process might be set in motion to negotiate a new international treaty that would better reflect existing realities, but this would be fraught with difficulties and would take years to accomplish. On the other hand, a peace process might be mounted for South Asia that would eventually result in India and Pakistan renouncing their nuclear weapons, but this, too, would be a difficult enterprise of long duration. In the meantime, the value of the NPT stands severely undermined as an instrument and as a global symbol in the struggle to contain and arrest the spread of nuclear weapons.

By their actions, India and Pakistan have not only weakened the NPT regime (and to a lesser extent the recent Comprehensive Test Ban Treaty to which they are not parties either), but have also set an example for other countries that may now or in future be led to contemplate the nuclear weapons option. That two countries as poor and as low ranking on the UN's Human Development Index as India and Pakistan should be able to produce usable nuclear weapons may well give pause to other better-endowed countries that may in the past have eschewed the nuclear weapons option on the grounds that it represented too formidable an economic or technological challenge.[8] The exemplar effect of the tests may be particularly relevant to East Asian countries such as Thailand, Malaysia, and Indonesia, which are seeking to come to terms with the rising military power of China, or to a Middle Eastern country such as Iran, which sees itself as being threatened by most of its Arab neighbours and is already reported to have a nascent nuclear weapons program. In the longer term, the Indian tests could also serve as a point of reference for Japan, South Korea, and Taiwan should they come to lose confidence in the security guarantees now provided them by the United States, for their security concerns *vis-à-vis* China are not qualitatively all that different from those of India.

By undermining the international non-proliferation regime and by the example they have set, India and Pakistan have contributed to weakening the barriers against the further proliferation of nuclear weapons in other regions of the world. This may well prove to be the most serious long-term consequence of their actions, since it seems almost self-evident that the larger the number of nuclear stockpiles dotted around the globe, particularly in areas of instability and conflict, the greater are the risks that they will actually be used, whether deliberately or through miscalculation. Their actual use would in turn have an impact well beyond the region in which they were detonated, since it would represent the first breach of a 50-year-old taboo that centres on two widely held beliefs: (1) the use of nuclear weapons is politically and morally unacceptable, and (2) nuclear weapons are useful instruments of deterrence, but their military value in any war-fighting strategy is dubious. Any such breach of the taboo, in Asia or elsewhere, would make the international security environment considerably more dangerous than it is today or than it has been in the recent past.

THE CANADIAN GOVERNMENT RESPONSE

The Canadian government's assessment of the implications of the tests highlighted their importance. In a statement to the Standing Committee on Foreign Affairs and International Trade, Foreign Minister Axworthy declared that 'thirty years of successful management of the nuclear proliferation threat has been undermined' and that the tests 'constitute a clear and fundamental threat to the international security regime and, thus, to Canada's security' (DFAIT, Statement, 1998: 1).

The Canadian government's policy response to the tests was a combination of condemnations, sanctions, and exhortations (DFAIT, Statement and News Releases, 1998). The principal elements may be summarized as follows: (a) strong to very strong criticism of the Indian and Pakistani governments;[9] (b) the discontinuation of Canadian non-humanitarian aid to the two countries; (c) support for the deferment of development projects funded by the international financial institutions; (d) the temporary withdrawal of high commissioners and the postponement or cancellation of certain government-to-government contacts; (e) a call to India and Pakistan to adhere to the NPT and CTBT; (f) a call to the nuclear weapons states to fulfil their nuclear disarmament obligations under the terms of the NPT; and (g) an undertaking to use 'soft power' to demonstrate that security is best built through co-operation.

When set against the Canadian government's assessment of the implications of the tests, the policy measures announced are underwhelming and are likely to prove singularly ineffective for several reasons:

- They address solely the symptoms as opposed to the causes of the problem.
- They totally ignore the Chinese dimensions of the problem.
- They fail to recognize the diminished usefulness of Canadian aid as a policy instrument in the wake of a decade of cuts in that aid to both India and Pakistan.[10]
- They equally fail to recognize that foreign aid now represents only a very small fraction of India's annual GDP (less than 2 per cent).
- They closely resemble the measures adopted by Canada following India's nuclear test in 1974 (DEA, Statements, 1974), the ineffectiveness of which is eloquently demonstrated by the latest series of tests.

Characterized as they are by inadequate analysis, weak sanctions, and strong rhetoric, the measures announced by the Canadian government seem caught in a time warp and hearken back to an earlier era in non-proliferation policy. The lessons of the 1990s suggest that successful non-proliferation efforts require very different ingredients: real political influence, sustained and skilful diplomacy, and large sums of money. All of these came to the fore in the approach of the United States to the problem of the nuclear weapons stockpiled in the Ukraine, an exercise that eventually cost the US some $800 million in aid and subsidies. The same was true of the American efforts to deal with the proliferation problems posed by North Korea's nuclear programs, an exercise expected to cost the US, Japan, and South Korea in the neighbourhood of $5 billion (Spector, 1995: 66–85). The contrast with the approach taken by the Canadian government to the proliferation issues in South Asia could not be more glaring.[11]

As well as being largely ineffective, the Canadian government's reaction to the tests is also counter-productive. After nearly two decades of allowing the Canada-India relationship to languish on the proverbial 'back burner', the Canadian government had begun to show a new interest in it in the mid-1990s. Recognizing the importance of the economic reforms implemented by the Indian government and the sheer size (200 million) of the Indian middle class as a consumer market, Canadian politicians, officials, and businessmen joined in a variety of endeavours to explore and exploit new opportunities for exports, investments, and joint ventures. Marshalling considerable political, bureaucratic, and private-sector assets, the government launched the 'Focus India' exercise in 1995 and a 'Team Canada' venture to the subcontinent in 1996 (Delvoie, 1998: 57–9). All of these sizeable investments of time and money now seem destined to go to waste, since a Canadian government policy stance characterized chiefly by denunciations and sanctions hardly seems likely to be very conducive to the development of a mutually advantageous economic relationship.

AN ALTERNATIVE CANADIAN APPROACH

In its response to the South Asian nuclear tests, the Canadian government could have pursued, and could still pursue, a far more positive and proactive policy. Such a policy would better reflect the Canadian interest in the issue while simultaneously achieving Canadian objectives.[12] It would involve Canada endeavouring to play a catalytic role in creating a coalition of influential countries to address the security problems of South Asia. To have any prospect of being effective such a coalition would have to bring together a group of countries with a real interest in regional stability and nuclear non-proliferation in South Asia and also in a position to exercise significant political, economic, and military influence in New Delhi, Islamabad, and Beijing. Such a coalition would ideally engage all of the members of the G–8 grouping of countries. The aim of the coalition would be to launch a sustained and systematic process of negotiation, involving India, Pakistan, and China, on all aspects of their mutual security relationships and on the other root factors that gave rise to the Indian and Pakistani nuclear weapons programs. The ultimate objective to be attained in stages and over a period of years would be to create conditions that would allow India and Pakistan to renounce their nuclear weapons programs and adhere to the NPT as non-nuclear weapons states.

In the course of what would be a highly complex process (but not necessarily any more complex than the ongoing Middle East peace process—Jerusalem and Kashmir are equally hard nuts to crack), the coalition would have to be prepared to deploy a variety of potentially costly inducements to the parties. These might include:

- improved access to G–8 markets, investment capital, and government-funded commercial credits;
- offers of co-operation in the nuclear energy field;

- offers of enhanced development assistance through both bilateral and multilateral channels;
- implicit threats of cuts in G–8 aid, investments, tariff preferences, and general market access;
- assistance in developing a comprehensive package of confidence-building measures and arms control measures in the India-Pakistan and India-China theatres;
- assistance in the verification and monitoring of arms control agreements and demilitarized zones; and
- holding out to India the prospect of a permanent seat on a reformed and enlarged UN Security Council.

The political and diplomatic challenges of building a coalition of influential countries are considerable and would require a sustained and creative effort on the part of the Canadian government over a long period of time. But these challenges would not seem insurmountable. It would not be a matter of starting from scratch, but of building on the areas of agreement that already exist among G–8 countries, as set out in their June 1998 communiqué. These include a shared assessment of the serious security implications of the South Asian tests, a shared conviction regarding the need for urgent action to confront the problem, and a shared willingness to assist India and Pakistan in achieving peaceful solutions to their problems (G–8 Foreign Ministers, 1998: 1–5). Thus, in undertaking this task the Canadian government could already rely on the existence of a fair degree of interest and harmony as to objectives on the part of the major external players. The task of Canadian diplomacy—in this case quiet, behind-the-scenes diplomacy—would be to identify further common ground and, where necessary, to foster common approaches, while recognizing that the complete harmonization of views is unlikely and not essential to the launching of a peace process. It would also involve 'selling' the merits of a multifaceted and comprehensive multilateral approach to achieve objectives that an overly long series of partial or unco-ordinated bilateral approaches have failed to achieve.

Canada is well placed to play a useful role as the instigator of a multilateral peace process for South Asia. In addition to its oft-touted skills in quiet diplomacy and coalition-building, Canada has direct access to the proven political consultation mechanisms of the G–8. It also now enjoys the status of a member of the UN Security Council and can legitimately claim a special voice on issues of international peace and security.[13] Canada does have standing, if not great influence, in South Asia as a generous contributor of aid for nearly 50 years, as a participant in all UN peacekeeping missions in the region, and as home to some one million people of South Asian origin. If and when the coalition came into existence and became operational, however, Canada's role would be essentially supportive and secondary to that of countries with major politico-military influence (the US, Russia) or with a large economic presence in the region (Japan, the US, Germany, France). Canada's contribution at that stage would primarily take the form of offers of economic assistance or of expertise in peacekeeping operations, in the design and implementation of confidence-building measures, and in the verification of conventional arms control agreements.

The policy approach briefly outlined above would seem to be fully consistent with (a) Canada's security interests; (b) the high priority traditionally attached to the proliferation of nuclear weapons and ballistic missile technology in Canada's international security policy; (c) the ever-increasing importance of the place occupied by the Asia-Pacific region in Canada's foreign and economic policies; (d) Canada's long-standing commitment to the socio-economic development of the nations and peoples of South Asia; (e) Canada's commitment to multilateralism in its approach to global and regional security issues; and (f) the limits of Canada's diplomatic, financial, and military resources. In taking the initiative to help resolve one of the most enduring and potentially most dangerous regional conflicts of the second half of the twentieth century, Canada would be serving both its national and international security interests. By helping to create conditions that would permit South Asia's absorption into the emerging economic and political architecture of the Asia-Pacific region, Canada would also be serving its political and economic interests, as well as the advancement of its altruistic ambitions for the peoples of South Asia.

CONCLUSION

The problems created by the nuclear weapons tests in South Asia are complex in their causes and serious in their implications. They are not amenable to easy or simple solutions. If Canada is to play a useful and positive role in the search for viable solutions, then the government will have to make a significant investment of intellectual, political, diplomatic, and financial resources in the enterprise (in the longer term it could also involve the deployment of military resources in peacekeeping or monitoring operations). Reaching such a decision would in turn require the government to reassess the relative priority of two concepts that now enjoy pride of place in its declaratory policy: 'soft power' and 'human security' (Hampson and Oliver, 1998; Nossal, 1998: A19).

There is certainly an important place for 'soft power' in Canadian diplomacy. It has been at the heart of Canada's public diplomacy for several decades in the form of cultural, academic, and media relations programs conducted by Canadian missions abroad. And it has repeatedly proved its value in furthering the attainment of Canadian objectives, e.g., in relation to the acid rain issue in the United States and to the fur trade issue in Western Europe. But it is not a panacea, suitable to all situations. Nuclear weapons are the ultimate expression of 'hard power', and decisions to produce, test, and deploy them go to the very core of a government's assessment of its national interests and its security needs. The modification of such decisions is not likely to be brought about by any array of 'soft power', but rather by the exercise of influence rooted in significant political, economic, and military capabilities of the kind possessed collectively by the leading members of the G–8.

The sorts of issues addressed under the heading of 'human security' are indeed ones that should be of concern to Canada. The types of initiatives to which they give rise certainly have a legitimate place in Canadian foreign policy, enjoy considerable support among the Canadian public, and can be of lasting humanitarian value, e.g., the movement to ban anti-personnel mines or the effort to create a standing international war crimes tribunal. That said, these are not issues that represent direct threats to the security of Canada and should not be given a higher priority than those that do, e.g., the proliferation of weapons of mass destruction and traditional interstate conflicts involving nuclear arsenals, such as those in South Asia. After all, it remains trite but true that the first responsibility of any Canadian government is to ensure the security of Canada and its citizens.

NOTES

1. Nehru was fundamentally opposed to the special status enjoyed by the five permanent members of the UN Security Council, but was realistic enough to

realize that there was little he could do about it given that India only achieved independence two years after the adoption of the Charter and the establishment of the UN.

2. India's foreign policy became progressively less genuinely non-aligned during the 1960s, culminating in the conclusion of its treaty of Peace, Friendship and Co-operation with the Soviet Union in 1971. This treaty brought in its wake a greatly intensified bilateral trading relationship and the supply of larger quantities of Soviet military equipment to India. Nevertheless, India continued to proclaim itself to be non-aligned and to play a leading role in the non-aligned movement.

3. India's position on Kashmir was equally ideological. For India to concede that Kashmir should become part of Pakistan simply because its population was predominantly Muslim would fly in the face of India's contention that it was a secular state in which peoples of all religions could coexist and enjoy equal rights; 'it would mean that Indian secularism was merely cosmetic and only religion could serve as the basis for a state in South Asia' (Ganguly, 1994: 10). This Indian contention, of course, belies the fact that the process of partition was based almost exclusively on religious affiliation, and that had Kashmir been included in the partition plan it would have been allocated to Pakistan.

4. Pakistanis are wont to point out that their nuclear weapons program was prompted by exactly the same reasons that led the NATO alliance to equip itself with nuclear weapons, i.e., the need to deter an adversary with substantially superior conventional forces.

5. This view is not based on any ideological attachment to democratic institutions, but is purely pragmatic. Indeed, it could well be argued that decision-making on military matters in the defunct Soviet Union was subject to more institutional checks and balances (Politburo, Central Committee, Defence Council, KGB, etc.) than is the case in contemporary Russia with its democratically elected president and Duma.

6. Proponents of the stable nuclear deterrence scenario also fail to recognize one significant geopolitical difference between the East-West situation and the South Asian situation: the former was essentially bipolar whereas the latter is tripolar, given China's intimate involvement. Establishing stable deterrence would seem a far more difficult proposition under these circumstances, given the possibility of third-party interference in any conflict involving one or other pairing of countries.

7. The fiction had already suffered a severe blow in the early 1990s with the revelation that South Africa had developed several nuclear warheads, but the international community largely chose to ignore the implications of these revelations when South Africa decided to destroy the warheads.

8. In 1995, Pakistan and India ranked 138 and 139 respectively on the UN's Human Development Index and had real per capita GDPs of $2,209 and $1,422. By way of comparison, Thailand and Malaysia ranked 59 and 60 on the HDI and had real per capita GDPs of $7,742 and $9,572 (UNDP, 1998: 20–1).

9. There is an interesting and unexplained difference in the terminology used in Canadian government statements in reaction to the Indian and Pakistani tests. In the case of India, the terms are 'very concerned', 'deeply disappointed', and

'strongly deplores'. In the case of Pakistan, the government sought to 'condemn' what is described as a 'highly irresponsible act'.

10. In the early 1970s Canada was one of the two or three largest contributors of aid to India. By the mid-1990s it ranked eleventh.

11. So far the only financial commitment made by the Canadian government consists of an $87,000 contribution to a group of Indian and Pakistani physicians to mount an advocacy campaign in favour of peace and disarmament (DFAIT, News Release No. 181, 1998).

12. What follows is a reformulated version of a proposal put forward in an earlier work (Delvoie, 1995: 40–3).

13. This is not to suggest that Canada should seek to get the UN involved in security issues in South Asia. This would be counter-productive. The UN has too much cumbersome historical baggage on the Kashmir question to be acceptable to India in any peace process. India has steadfastly rejected any role for the UN in its relationship with Pakistan since the conclusion of the Simla accords of 1972.

REFERENCES

Bajpai, K.P., and S. Cohen. 1993. *South Asia after the Cold War*. Boulder, Colo: Westview Press.

Bradnock, R.W. 1990. *India's Foreign Policy since 1971*. London: Royal Institute of International Affairs.

Delvoie, L.A. 1995. *Hesitant Engagement: Canada and South Asian Security*. Kingston: Queen's University Centre for International Relations.

———. 1996. 'The Islamization of Pakistan's Foreign Policy', *International Journal* 51, 1: 126–47.

———. 1998. 'Canada and India: A New Beginning?', *The Round Table* 345 (Jan.): 51–64.

Department of External Affairs. 1974. Statements (unnumbered). Ottawa, 22 May.

Department of Foreign Affairs and International Trade (DFAIT). 1998. Statements. Ottawa, No. 98/40, 26 May.

———. 1998. News Releases. Ottawa, No. 116, 11 May; No. 120, 12 May; No. 136, 28 May; No. 140, 30 May; No. 181, 27 July.

Ganguly, S. 1994. *The Origins of War in South Asia*, 2nd edn. Boulder, Colo.: Westview Press.

Ghoshal, B. 1996. *Diplomacy and Domestic Politics in South Asia*. New Delhi: Konark Publishers.

Gopal, M. 1974. *India as a World Power: Aspects of Foreign Policy*, 2nd edn. New Delhi: Sagar Publications. First edition published in 1948.

G–8 Foreign Ministers. 1998. Communiqué on Indian and Pakistani Nuclear Tests. London, 12 June.

Hampson, F.O., and D. Oliver. 1998. 'Pulpit Diplomacy: A Critical Assessment of the Axworthy Doctrine', *International Journal* 53, 3: 379–406.

IDSA. 1998. *Strategic Digest* 28, 7 (July).

Ispahani, M. 1990. *Pakistan: Dimensions of Insecurity*. London: International Institute for Strategic Studies.

Kapur, A. 1995. 'India and Pakistan: Nature and Elements of Nuclear Deterrence between Two Regional Rivals', *Occasional Paper* No. 28. Winnipeg: University of Manitoba Centre for Defence and Security Studies.

Mehta, P.B. 1998. 'India: The Nuclear Politics of Self-Esteem', *Current History* 97, 623 (Dec.): 403–6.

Morrison, B., and D. Page. 1974. 'India's Option: The Nuclear Route to Achieve Goal as World Power', *International Perspectives* 25, 9 (July-Aug.).

Munro, R.H. 1993. 'The Loser: India in the Nineties', *Strategic Studies* 26, 1–2 (Autumn-Winter): 80–9.

Nehru, J. 1961. *India's Foreign Policy*. New Delhi: Government of India Publications Division.

Nossal, K.R. 1998. 'Foreign Policy for Wimps', *Ottawa Citizen*, 23 Apr.

Sarhadi, A.S. 1979. *India's Security in a Resurgent Asia*. New Delhi: Heritage Publishers.

Sherwani, L.A. 1964. *Foreign Policy of Pakistan*. Karachi: Allies Book Corporation.

Singh, Jasjit. 1996. 'India and the CTBT', *Strategic Analysis* 19, 6: 835–50.

Singh, Jaswant. 1998. 'Against Nuclear Apartheid', *Foreign Affairs* 77, 5: 41–52.

Spector, L. 1995. 'Neo Non-Proliferation', *Survival* 37, 1: 68–85.

The Economist. 1998. 'India and Pakistan: Can they arrange a cold war?', 3 Oct., 46.

Thomas, R.G. 1993. *South Asian Security in the 1990s*. London: International Institute for Strategic Studies.

Tucker, N.B. 1998. 'A Precarious Balance: Clinton and China', *Current History* 97, 620 (Sept.): 243–49.

UNDP. 1998. *Human Development Report 1998*. New York: Oxford University Press.

Wolpert, S. 1993. *Zulfi Bhutto of Pakistan*. New York: Oxford University Press.

13

Small Arms: Testing the Peacebuilding Paradigm

ERNIE REGEHR

When Foreign Affairs Minister Lloyd Axworthy described peace-building as 'casting a life line to foundering societies struggling to end the cycle of violence, restore civility and get back on their feet' (Axworthy, 1996), small arms did not yet have a place of prominence on the international arms control agenda. With the emergence of peacebuilding and human security as prominent paradigms of inter-national diplomacy, however, it was inevitable that the global small arms problem would become a top contender to succeed landmines as an issue to galvanize the international community's continuing efforts to come to terms with a post-Cold War order that displayed little evidence of the anticipated peace dividend. The cycles of vio-lence that destroy civility and cause societies to founder are sustained in no small measure by the hundreds of millions[1] of military-style small arms and light weapons[2] that circulate from war to war and are diffused[3] to permeate all levels of troubled, insecure societies.

At the December 1997 landmines signing conference both Axworthy and Red Cross President Cornelio Sommaruga identified an urgent need to build on the success of the landmines campaign. Together they urged active collaboration among like-minded governments and civil society to address the devastating impacts of small arms and other weapons of war that are widely and readily used against civilians. At a post-conference lessons-learned workshop, a non-governmental organization-inspired proposal for a convention to prohibit civilian access to military-style small arms and to restrict intergovernmental transfers was proffered as a successor to the landmines convention just signed.

But the small arms issue was not invented by landmines diplomats or NGOs looking for meaning and purpose in a post-landmines convention world. Ongoing attention to efforts to control the trade in conventional arms has always included small arms. Two decades ago a significant discussion of 'repression technology' addressed the role of small arms in propping up repressive regimes. In the current round of renewed interest, the British American Security Information Council convened an informal network of researchers and NGO representatives in the early 1990s to address small arms issues. The group produced an anthology in 1995 (Singh, 1995), complementing the publication earlier that year of a collection of essays that has become a primary reference point (Boutwell, Klare, and Reed, 1995) for small arms research and policy development. In the same year the United Nations General Assembly instructed the Secretary-General to appoint a panel of governmental experts to prepare a report on small arms (in part to fill the gap left by the UN Register of Conventional Arms, developed in the early 1990s, which for technical and especially political reasons had excluded small arms).

Axworthy's December 1997 public expression of interest and concern did not represent the introduction of the small arms issue to the Department of Foreign Affairs and International Trade (DFAIT). Canada had already participated in the UN panel (reporting in August 1997) on the basis of a particular interest in exploring ways in which UN peacekeeping missions might become more effective in carrying out post-conflict disarmament and weapons collection, thus preventing the unrestrained circulation of surplus arms in fragile societies just emerging out of prolonged war. By 1995 Canada was in the midst of a major domestic overhaul of its internal gun control laws, which included preventing civilian access to any military-style weapons as well as a comprehensive registration system, two elements that DFAIT was keen to take into international discussions. With technical leadership from the Department of Justice, Canada also became active as co-ordinator of the project team of the United Nations International Study on Firearm Regulation.

These developments occurred well in advance of the international focus on landmines, but the success of the landmines campaign gave new impetus and energy to small arms control efforts. Shortly after the landmines conference, in early 1998, Canada co-sponsored resolutions in the Commission on Crime Prevention and Criminal Justice and the Economic and Social Council (ECOSOC) calling on states to 'work towards the elaboration of an international instrument to combat the illicit manufacturing of and trafficking in firearms, their parts and components and ammunition within the context of a United Nations convention against transnational organized crime' (ECOSOC, 1998). The resolution, though focused on crime prevention and on the regulation of non-military, civilian-owned firearms (essentially including all long guns and handguns, a much broader definition than the one used by the UN panel), acknowledges that 'international illicit trafficking in and criminal misuse of firearms have a harmful effect on the security of each State and endanger the well-being of peoples and their social and economic development.'

The ECOSOC reference to an 'international instrument' to control illicit trafficking cited another initiative with prominent Canadian involvement, namely, the November 1997 Inter-American Convention Against the Illicit Manufacturing of and Trafficking in Firearms, Ammunition, Explosives, and other Related Materials.

It is no wonder that Canadian interest in addressing small arms predated its landmines activism. The devastation wrought by these small weapons dwarfs that of anti-personnel landmines. In the past decade, the continuous worldwide prosecution of some three dozen local wars,[4] in which the majority of the killing is by small arms, has claimed as many as three million lives; and the figure for firearm deaths might well be doubled if worldwide firearm killings and suicides outside war zones were taken into account (Cukier, n.d.: 2).

In the context of political conflict, the availability of arms is the pre-eminent condition that transforms political and social conflict into war, as it has, for example, transformed cattle raiding between Pokot and Marakwet pastoral communities in Kenya's Rift Valley province into a full-scale local war. The traditional bows and arrows have been replaced by AK–47s, mortars, and hand grenades, with hundreds killed, including security officers, and many more forced to abandon productive agricultural lands and seek refuge in forests. In the past cattle rustling was confined to sporadic raids in which small numbers of animals were taken, but the arrival of sophisticated arms has transformed cattle rustling into a major racket. In other contexts, the level of violence is much higher, involving a more sophisticated range of weapons. Consider some of the weapons in the arsenal of the Tamil Tigers, the guerrilla army waging a war for an independent state on the island nation of Sri Lanka: surface-to-air missiles from Cambodia, assault rifles from Afghanistan, mortar shells from the former Yugoslavia and Zimbabwe, and assorted explosives from Ukraine. Tamil Tigers have bought arms from dealers in Hong Kong, Singapore, Lebanon, and Cyprus; from corrupt military officers in Thailand and Burma; and directly from governments, including Ukraine, Bulgaria, and North Korea.

A particularly pernicious characteristic of landmines is that they linger long after the war, arbitrarily claiming hapless victims for years and even generations to come. Small arms also linger, and in much greater numbers. Indeed, it is the testimony of many communities that peace agreements and the termination of armed conflict in political disputes leave the incidence of gun deaths virtually undiminished. Surplus arms, a lack of economic opportunity, and less than reliable security systems combine to transform political conflict and economic failure into criminal conflict, leaving communities as vulnerable as they were during the war.

Indeed, the uncontrolled circulation of small arms in and out of war zones is foremost among the conditions that frustrate the 'agenda for peace' that the international community had expected to pursue in the new post-Cold War era. Against the commitment to war prevention, the easy availability of small arms conspires to continue to make the violence option readily accessible to the disaffected. The abundance of weapons undermines peacemaking efforts, prolongs violent conflict, and makes such conflict much more lethal and destructive. The post-Cold War outburst of warfare in the former Yugoslavia and the former USSR, and the continuing high levels of warfare in Africa, Asia, and the Middle East, confirm the tragic reality that domestic political conflict, in states that have failed to produce trusted social and political institutions to mediate the conflicting interests and sensibilities that are necessarily a part of ethnically and economically diverse states, is quickly transformed into armed conflict where the hardware of violence is readily at hand. Combinations of frustration, desperation, malice, and, most notably, abundant supplies of user-friendly weapons of war make it increasingly difficult to avoid the descent into social chaos and finally war—war that in almost 20 per cent of states remains a form of deadly politics by other means.

HUMAN SECURITY AND THE CANADIAN INTEREST

While the arguments for urgent international attention to small arms diffusion are convincing enough, not all the inhabitants of the Pearson Building in Ottawa are convinced that Canada has a particular role to play. Canada, it is argued, has no special links to the issues. We are neither a major supplier, nor do we have an extraordinary domestic small arms or firearms problem. But it is more likely that the lack of consensus within DFAIT on a response to small arms reflects a more profound lack of consensus about the changing objectives of security diplomacy—namely, the gradual progression from the primary pursuit of a politically compelling national interest (an interest understood as advancing the well-being of its citizens) to the international pursuit of human security or the well-being of persons as a primary objective.

The clearest distinction between the two perspectives is not that the central object of security under a human security approach switches from maintaining the integrity of the state to protecting the welfare of the person (for which credible state institutions are obviously essential). A human security approach certainly assumes that the security of persons, and not regime survival, is the focus of state security measures, but the truly radical dimension of human security is the understanding that states have an obligation for the welfare and protection of persons wherever they are, not only the persons within the state's own borders. When individual states fail to meet the needs and respect the welfare of persons within their jurisdiction, then the international community, made up of states and an international civil society, has an obligation to meet certain basic needs and to ensure that state sovereignty is not a barrier between vulnerable populations and international protection. As has been frequently noted, what drove Canada's landmines activism was not any

strict national interest, but a broadly acknowledged national obligation—or, not 'pragmatic and rational military concerns', but 'ethical,
specifically humanitarian, concerns' (Dolan and Hunt, 1998: 398).

In practice, the gap between national interests and national obligations is not as wide as might be expected. Obligations to the international community are such that, to meet those obligations, in
co-operation with others, is to build the quality and stability of international life to the benefit of one's own place in that international
community. In a sense, policy initiatives based on principles of the
security and well-being of persons wherever they are must necessarily be the focus of middle-power states, for they lack a credible
capacity to pursue their own narrow national security interests on
their own, and they depend on international standards to build sustainable global environments that serve their national needs.

The other reality of middle powers, unable to single-handedly
advance national interests, is that they also cannot single-handedly
advance international standards that serve national needs. Hence the
need for niche contributions and the development of coalitions of the
like-minded within which to work co-operatively. As a result, Canada
is drawn to become engaged in the small arms issue due largely to a
developing level of comfort in working in government/NGO alliances,
the capacity to mobilize and work within alliances of the like-
minded, and the respect for and capacity to work within multilateral
institutions. All factors point to Canada as a significant actor in small
arms diplomacy efforts.

Canada's approach to small arms is essentially a combination of
peacebuilding and arms control measures, defined in an October
1998 *Strategic Framework* document as a three-track approach. The
paper notes that increased international attention to the effects of
small arms proliferation, including protracted and intensified armed
conflicts and their impacts on children, has generated new political
will to curb the flow of small arms. It then identifies a threefold
response: to address the roots and consequence of small arms proliferation through measures to build sustainable peace, to contribute
to more effective efforts to control legal arms transfers, and to contribute to efforts to eliminate illicit trafficking.

Peacebuilding measures attend to the roots of social-political conflict and to conditions that generate demand for weapons with the
aim of reducing demand. Arms control measures are designed to limit
availability. Controlling availability addresses domestic gun controls,

illicit trafficking, military export controls, and disarmament (notably
the collection of surplus weapons in post-conflict situations). The
peacebuilding component responds to the stark reality that efforts to
control the supply of small arms are likely to founder as long as the
demand for them remains buoyant. Reducing demand means building stable and sustainable societies with social, political, and economic conditions conducive to a durable peace and individual
security. In other words, no campaign to control small arms will be
fully credible unless it includes significantly expanded resources
committed to the advancement of economic development, democratic structures that enjoy a credible level of public confidence, respect
for human rights, and environmental sustainability. In addition to stable states, reduced demand will follow on regional structural stability, which relies on institutions and habits of co-operative security,
common approaches to limiting weapons imports, mutual respect for
borders and norms against destabilization tactics, and co-operation
among regional law enforcement and customs officials.

Good governance is in fact key to small arms control. The international arms control community has not been accustomed to linking arms control to issues of good governance. In a very real sense,
traditional arms control measures with regard to major conventional
weapons, as well as weapons of mass destruction, have been assumed
to rely on authoritative (even authoritarian) governments capable of
making and carrying out decisions relating to their military institutions and forces. Similarly, the implementation of the ban on anti-
personnel landmines is not dependent on the kind of governance
structure and practice that obtains in signatory states. The governance
question may best illustrate the necessary difference in approaches
to addressing landmines and small arms.

In the case of landmines, for example, it was possible for authorities in a state such as Kenya to sign on to the landmines treaty and
to implement the commitments and obligations of the treaty. The
Kenyan government is in control of its armed forces and clearly has
the capacity to decide not to use landmines and to carry out that decision by disposing of any stocks and by changing armed forces planning and training accordingly. But what would happen in the case
of a convention to prohibit civilian possession of military-style automatic assault rifles? How would such a government carry out that
decision? In fact, the same Kenyan government would have little
capacity to meet the conditions of such a convention. It is not

capable of policing large areas of the country. Borders are porous and impossible to patrol and guard for their full length. In urban centres the police are frequently corrupt. Above all, the social and economic (human security) conditions are such that there will continue to be a high demand for small arms among civilians, whether for personal security, for communal security, or for criminal purposes.

Small arms control requires social conditions of minimal human security and state governments with certain basic, minimum capacities and, notably, with the confidence of the people. Without that, control or regulatory measures will be ineffective and the demand for small arms will escalate.

THE DEMANDS OF THE MARGINALIZED

Controlling the demand for weapons requires social and governmental transformation. In other words, the small arms problem calls for a broad peacebuilding approach in a way that other arms control agreements have not. The small arms problem will probably be a key test of whether peacebuilding is more than a slogan or paradigm and actually represents a set of policies and programs that can be implemented.

The absence of good government, or the failure of states to meet the minimal requirements of human security, is the fundamental condition that generates demand for small arms. The demand for small arms is buoyant in the United States and it may seem to stretch credibility to claim that the local American demand for small arms is a function of state failure. In parts of Los Angeles and Miami, however, it is not a notion to be dismissed out of hand. Social conditions, even in American cities, are not irrelevant to the level of demand.

It is less surprising that the chronically marginalized, whether politically or personally, or those driven to desperation for whatever reason, should find in user-friendly weapons, if not hope, at least a kind of dark resolve. Put another way, guns significantly expand political and personal options. Parties to intractable political conflict, when they run out of options, do not usually give up. They turn to more dramatic means of gaining access to a credible political process. Former combatants in any of the dozens of recent wars, if they are not effectively reintegrated into post-conflict societies, frequently turn to one of the few skills they can claim with confidence, the menacing operation of firearm technology.

The result in troubled societies is growing insecurity, communal and personal, and the acculturation of violence. Worsening social-political conditions generate their own demands. Transforming these conditions into those that promote stability is the long-term challenge of peacebuilding and a prerequisite to small arms control.

A significant factor in generating demand for and facilitating illegitimate use of small arms (either towards political objectives or in criminal actions) is their availability. It is not inappropriate to speak of the phenomenon of domestic arms races—a process whereby criminal acquisition of weapons encourages citizenry to acquire weapons, leading criminals to upgrade theirs, and so on. Similarly, in political conflicts the availability of arms to non-state actors leads to the armed resistance option, which, in turn, generates governmental demands for an escalation in the counter-insurgency struggle. The provision of weapons to one communal group may also induce the rival group to acquire its own. A political and social climate of instability and insecurity sustains a demand for weapons that, in the final analysis, is accelerated simply by their availability. In political and social conflict this availability advances the military option and expands the options of the disaffected and criminals alike, which in turn generates a process of weaponization that increases demand still further. The point is that measures to limit the supply of weapons contribute to the mitigation of demand, just as measures to promote conditions of social stability, security, and the peaceful resolution of conflict and to enhance government capacity will contribute to efforts to control the supply of arms.

Canada's *Strategic Framework* for addressing the small arms issue acknowledges that the key challenge is to convert a peacebuilding approach into concrete action. Such actions in turn 'entail the rebuilding of State and civil society capacities to contribute to the security of all, and processes by which to tackle the political, economic and social causes of deep-rooted tensions' (DFAIT, 1998a: 4).

Peacebuilding measures are focused on four kinds of initiatives: post-conflict disarmament and the demobilization and reintegration of former combatants; local-level micro disarmament projects; strengthening efforts to meet the governance challenges of small arms proliferation; and raising awareness of the impacts and available operational responses of small arms proliferation. The peace-building initiative has provided funding for a variety of measures, including case studies, public awareness projects, and local 'goods for guns' buy-back programs, as well as for national and regional initiatives such as the proposed West African small arms moratorium.

THE POLITICAL ECONOMY OF SUPPLY

The supply of small arms is certainly plentiful. Economic motives play a part as states insist on what they regard as their sovereign right to export whatever they wish, including the profitable disposal of surplus arms. So there are, of course, those who profit from arms sales—producers, brokers, dealers, and corrupt officials. But small arms, in macroeconomic terms, are not key to anyone's successful military-industrial complex. For governments within regions of conflict, supplying arms is more politics than economics, although a number of northern states are happy to sell off post-Cold War surpluses. Canadian exports, largely to the North Atlantic Treaty Organization (NATO) allies, are primarily economically motivated. An automatic rifle manufacturing facility was set up to supply Canadian forces and is now kept busy and viable through export orders.

During the Cold War, the superpowers used the supply of major conventional arms, and small arms, in the effort to manage security conditions within and between their respective spheres of influence. In the post-Cold War world, virtually any state can use the abundant supplies of small arms to manipulate, or at least interfere in, neighbouring domestic and subregional political/security conditions. The politics of domestic conflict management even involves governments arranging to get arms into the hands of selected groups of their own citizens (Lata, 1996). Communal groups, for example, may be armed to combat or discipline their traditional rivals, either because the latter have fallen out of favour with the government of the day or simply as a means of fostering chaos to keep opponents of the government divided and fighting among themselves. Sometimes communal groups organize themselves into militias, but without the benefit of either military training or the discipline of commanded military units. They are simply civilian communities that are given or by some means acquire arms that they then use to advance the interests of their own community. In parts of Africa in particular, as already noted, such groups also use state-supplied weapons to pursue traditional practices such as cattle raiding—or to protect their livestock from the raiding of others, or to manage relations with rival communal groups over access to land and resources. Of course, once arms enter the civilian political economy they don't remain among a select few for very long. The supply to one group generates new demand (and a market) in others.

The need to prevent military weapons from finding their way into civilian hands has been a particular concern of Foreign Affairs Minister Axworthy. In mid-1998 he put forward for discussion a proposed measure to block legal transfers from states to non-state actors. The proposal was of interest not only for its substance, but also for the extent to which it countered the popular perception that Canada, still flushed from the landmines high, would quickly try to position itself to assume the moral and tactical leadership of the international small arms effort. While the proposed convention prohibiting small arms transfers to non-state actors signalled an intention to play a noticeable role, the measure was sufficiently narrow and limited within the overall small arms agenda to make it clear that it was regarded as one measure among many that others might advance— it was not regarded as a central, high-profile action.

A Proposed Global Convention Prohibiting the International Transfer of Military Small Arms and Light Weapons to Non-State Actors would oblige signatory states 'not to transfer military small arms and light weapons that originate from their territory to any recipient other than a state, state actor, or persons or organizations lawfully authorized to receive the transfers by a state or state actor.' Despite the fact that DFAIT has consulted widely on the proposal, to date it has not been broadly endorsed and has received considerable critical comment from the NGO sector.

NGOs expressed concern that such a convention could make too simple a distinction between state actors as legitimate and non-state actors as illegitimate recipients. They pointed out that many states are in substantial violation of humanitarian law and human rights standards and ought not to be entitled to receive arms simply by virtue of being states. Sovereignty and the right to self-determination are linked to obligations, and states that consistently and seriously ignore those obligations should also face restrictions in gaining access to small arms. Many NGOs argued that the supply of weapons to states for the purpose of carrying out wrongful acts should itself be defined as a violation of international humanitarian laws and standards. Canadian officials, in turn, pointed out that restrictions on the legal trade of small arms to human rights violator countries are intended to be addressed by national export regulations and international codes of conduct designed to set international standards for the control of such sales.

At the same time, the Canadian proposal does helpfully, in effect, affirm the principle of state monopoly on the use of lethal force. While background notes to the draft acknowledge that civilian populations must be able to defend themselves against unlawful states, they go on to argue that the primary defence of civilian victims of criminal states should come via the international community's pressure on states to conform to international laws and standards, rather than by putting the burden of self-defence on individuals or groups of civilians. In defence of the proposed convention, Canadian officials, backed by the minister's own comments, make the compelling point that Canada and many other states do not regard armed resistance to oppression as an effective means of toppling unlawful governments or of protecting vulnerable civilians. Rather, it tends to expose civilians to even greater danger. In fact, much of the work by NGOs against small arms is based on that very understanding—that armed resistance may ultimately topple unlawful regimes, but it is a process that invariably kills many civilians and leaves in its wake extraordinary legacies of weaponized, traumatized cultures for generations to come. The obligation on the international community therefore is not to arm non-state victims of oppression, but to require oppressive regimes to conform to international laws and standards. It is the international community's failure to meet that responsibility, rather than the lack of armed civilians, that accounts for the impunity some criminal regimes continue to enjoy.

The proposal also carries with it at least an implied prohibition on transfers to private security or mercenary firms. Mercenary firms, which by definition operate in states that themselves lack the capacity to regulate and control, are an emerging threat to the state monopoly on force and the proposed convention has the potential to contribute to control these groups.

The proposal, as of early 1999, was primarily a device for generating discussion on appropriate measures for expanding the legal constraints on small arms diffusion. Indeed, it was regarded as a successful device inasmuch as the European Union's policy on small arms had incorporated the core of the proposal through its declared principle that EU states would 'supply small arms only to governments (either directly or through duly licensed entities authorized to procure weapons on their behalf) in accordance with appropriate international and regional restrictive arms export criteria' (Article 3.b.: L9/2).

In the meantime, much of the international community's attention continues to focus on controlling the illicit trade in small arms. The Organization of American States (OAS) convention and the ECOSOC initiative to develop an international instrument modelled on the OAS convention address the small arms issue in the context of crime. The US and the G–8 have pledged to work towards the development of an international convention to universalize the essential provisions of the OAS convention, but the US, with the National Rifle Association looking over its shoulder, is obviously much more comfortable with law enforcement measures than with expanding legal restrictions on transfers. US Secretary of State Madeleine Albright gave a spirited endorsement in late 1998 of the need to control small arms, but with a major qualification: 'The culprit is not the legitimate international trade in arms, nor the sale of individual sport weapons to sportsmen, collectors, businesspeople and homeowners.' Her focus was on the illicit trade: 'The problem is the unregulated and illegitimate sale of large quantities of weapons, often via middlemen, to places unknown, for purposes unasked, to end-users whose identities are not investigated. It is a trade carried out by profiteers, abetted by corruption, creating a bottomless armory for rogue militias, criminal empires and bands of thugs' (Albright, 1998).

AN EMERGING CONSENSUS

Although small arms threaten the security of individuals and communities in a variety of contexts, most fall within the two broad categories of political conflict and social instability. In the context of political conflict, the focus is on local, national, and international political disputes that threaten to degenerate into armed conflict and full-scale war if peaceful means of resolving them are not found. Internal political disputes involving the denial of fundamental rights and freedoms and the exclusion of citizens from participation in the political process are especially vulnerable to disruption through small arms. The marginalized, by definition, are denied other options, but with weapons in hand they acquire both new attention and some new options. At the same time, small arms acquired by states aid governmental repression and the further marginalizing of the disaffected. Opposition groups acquire weapons in the effort to press for basic rights, to gain access to the political process from which they are excluded, or simply to destabilize an unpopular regime. As tensions escalate, the availability of weapons on both sides fuels conflict and converts political conflict into armed conflict or actual war.

Naturally, not all political disputes are strictly between governments and marginalized groups. Political conflicts between communal groups, none of which is linked to a national government, are also a prominent contemporary phenomenon. The international response is focused on the pursuit of a political settlement and war prevention, a prominent element of the latter being efforts to control access to small arms.

In the second broad context, social instability, the focus is on the domestic order and the safety and well-being of individuals and communities, rather than on political disputes *per se* either with governments or between communities. Here, too, in addition to weapons being acquired to advance organized crime, the socially and economically marginalized also find in small arms new personal options. The exercise of those personal options manifests itself in advancing social disintegration and rising urban violence and crime. The primary response in this context has been enhanced law enforcement capacity and, again, control of small arms and small arms trafficking.

Of course, the distinctions between these two basic contexts (political and social) are frequently, indeed usually, blurred. In various civil conflicts different groups pursue not only political aims but also criminal aims (especially in long, drawn-out conflicts where external support for combatants is not available). On the other hand, in societies plagued with pervasive urban violence and social disintegration, high levels of criminal violence are, at the core, also responses to social, economic, and political marginalization. That is to say, criminal violence in extreme forms must also be understood as fundamentally a response to political and social exclusion. Of course, the wide circulation of weapons as a result of politically motivated armed conflicts or of organized international crime (e.g., the drug trade) spills over into social and urban settings and exacerbates social conditions and fuels local violence and crime.

The inescapable links between basic political and social conditions and political and social violence are acknowledged in the growing international recognition that peacebuilding, the effort to halt violence and restore civility, is the core tool for addressing the problems of small arms diffusion. Small arms control is fundamentally a peacebuilding effort. If weapons are acquired to expand political and personal options, the policy objective must be to provide real options by other means—by peacebuilding measures designed to promote human rights, economic development, enhanced attention to democracy, and disarmament.

Current international initiatives and proposals are heavily focused on controlling the supply and availability of weapons, rather than on mitigating demand by promoting conditions more conducive to meeting basic needs and stability. Supply-side controls tend to be emphasized partly because they are concrete measures that can be implemented in the short term, whereas demand-side remedies are general and depend on a long time line, measured more in decades than years. But another reason that supply-side solutions are preferred over demand-side solutions is that arms control measures are more readily universalized. When you try to devise a small arms solution applicable both to street gangs in Los Angeles or Rio and to communal warfare in Kenya or Ethiopia, the tendency is to focus on the one thing that the two situations have in common—the weapons themselves. Hence, the solutions are directed at the weapons and on efforts to control them. Those are supply-side solutions. But if you separate out those two contexts it is possible to go much more directly to the core of the problem, which is not fundamentally the weapons themselves but rather the conditions that give rise to weapons use (whether they are weapons culture and values, or economic and social vulnerabilities). In other words, distinguishing clearly between the contexts helps to generate demand-side solutions and to tailor supply-side controls to specific situations.

A broad international consensus around the minimum requirements for effective small arms action is beginning to emerge. It includes the recognition that a peacebuilding approach is essential to address the political and social roots of conflict, but the concrete proposals still tend to focus more on measures to control the supply or availability of arms.

For example, there is broad recognition that there must be a clear distinction between the kinds of weapons legitimately available to military and law enforcement officers and those available to civilians. Just what that distinction should be, however, is less clear. Generally it is agreed that military-style weapons should be kept out of the hands of civilians, but there are wide differences on what that means, as is evident in the contrasting approaches to gun control in Canada and the United States. The matter is further complicated by the recognition that the distinction between legitimate and illegitimate use of military-style small arms is not as simple as distinguishing between official and civilian use. In too many contexts official use of such weapons is far from legitimate, whether by undisciplined Canadian peacekeepers in Somalia, corrupt police in Colombia, or repressive Indonesian military forces in East Timor. The OAS gets around the problem by simply asserting the need for national laws to regulate availability, but without setting a regional international standard (the same non-committal formula is destined to be repeated in the ECOSOC instrument currently being developed with G–8 support).

National gun registration in aid of domestic gun control legislation is also broadly accepted. State-based licensing arrangements for all weapons, including sporting guns and others that are legitimately owned and used by civilians, should be registered with a public authority.

In addition to the need for domestic restrictions on access to small arms, another area of broad consensus is an agreed need to strengthen international norms against the supply of small arms to military and law enforcement agencies in states with significant human rights violations. The responsibility of states to establish and maintain effective controls over the export of weapons is also widely accepted. While the criteria for such controls are not universally agreed upon, there is broad recognition that states should apply the greatest constraint in the supply of any weapons to states in conflict and where human rights violations are common. In addition, in the case of small arms, states are understood to have a responsibility not to supply small arms to states that lack adequate provisions for licensing and regulating small arms and for preventing their diversion for illicit purposes.

To support implementation of both domestic and international transfer regulations, weapons must be trackable, and most small arms control proposals include provisions for marking all weapons (showing, for example, the year and place of manufacture, as well as current ownership) so that records can be maintained and each weapon's movement traced.

Another widely accepted requirement is that all states establish regulations governing safe and secure storage of weapons and provide training for their safe operation. Also within the emerging international agreement on small arms control is acceptance of the need for a high degree of transparency in small arms management and control. Adding small arms to the UN Register of Conventional Arms and/or the establishment of regional registers are among the various measures that have been discussed.

Perhaps the most urgent problem is to find ways of dealing with the hundreds of millions of small arms already out there. There is an emerging consensus on the importance of measures to collect and destroy surplus weapons. Such measures are particularly urgent in immediate post-conflict situations. It is widely agreed, in principle at least, that peacekeeping personnel need to be given the necessary training, means, and mandates to make disarmament a key element of post-conflict patrols. Amnesty programs and weapons buy-back schemes are also frequently mentioned, with the additional provision that collected weapons must actually be destroyed, not merely stored (with the attending risk of future use or unlawful diversion).

Finally, another measure that finds wide agreement is providing support to law enforcement efforts in states where the illicit use of weapons is most severe. Law enforcement training and technical support are frequently noted, and it will most certainly become necessary to include training in the requirements of international humanitarian law and human rights standards.

As yet there is no consensus on what an effective, global small arms campaign might best focus on. But it is possible now to discern an emerging appreciation about the scope of the small arms problem and the broad sweep of actions that will be necessary to address the problem effectively. Furthermore, the issue now also has a place of prominence on the international political agenda. The Norwegian government hosted a meeting in mid-1998 of 21 like-minded states and issued a general statement of common understanding that emphasized efforts to prevent the illicit spread of small arms, greater restraint in the legal trade, and redoubled efforts to control or destroy surplus weapons in post-conflict environments. Later in the year, Brussels hosted a much larger gathering of governments and NGOs that linked the idea of sustainable development to sustainable disarmament, and called for greater attention to human security, human rights, and development programs with weapons collection and security assistance. Small arms continue to be on the annual agenda of the United Nations General Assembly (UNGA) First Committee, and in 1998 the UN agreed to convene an international conference on the illicit arms trade not later than 2001. A global convention to combat the illicit manufacturing of and trafficking in firearms is currently under development through the Economic and Social Council and the UN Crime Commission. It is generally to follow the model of the OAS convention and has received the endorsement of the G–8 (at the Birmingham summit in May 1998).

Confirmation of growing international support for addressing the small arms problem came in the form of the entry into force of two regional agreements, the OAS convention and the West African moratorium. Lora Lumpe, a senior researcher with the Norwegian Initiative on Small Arms Transfers, emphasizes the importance of committing the resources needed to make these agreements real and effective. Canada has supported the development of the West African moratorium on the import, export, and manufacture of small arms and light weapons, but more money is needed for disarmament and demobilization programs, to generate economic opportunities as a counter to armed banditry, and to facilitate gun collection and destruction programs. Similarly, southern OAS states will require extensive support to establish the domestic legislation and control mechanisms called for in the agreement (Lumpe, 1998: 3).

Also in 1998 Canadian NGOs hosted an international NGO gathering to launch the International NGO Action Network on Small Arms (IANSA). The Canadian meeting followed a number of regional gatherings and adopted a preliminary policy framework to advance the core elements of the program needed to come to terms with the global small arms problem: greater restraint in legal transfers, more effective measures to prevent illicit trafficking, collection of surplus weapons, and greater transparency. In addition, NGOs place a high priority on measures to reduce demand. Recognizing that the primary impediments to effective small arms control are the widespread debilitating social and economic conditions that fuel demand, the NGOs point out that 'positive, economic, political, and social environments are necessary to reduce the demand, and policies designed to limit the availability of small arms should therefore be pursued in parallel with a wide range of efforts to promote human security as well as social/political security and stability—notably efforts in support of peacebuilding, conflict prevention, nonviolent conflict resolution, human rights and good governance, and social and economic development' (Project Ploughshares, 1998: 7).

It is an exhausting, if not exhaustive, list, and the challenge facing the international community is to convert those grand, and surprisingly widely shared, intentions into practical political action. By virtue of the peacebuilding/human security paradigm appropriated by DFAIT, Canada has acknowledged the obligation to contribute to efforts to remove from the global security environment one of the chief mechanisms for transforming political conflict into violent armed conflict. The degree to which we, in the company of other like-minded communities, succeed will be the degree to which peacebuilding is finally able to evolve from political paradigm to practical accomplishment.

NOTES

1. Counting small arms is less than an exact science. No systematic research has to date documented firm numbers. The figure of 500 million has gained a certain currency in the literature. Jasjit Singh of the Institute for Defence Studies and Analyses of India noted in 1995 that '500 million guns . . . are in circulation in the world, including 55 million Kalashnikov automatic assault rifles' (Singh, 1995: IX). Michael Renner of World Watch noted in 1997 that 'although the information available is still sparse, mounting evidence indicates that the quantities involved are enormous.' He cites Singh, saying, 'there may be about 500 million military-style firearms, in addition to many hundreds of millions of guns designed for police forces or for civilian use' (Renner, 1997: 6).

2. Although these are broad terms, there is also broad agreement among governments and NGOs alike as to what they include. For example, NGOs coming together in the International NGO Action Network on Small Arms have agreed to use the term 'small arms' to mean small arms, light weapons, and ammunition and explosives as defined in the 1997 report of the United Nations Panel of Governmental Experts on Small Arms. Generally, small arms can be described as those that can be operated by one or two persons and can be carried by one or two persons or by a pack animal or light vehicle. The August 1997 UN report (UN, 1997b) offers the following definitions: *small arms* includes revolvers and self-loading pistols, rifles and carbines, sub-machine-guns, assault rifles, and light machine-guns; *light weapons* includes heavy machine-guns, hand-held under-barrel and mounted grenade launchers, portable anti-aircraft guns, portable anti-tank guns, recoilless rifles (sometimes mounted), portable launchers of anti-aircraft missile systems (sometimes mounted), and mortars of calibres less than 100 mm; *ammunition and explosives* includes cartridges (rounds) for small arms, shells and missiles for light weapons, mobile containers with missiles or shells for single-action anti-aircraft and anti-tank systems, anti-personnel and anti-tank hand grenades, landmines, and explosives.

3. The pattern of weapons circulating, moving from conflict to conflict and becoming infused into the social fabric of certain countries and communities, has led Michael Klare to refer to the 'diffusion' of small arms: 'I use the term "diffusion" rather than "proliferation" because it better describes the spread of arms throughout the world and all levels of society. While "proliferation" suggests

an *increase* in the number of weapons possessed by certain governments, or in the number of states possessing a particular weapon system, "diffusion" suggests the *dispersion* of arms *within* societies, extending not only to governments and state-owned entities but also to private armies and militias, insurgent groups, criminal organisations and other non-state actors' (Klare, 1995: 3).

4. If war is defined, as it is in the annual *Armed Conflicts Report* published by Project Ploughshares, as a political conflict in which armed combat involves the armed forces of at least one state (or one or more armed factions seeking to gain control of all or part of the state), and in which at least 1,000 people have been killed by the fighting during the course of the conflict, then there have been at least three dozen wars ongoing at all times since the mid-1980s. That level increased to more than 40 in the early years after the end of the Cold War, during the time of the wars in the former Yugoslavia, but by 1997 fighting had returned to earlier levels with 37 armed conflicts fought on the territories of 32 countries.

REFERENCES

Albright, Madeleine. 1998. Speech in New York to the International Rescue Committee Freedom Award Ceremony, 10 Nov.

Axworthy, Lloyd. 1996. Speech to York University announcing the Peacebuilding Initiative, Oct.

———. 1997. Speech to the United Nations General Assembly, 25 Sept.

———. 1998a. Speech to the NGO Conference on Small Arms (organized by Project Ploughshares), 19 Aug.

———. 1998b. Speech to Seminar on Small Arms and Light Weapons (sponsored by BASIC), 25 Sept.

Boutwell, Jeffrey, Michael T. Klare, and Laura W. Reed, eds. 1995. *Lethal Commerce: The Global Trade in Small Arms and Light Weapons*. Washington: American Academy of Arts and Sciences, Committee on International Security Studies.

Cukier, Wendy. n.d. *International Small Arms/Firearms Control: Finding Common Ground*. Ottawa: Canadian Centre for Foreign Policy Development.

DFAIT. 1998a. *Small Arms Proliferation and Peacebuilding: Strategic Framework*. Ottawa, 28 Oct.

———. 1998b. *An International Register of Small Arms and Light Weapons: Issues and Model*. Ottawa, Oct.

———. 1998c. 'Canada-EU Statement on Small Arms and Anti-Personnel Mines', 17 Dec.

Di Chiaro III, Joseph. 1998. *Reasonable Measures: Addressing the Excessive Accumulation and Unlawful Use of Small Arms*. Bonn: Brief 11, Bonn International Center for Conversion.

Dolan, Michael, and Chris Hunt. 1998. 'Negotiating in the Ottawa Process: The New Multilateralism', in Maxwell A. Cameron, Robert J. Lawson, and Brian W. Tomlin, eds, *To Walk Without Fear: The Global Movement to Ban Landmines*. Toronto: Oxford University Press, 392–423.

Economic and Social Council (ECOSOC). 1998. Document E/CN.15/1998/L.6/Rev.1, 28 Apr.

EU Programme for Preventing and Combatting Illicit Trafficking in Conventional Arms. Joint Action of 17 December 1998 adopted by the Council on the basis of Article J.3 of the Treaty on European Union on the European Union's contribution to combating the destabilizing accumulation and spread of small arms and light weapons (1999/34/CFSP), in *Official Journal of the European Communities* 15.1.99, L9/1–L9/5.

European Union, Council of the European Union. 1998. Code of Conduct. Brussels, 8 June.

Goldring, Natalie J. 1997. *Overcoming Domestic Obstacles to Light Weapon Control*. Washington: British American Security Information Council, Project on Light Weapons, Apr.

Greene, Owen. 1997. *Tackling Light Weapons Proliferation: Issues and Priorities for the EU*. Saferworld Report. London, Apr.

Inter-American Convention Against the Illicit Manufacturing of and Trafficking in Firearms, Ammunition, Explosives and other Related Materials. 1997. Permanent Council of the Organization of American States, Nov.

Klare, Michael T. 1995. 'Light Weapons Diffusion and Global Violence in the Post-Cold War Era', in Jasjit Singh, ed., *Light Weapons and International Security*. New Delhi: British American Security Information Council, Indian Pugwash Society, and Indian Institute for Defence Studies and Analyses, 1–40.

————. 1997. 'The International Trade in Light Weapons: What have we learned?', prepared for the Workshop on Controlling the Global Trade in Light Weapons, Washington, 11–12 Dec.

Lata, Leenco. 1996. 'Small Arms Diffusion in the Horn of Africa: Result and Cause of Instability', paper presented to the International Resource Group on Disarmament and Security in the Horn of Africa Conference on Peace and Security in the Horn of Africa, Mombasa, 6–9 Nov.

Laurance, Edward J. 1997. 'Small Arms and Light Weapons as a Development and Disarmament Issue: An Overview', presented to the Conference on Converting Defence Resources to Human Development, Bonn, Nov.

————. 1998. *Light Weapons and Intractable Conflict: Early Warning Factors and Preventive Action*. A report to the Carnegie Commission on Preventing Deadly Conflict, July.

Lumpe, Lora. 1998. 'Controlling Small Arms: Progress and Priorities', *Disarmament Diplomacy* 32 (Nov): 2–7.

Project Ploughshares. 1998a. *Armed Conflicts Report*. Waterloo, Ont.

————. 1998b. *Report on An International NGO Consultation on Small Arms Action*. Waterloo, Ont.

Renner, Michael. 1997. *Small Arms, Big Impact: The Next Challenge of Disarmament*. Washington: World Watch Paper 137, Oct.

Singh, Jasjit, ed. 1995. *Light Weapons and International Security*. New Delhi: British American Security Information Council, Indian Pugwash Society, and Indian Institute for Defence Studies and Analyses.

'Small arms, Big problems'. 1999. *Bulletin of the Atomic Scientists* 55, 1 (Jan./Feb).

United Nations. 1997. *Report of the UN Panel of Governmental Experts on Small Arms*. UN Document A/52/298, 27 Aug.

————. 1998. *Report of the UN Commission on Crime Prevention and Criminal Justice*. E/CN.15/1997/CRP.6, 25 Apr.